JUNE PLATT'S

Party Cookbook

JUNE PLATT'S

Party Cookbook

WITH ILLUSTRATIONS

HOUGHTON MIFFLIN COMPANY · BOSTON

The Riverside Press Cambridge

The Riverside Press

CAMBRIDGE · MASSACHUSETTS

PRINTED IN THE U.S.A.

DEDICATED TO
AGNES WRIGHT
AND
DICK WRIGHT

Preface

I<small>F</small> YOU were to ask me why and how I came to write this cookbook, I should lay the blame or thanks, as the case may prove to be, on a simple but excellent, if I do say so, Canard aux Navets which I happened to cook and serve, on a moonlight night, at a gay little table, on a narrow little porch, away back in the country, some two years ago, to two most appreciative, and, I have no doubt, hungry, week-end guests to whom this book is appreciatively and fondly dedicated.

Had the moon been less brilliant, the wine less fragrant, the guests unappreciative, and the duck not so tender — who knows ——

Were you to ask me the aim and purpose of this book, I should answer that it is written for the special benefit of people who, like myself, not only love to eat, but love to cook, who are certainly chefless and possibly cookless, and who are willing to go to any amount of trouble and care to achieve the delight of serving a perfectly prepared meal for friends worthy of this attention.

This wouldn't be a cookbook preface if I didn't quote from Brillat-Savarin; so here is my favorite one: 'He who gives a dinner for a group of friends, without giving it his personal attention, is unworthy of having friends.'

If you are a natural-born gourmet, but through force of circumstances have been unable to acquire a wider knowledge of food in its perfection, this book may help you to attain more variety and elements of surprise in the meals you serve. In my experience cooks, amateur or professional, are often not better cooks simply because they have never had the good fortune of serving or dining in houses where superlative meals were served: it is only by comparison that we can appreciate degrees of perfection.

Good ingredients and their lavish use are necessary for gourmet cooking. It is better, in my opinion, to eat simply a good soup and a fruit than a mediocre banquet.

It has always been a joy to me to write down in a little book good menus, and good dishes whenever encountered, whether enjoyed at restaurants abroad or at private tables; so that when Mr. Wright asked me to write a food article for *House and Garden*, after partaking of the aforementioned Canard aux Navets, I was delighted to be able to accept. The result was a series of articles over a period of two years, and the result of that — this book.

I have made a special effort to describe in detail the process of accomplishment of the various recipes, step by step, which may occasionally give them an air of complication. I hope you will not let this discourage you, for I really believe that even an inexperienced cook should have fortunate and successful results with them all.

In giving a party, be lavish with pink roses and lilies; choose the wine with care; chambré it, or cool it, as the case may be. Cook the meal yourself or at least supervise it with care. Be sure the dining-room is well aired, the plates hot, the silver and glasses shining brightly. Put on your favorite dress, powder your nose, light the candles and fire — and relax. The party will be a success.

Contents

INTRODUCTION, BY JULIAN STREET — xi

I. HORS D'OEUVRES AND FIRST-COURSE DISHES — 1

II. SOUPS, THIN AND THICK — 9

III. FISH — 27

IV. EGGS — 47

V. FOWL — 63

VI. MEAT — 99

VII. ALMOST NO MEAT — 121

VIII. VEGETABLES — 129

IX. SALADS — 145

X. FILLING AND FATTENING FOODS — 157

XI. CUSTARDS AND PUDDINGS — 167

XII. FRUIT DESSERTS — 187

XIII. SPECIALTIES OF MY FRIENDS — 209

XIV. TEA AND COCKTAIL PARTY ACCESSORIES — 225

XV. HOT DRINKS — 239

XVI. MENUS — 249

CLASSIFIED INDEX — 263

ALPHABETICAL INDEX — 269

Introduction

Experience with recipes published in newspapers, magazines, and books has led me to believe that often those who sponsor them have not tried them, or that they have written them carelessly, or that they do not themselves understand the art of cookery or the proper composition of a meal.

It is the more a pleasure to me, then, to have an introductory finger in this pie of June Platt's, for I am convinced of its high merit.

June Platt, though a matron distinctly young, is wise beyond her years in matters culinary. She has been a practical and practicing cook since early childhood; her background, as a first-rate culinary background must inevitably be, is international; and she is above all an artist, whether in painting mural decorations, in choosing the costumes she wears so beautifully, in arranging a dinner table and a menu, or in preparing the dishes of which that menu is composed. She is, in short, a prodigy.

Her first sharp awareness of the importance of food and drink came, she tells me, when as a very little girl she was placed in a convent school in Paris while her mother was studying miniature painting in that city. The fare at the convent consisted of cabbage soup for breakfast, cabbage soup and hard red wine for lunch, and cabbage soup and hard red wine for dinner. There is some significance, perhaps, in the fact that none of the twenty-seven soups for which she here gives recipes is made from cabbage.

From the convent school she went to live for a year as the guest of an English family at Ripon, Yorkshire. Here she became kitchen-conscious, spending much time with the cook and watching her prepare stolid British meals in which principal items were roast beef, Yorkshire pudding, hard-boiled egg salad and Devonshire cream.

At seven she went for a long visit to her grandmother in Bloomington, Illinois, and a principal memory of that visit is of the miniature soda biscuits she was allowed to cut from scraps of dough with her grandmother's gold thimble.

When she was eight her mother turned her loose with a cookbook in the kitchen of a little apartment in New York. It was not long before she graduated from the White House Cook Book to a little French cookbook, and by the time she was ten she and her sister Lucy could together cook and serve a creditable course dinner for guests.

Moving again to France — the glories of the higher French cuisine began to unfold themselves to our author, and she spent much time in concocting imitations of various delectable dishes tasted in Parisian restaurants. This went on for several years, and when the war drove the family home and June went to high school in New York she reached the low spot in her life, for there were 'French lessons from a German who couldn't speak French, and compulsory cooking lessons in which we were taught the fundamentals of potato peeling and how to make cakes with a quarter of an egg.'

Two happy years at an art school followed; then marriage and babies and another glorious period of residence in Paris with a painter husband who was likewise an epicure, good cooks who taught her a great deal, and finally a course in cooking at the famous Cordon Bleu.

In Paris, and subsequently in New York, the Platts have entertained extensively. Many of their friends are gourmets (see Chapter XIII), and invitations to their dinners are much coveted. Two or three years ago Richardson Wright, author, who is also editor of *House and Garden*, spent a week end with them at their place in the country, and having dined upon a *canard aux navets* prepared by the hostess, was so overcome as to lose his editorial reserve and beg her to write an article upon cookery for his magazine. This she did, and she has kept on writing them ever since. Hostesses with literary aspirations will find the recipe for *canard aux navets* on page 67.

'The only criticism I have heard of June Platt's articles,' Mr. Wright said to me recently, ' is that some of her recipes call for a good deal of work. Therein, I think, lies her genius, and the greatest difference between any genius and a "flop." A hostess who wants to serve a perfect meal cannot escape a lot of planning and hard work.'

That, of course, is entirely true, and it seems to me that since wines have become legally available, the tone of American dining has vastly improved — for there can be no fine dining without wine. Many hostesses, I am sure, are ready and glad to plan and to work hard in order to make their luncheons and dinners as good as they can be made. It is to such women, I take it, that this book is addressed, and I am confident that those who use it will feel a profound sense of indebtedness to its author, for it is indeed a cookbook that belongs in the top flight.

PASADENA, CALIFORNIA   JULIAN STREET
March the first 1936

I. HORS D'ŒUVRES AND FIRST-COURSE DISHES

Sometimes it is fun not to start the meal with a soup. What could be better than hot or cold hors d'œuvres? A few do's and don't's though. Don't serve too much of it if a big meal is to follow; and if this is not to be the case, serve plenty of it. Italian or French bread with coquilles de beurre should accompany most of them. If melon is served, the French believe it is pure poison unless accompanied by at least half a glass of Madeira — or Marsala — and salt and pepper.

GRILLED SARDINES ON TOAST *(for eight)*:

Slice white bread a quarter-inch thick and cut into 8 strips 3 inches by 1½ inches. Toast lightly; make a paste of 5 sardines, boneless and skinless, 1 teaspoon of grated onion, 1 teaspoon of Gulden's mustard, 3 level tablespoons of butter, 1 teaspoon of vinegar and half a teaspoon of salt. Spread the toast lightly with this and lay a whole sardine on each. Squeeze a little lemon juice over all and put under a very hot grill for a few minutes. Serve at once.

HONEYDEW MELONS À LA VENISE *(for twelve)*:

In our crystal-chandeliered, damask-hung, marble-trimmed, hotel room, on the Grand Canal in Venice, we ordered melon for breakfast, and this is the way they served it to us:

Two honeydews are cut in six parts, the seeds carefully removed and the melons put together in their original forms, the centers being first filled with crushed ice. Serve them on a bed of crushed ice on deep glass platters with quartered limes around the edge, the idea being to try to make the melons look like bubbling fountains. This is devilishly hard to accomplish, but gratifyingly pretty if you do.

CANTALOUPE WITH PARMA HAM (*any number*)·

Scoop out the meat of several cantaloupes in quarters with a silver spoon, and serve with thin slivers of Parma smoked ham.

RADISHES, CUCUMBERS, AND GREEN PEPPERS (*for eight*):

On our first trip to the south of France, very hot, and very dusty, and very tired, we stopped at a gay café in Aix en Province for lunch. We started the lunch with this — and the memory lingers on:

Wash and stem a bunch of tender radishes. Peel 2 tender cucumbers, slice them paper-thin, and put them to soak in ice-water. Wash 2 tender green peppers and remove the seeds. Make a good French dressing. Drain the cucumbers on a teacloth. Place them on a shallow oblong dish and slice over them the green peppers in paper-thin slices, and also the radishes. Pour the dressing over them fifteen minutes before serving. Serve with this, French bread and coquilles de beurre, made by scraping ice-cold butter with a curved, dented knife sold especially for this purpose.

MARINATED MUSHROOMS (*for eight*):

Peel, trim, and wash well 1 pound of small mushrooms. Boil them for five minutes in salted water, in which you have put the juice of 1 lemon. In an enamel saucepan boil for five minutes 1 cup of vinegar with half a clove of garlic, 1 bay leaf, a pinch of thyme, 1 teaspoon of salt, some freshly ground pepper, and 2 shallots, cut up. Cool, remove garlic; then add three quarters of a cup of olive oil and a tablespoon of tomato catsup. Drain the mushrooms well and put them in a deep bowl. Pour the dressing over them and let them marinate in it for several hours in the refrigerator. When ready to serve, put them in a shallow dish, sprinkle with chopped chervil, and pour over them the dressing, which you have strained through a fine sieve.

CANNED RED PIMENTOS STUFFED WITH RICE AND PEAS AND HAM (*for twelve*):

Chop 3 slices of cold boiled ham. Grate 1 white onion and put it in a saucepan with 2 tablespoons of butter, cook without browning for a minute, then add the ham and continue to cook, letting the ham brown ever so lightly. Remove from the fire and add 2 cups of flaky boiled rice and 1 cup of freshly cooked peas, a little more butter, salt and pepper to taste, and 1 cup of freshly grated Parmesan cheese. Stir for a minute or so over a low fire, then stuff 12 canned red pimentos with the mixture. Place in a pyrex dish lightly buttered, with a few drops of water, and put in the oven just long enough to heat through. When cool, pour some good French dressing over them, and put in the refrigerator until ready to serve.

CURRIED HARD–BOILED EGGS (*for twelve*):

Hard-boil a dozen eggs. Slice in two lengthwise. Remove yolks and put through a fine sieve. Mix 2 teaspoons of curry powder with 2 tablespoons of tarragon vinegar. Squeeze through muslin cloth and mix with 3 tablespoons of mayonnaise. Add this to the egg-yolks and stir into a paste. Add 1 tablespoon of chopped tarragon leaves and salt and pepper to taste. Fill the centers of the whites with this and stick the eggs together. Lay them in a dish and cover lightly with mayonnaise, which has been thinned with cream and lemon juice.

HONEYDEW MELON WITH POWDERED GINGER (*for eight*):

Having spent the day drinking in the beauty of Oxford, we stopped for the night in a very unprepossessing hotel somewhere on the way to somewhere else. To our amazement, the dinner proved to be very good, starting out with melon served like this:

Pick some leaves from the grapevine, wash them well and put them in the refrigerator to cool. Cut a circular piece out of the top of a honeydew melon which has been thoroughly chilled. With a spoon, remove the seeds carefully and fill the melon with pounded ice. Place the melon on a large platter, which has been covered with the grape leaves. (You may have to remove a tiny slice from the bottom so that it will stand up.) Put a sprig of fresh mint in the ice, and place limes cut in quarters around the bottom of the melon. The melon is cut at the table; the ginger, which has been put into a pepper-shaker, is sprinkled by each person lightly over his melon with a few drops of lime.

ALLIGATOR PEARS À LA TAHITI (*any number*):

Crossing the ocean alone (tourist), I was invited to have dinner at the Captain's table. Alligator pears were served halved with the usual French dressing. The man on my right from Tahiti assured me that this was all wrong. The Tahitians eat them this way — I took his word for it — and jotted it down in my little memory book to be tried on dry land. I liked it:

Cut in halves ice-cold alligator pears, remove the pit and brown skin, and pour a little good rum with powdered sugar into the center of each.

STRAWBERRIES WITH POWDERED SUGAR (*any number*):

Place luscious ripe strawberries all around the edge of glass plates, with a little inverted mold of powdered sugar in the center. To do this, fill tiny little thimble-shaped liqueur glasses with powdered sugar. Pack it well in, and place in the refrigerator for an hour or so. Just before serving, turn them upside down in the center of each plate and remove the glasses carefully.

TOMATO JUICE FRAPPÉ:

Open several cans of your favorite tomato juice, and freeze it to the mushy stage in a refrigerator compartment, or, better still, in a real freezer. Serve in glasses with a slice of lemon sticking out of the middle.

BAKED SPICED ONIONS (*for twelve*):

Peel and wash 2 dozen onions and parboil them. Drain well and sauté in a frying pan with a little butter and a teaspoon of sugar until glazed. Stick 2 whole cloves in each one and arrange them neatly in a small oblong pyrex dish. Make a very thin cream sauce with a teaspoon of butter and a teaspoon of flour and a cup of thin cream; salt and pepper. Add 2 tablespoons of thick cream and pour over the onions. Bake fifteen minutes. Serve hot.

SMOKED SALMON ON TOAST WITH OLIVE OIL AND COARSE BLACK PEPPER (*for eight*):

Having once crossed the ocean with a smoked salmon, bought for a million dollars at Selfridge's in London as a coming-back-from-Europe present for friends in America, I decided definitely that I hated smoked salmon. I was recently confronted with it, however, at a very exclusive small dinner where there was nothing to do but at least pretend to eat it. To my astonishment, the first bite won me over, and I am now a smoked-salmon addict. Just the same I'm never going to travel with one again. By the way, in buying smoked salmon, choose the pale pink variety, if possible.

Toast 8 slices of white bread from which the crust has been removed. Cover the toast with thinly sliced smoked salmon which is good and cold and serve at once. Pass a pepper-grinder and a cruet of olive oil. A little olive oil is first poured over the salmon and then a sprinkle of freshly ground black pepper.

CAVIAR WITH TOAST AND TRIMMINGS

Please notice that I don't say caviar *on* toast. It is quite impossible to spread caviar on toast ahead of time and not have the toast limp and tough. The proper way to serve it is in a glass dish in another glass dish completely surrounded by ice. This must be done well ahead of time so that the caviar when served shall be ice-cold. The toast, on the other hand, is brought in piping hot and crisp, lightly buttered or not, as you prefer. The caviar is heaped on the toast by the guest himself, and a tray containing quartered lemons, chopped onion, the chopped whites of hard-boiled eggs, and the powdered yolks, is passed immediately. The result being ice-cold caviar on hot toast with or without trimmings, as each guest desires.

II. SOUPS, THIN AND THICK

Soup (to quote Grimod de la Reynière) is to a dinner what an overture is to an opera. It is not only the commencement of the feast, but should give an idea of what is to follow. So, if we want our guests to anticipate a delectable dinner, we should start with a delectable soup, bearing in mind, of course, that if the soup is to be followed by a rich fish or meat or both, the soup should be light. If, on the other hand, the rest of the dinner is to be light, a hearty soup may be indulged in. The very most important thing of all, however, is to be sure that the soup is served scalding hot if meant to be hot — and ice-cold if it is to be cold.

THIN SOUPS

CONSOMMÉ (*for twelve*):

Wash 1 chicken carefully, put it into a large soup pot, add 2½ pounds of shin of beef, and cover well with 6 quarts of cold water. Let stand for a half-hour, then put on the fire and bring slowly to a boil. Remove the scum, add half a glass of cold water, and bring to a boil again. Repeat this process twice. Simmer very slowly for an hour, then add 2 large carrots, 2 white onions, 2 leeks, parsley, thyme, 1 clove of garlic, 1 laurel leaf, 2 cloves, salt and pepper, and simmer for seven hours. Strain through a fine sieve and then through wet cheesecloth. When cold, carefully remove the grease. When ready to serve, heat to boiling point and serve in soup plates. A few cubes of alligator pear added to each plate are a happy elaboration.

BEEF STOCK (*for twelve*):

Clean one fourth of a pound of beef liver and 2 chicken livers; peel and wash 5 carrots, 2 small white turnips; 6 pea pods dried brown in oven, 1 pepper, 4 leeks (white part), 1 small parsnip in which stick 2 cloves, and 1 stalk of celery. Make a bouquet of the celery, parsnip, a pinch of thyme, the leeks, 1 small clove of garlic, and one fourth of a laurel leaf. Put 4 pounds of shin of beef (bones well cracked) into a big enamel soup pot. Salt and pepper and cover with 4 quarts of cold water. Soak for a half-hour, then put on the fire and bring slowly to a boil. Skim carefully, add the green pepper and the bouquet, the carrots, the browned pea pods, the turnips, and a teaspoon of caramel, which is made by browning a tablespoon of sugar in the bottom of a pan, adding a small cup of bouillon to it, and then boiling until the caramel is melted.

Simmer the stock for three hours. Then add the beef and chicken livers and simmer for another two hours. Pass through linen and remove the grease when cold

CHICKEN BROTH (*for eight*):

Wash a 4- or 5-pound fowl, cut up, then put it to soak with a half-pound of ham for an hour in 3 quarts of cold water. Put on the fire and bring slowly to a boil. Skim and add 2 large carrots, 2 leeks, 2 stalks of celery, some parsley, salt and pepper. Boil slowly for three hours. Strain, cool, and remove fat.

VEAL BROTH, TAPIOCA (*for eight*):

Put a knuckle of veal and 1 pound of solid veal in 3 quarts of cold water. Let stand for a half-hour. Bring slowly to a boil. Skim carefully, add salt and pepper, 4 carrots, 2 onions, and 1 white turnip. Simmer for three hours or more. Strain and remove fat. A few minutes before ready to serve, bring to a boil, and add gradually 2 tablespoons of minute tapioca and cook until tapioca is transparent.

MADRILÈNE (*for twelve*):

Peel and wash 2 carrots, 1 small white turnip, 1 small parsnip, in which stick 2 cloves and 1 stalk of celery. Put a knuckle of veal to soak in 5 quarts of cold water for a half-hour. Add 1 large can of tomatoes, 1 clove of garlic, the soup greens, 1 laurel leaf, some parsley, 2 teaspoons of rock salt and pepper, and bring slowly to a simmer. Simmer for five to six hours, being careful to skim when necessary. Strain carefully through fine wet cheesecloth, cool and remove grease. Color to pale red with the juice from a small can of beets. Season to taste. This may be served ice-cold in bouillon cups, with a thin slice of lemon, or hot with a little chopped parsley, or tiny cubes of preserved ginger, or cubes of alligator pear may be added.

DIET VEGETABLE SOUP (*for eight*):

Having been put on a diet, where practically everything edible was denied, I evolved this soup. It is really not bad, and has the advantage that it may make you bright-eyed, pink-cheeked, and beautifully thin.

Make it a practice to save the water from any vegetables

you may cook the day before you expect to make vegetable soup. Use this vegetable water instead of plain water.

Peel, wash, and cut up very fine 2 carrots, 1 white turnip, a handful of green peas, a handful of string beans, a handful of lima beans, 2 onions, 1 heart of celery, 2 peeled and seeded tomatoes, the heart of 1 leek, 2 small white potatoes, and some parsley. Cover with the vegetable water and add some Vegall salt — which is a salt made from vegetables that is being recommended by diet specialists at the moment. Boil the vegetables for about an hour, or until they are quite tender. Add 1 level teaspoon of Savita, which is a vegetable extract and which gives the soup a little color. If carefully made, this soup is delicious, light, and very good for you.

BEEF BROTH WITH CABBAGE TOASTS AND CHEESE
(*for twelve*):

This soup I had while visiting the daughter of a very, very famous French painter, living in Giverney, France.

Shred the tender part of a small half-pound green cabbage very fine. Boil some water. Add the washed shredded cabbage, a pinch of soda and some salt. Cook for five minutes. Drain thoroughly. The cabbage should be tender and green, not soft and mushy and brown.

Slice several rolls in thin slices and toast to a delicate brown. Butter them well, pile a little cabbage neatly on each, and sprinkle liberally with 1 cup of grated Parmesan cheese. Put a tiny piece of butter on top of each one, and set under the grill in a hot oven until cheese and butter have melted together to a light brown. In the meantime, heat 2 quarts of beef broth to the boiling point. Pour into a hot tureen and sprinkle with a little parsley. Place the tureen in front of the hostess and bring the cabbage toasts piping hot on a separate platter. The hostess then places two or three of the cabbage toasts in each soup plate as she serves them, and pours over them a ladleful of the hot broth.

THIN PEA SOUP (for eight):

Peel 6 onions and slice them. Cook in a tablespoon of butter and a little water until quite tender. Shell 4 pounds of green peas and put them into a small quantity of boiling water in which is a tiny pinch of soda. Boil until tender, then drain off and keep the juice. Keep out about 4 table-spoons of the peas and keep them warm in the juice. Add the cooked onions and pass the rest through a sieve. Make a thin cream sauce by melting 4 teaspoons of butter; add 4 teaspoons of flour and 1 pint of thin hot cream. Add the purée of peas and onions and keep warm in double boiler. When ready to serve, salt and pepper to taste and add the juice and the whole peas.

SPRING SOUP (for eight):

Wash thoroughly half a bunch of asparagus and cut the tender parts only into tiny pieces the size of a pea. Shell a pound of tender baby peas. Wash and cut up fine 2 dozen wee spring onions and 3 baby carrots. Put 3 tablespoons of butter into a saucepan and cook the vegetables in it over a very slow fire until they begin to get tender. Be careful not to brown them. Now add 2 quarts of good broth and sim-mer gently for about an hour.

COLD TOMATO AND CUCUMBER SOUP (for eight):

Wash and peel 8 raw beets. Run them through the meat-grinder, carefully saving all the juice which runs out. Place the beets in a bowl and pour a little warm water over them. Let them stand a few minutes, then strain through a fine sieve. This should give you about 2 cups of good beet juice. Simmer in an enamel pan for a half-hour 2 large cans of tomatoes with 1 onion chopped fine and a little celery and 2 cups of cold water. Strain the juice off, but don't push any of the pulp through. Put this in the refrigerator.

Peel 2 tender medium-sized cucumbers, being careful to remove enough skin, so that none of the green is left. Remove seeds if at all tough. Cut in small dice and put to soak until crisp in ice-water — no salt. Mix some French dressing, using white vinegar or lemon juice. Mix beet juice with tomato juice, and add enough French dressing to flavor well. Season to taste with salt and pepper. Put a lump of ice into this just before serving and beat with an eggbeater until the oil is well incorporated. Serve at once in cold soup plates — preferably clear glass; and just before sending to the table, add a tablespoon of the diced cucumbers and a few small bits of ice to each plate.

THICK SOUPS

PEA SOUP WITH WHIPPED CREAM AND CROUTONS (for twelve):

Peel and cut fine 4 or 5 white potatoes and 6 white onions. Place a large piece of butter in an enamel pan; add the potatoes and onions and a little boiling water and cook until quite soft. Cook 3 pounds of fresh peas separately in not too much water, and be careful that they remain green. A small pinch of soda is, of course, the trick. When the peas are tender, pour off the juice, but don't throw it away — you will need it later. Add the peas to the potatoes and put all of this through a fine sieve. Place in a double boiler and keep hot on the back of the stove. When ready to serve, add 1 pint of thin cream and as much of the juice from the peas as will make the soup of the right consistency; and salt and pepper to taste. Serve piping hot in hot soup plates with a tablespoon of whipped cream, a few tiny croutons, and a pinch of chopped parsley.

A variation of this soup is made by serving buttered toasted crumbs instead of the croutons; in which case the crumbs are passed separately in a bowl.

CREAM OF SOY BEAN TAPIOCA SOUP (for twelve):

Wash 2 pounds of soy beans thoroughly and throw out any black ones. (Soy beans may be bought in health food shops.) Soak overnight. Put them to boil in the water in which they have soaked, until they are perfectly tender (about four hours), adding more hot water, if necessary. When cooked, allow them to boil almost dry, and at this point, add a half-pound of sweet butter, a half-cup of water, three fourths of a cup of white wine, and salt and pepper. Let them simmer for twenty minutes and then mash through a sieve. When this is done, put the purée through a very fine sieve. In the meantime, cook 3 tablespoons of Pearl tapioca in 1½ quarts of strong chicken broth, until transparent. (This takes about an hour.) Then add the purée to the broth. When ready to serve, put the yolks of 3 eggs into the bottom of a soup tureen and beat them well with a fork. Add 1 cup of cream, then pour in very slowly, beating all the time, the very hot broth purée. Mix well, complete the seasoning to taste. Serve at once.

CREAM OF TAPIOCA VEAL BROTH (for eight):

Heat 2 quarts of strong veal broth to boiling point, and then slowly add 4 tablespoons of minute tapioca, stirring all the time. Continue boiling until the tapioca is cooked and the broth is thick. Put 3 egg-yolks in the bottom of the soup tureen. Beat well with fork and add 1 cup of thick cream. Pour gradually onto this the boiling broth, stirring furiously the while. Continue to stir for a minute, then serve at once, garnished with a little parsley chopped fine.

MINESTRONE (*for eight*):

Soak 1 cup of dried beans overnight. Then cook them in a quart of water. Peel 1 large white onion and slice it thin. Brown it carefully in bacon fat. Add one eighth of a pound of lean salt pork, cut in tiny squares. Put in 3 large tomatoes, 3 carrots cut fine, one half of a small cabbage cut not too fine, 1 white turnip peeled and cut fine, 1 summer squash peeled and sliced fine (the seeds removed, of course), and then add to all this the beans and their water, a pinch of thyme, 1 laurel leaf, salt and pepper, and 2 cups of hot water. Cook for at least an hour, adding more hot water, if necessary. Serve with Italian breadsticks and grated Parmesan cheese.

WATERCRESS AND POTATO SOUP (*for eight*):

Peel and wash 3 pounds of white potatoes, cut them up fine, boil 2 quarts of water, add salt and potatoes, and cook until soft. In the meantime, wash 2 bunches of watercress, carefully cutting off the thick stems. Chop and add to the potatoes and one eighth of a pound of butter. Cook for ten minutes and put through a sieve. Put the yolks of 2 eggs in the bottom of the soup tureen, beat well with a fork, add 1 cup of cream, and pour slowly into this the hot potato and cress soup. Season to taste, add one eighth of a pound of butter, stir, and send to the table at once.

VICHISOISE MEADOWBROOK (*for eight*):

Ask a hundred people what Vichisoise is made of and ninety-nine of them will say, 'Oh, yes, that wonderful soup made of carrots and potatoes and cream,' and ninety-nine out of a hundred of them will tell you that they have the original recipe for it tucked away somewhere. Well, I don't know who invented it, but I do know that I am positive it should not have carrots unless possibly you count the one which should have been in the chicken broth in its making.

Cut all the green part off 6 hearts of leeks and split them down the center. Wash thoroughly to remove all the sand. Peel 2 white onions. Chop the leeks and onions very fine. Melt one fourth of a pound of sweet butter in an enamel pan and cook the onions and leeks very, very slowly in the butter, adding a few spoonfuls of water if necessary to keep them from browning. Add 2 quarts of chicken consommé and 1 pound of white potatoes, which have been peeled and cut up very fine. Add salt and pepper and cook until the potatoes are thoroughly done. Put through a very fine sieve. Add another quarter-pound of sweet butter and stir until melted. When ready to serve, add 1 pint of cream and heat in a double boiler. Never let it boil, once the cream has been added.

This soup is equally good served cold; but in this case, use fewer potatoes.

BLACK BEAN SOUP (*for twelve*):

Wash 1 pint of black beans. Soak overnight in cold water. Cook in water until tender and drain through a colander. Add 4 quarts of beef stock, a half-teaspoon of cloves, 1 teaspoon of nutmeg, and 1 tablespoon of catsup, and boil for half an hour. Then add 1 glass of sherry.

Put through a fine sieve. Make a brown roux of 2 table-spoons of flour and 2 tablespoons of butter and pour the soup into it. Boil for ten minutes more. In the meantime, hard-boil 2 eggs and slice them. Slice 1 lemon very fine. Season the soup to taste with salt and pepper, put eggs and lemon in soup tureen and pour hot soup over them. Serve at once.

PUMPKIN SOUP (*for twelve*):

Peel 6 pounds of yellow pumpkin, remove seeds, cut up fine, and put into a saucepan with 4 ounces of butter. Add a pinch of salt, 2 ounces of granulated sugar, and 2 tumblers of water. Boil until soft and put through a fine sieve. Add 6 glasses of rich boiled milk. Prepare some tiny fried croutons. Put the yolks of 4 eggs in the bottom of a soup tureen, beat well, and pour over them, gradually, the hot pumpkin soup. Season to taste, sprinkle with parsley, add the croutons, and place in front of the hostess to be served at once.

OYSTER STEW (*for eight*):

This soup was the specialty of a colored chef on the private car 'The Bright Star,' who taught a very famous banker how to make it, who taught my pretty mother how to make it, who taught me how to make it, at the age of twelve, so that she wouldn't have to make it herself:

Make a cream sauce by melting 2 tablespoons of butter, add 2 heaping tablespoons of flour, stir well, and gradually pour in 2 cups of scalded milk. Keep warm in a double boiler. Peel 4 small carrots, 2 turnips, and 4 small white onions, and scrape 4 hearts of celery. Wash them carefully and then cut them up very, very fine. Chop some parsley. Take 2 more tablespoons of butter and place them in a frying-pan, then add the chopped vegetables and fry to a golden brown, being very careful not to burn them. Next put 2 dozen oysters and their juice into an enamel saucepan with 2 more tablespoons of butter, salt lightly and add freshly ground pepper. Heat 1 pint of cream.

When ready to serve, put the oysters on the fire and heat them until they curl at the edges. Now add the chopped vegetables to the cream sauce, then the hot cream to the sauce, and, last of all, the oysters and a little of their juice. Put at once into a soup tureen, sprinkle with a little parsley chopped fine and a dash of paprika.

CREAM OF CHICKEN SOUP (*for eight*):

Order a 6-pound fowl cut up as for frying. Wipe the pieces with a wet cloth and put into a pot with 3 quarts of cold water, 3 carrots peeled and cut up, 2 white leeks, 1 onion, several branches of celery and some parsley. Cook until the meat is tender, then remove the breasts, put them into a bowl and cover them with part of the bouillon. Continue to cook until there are only 3 cups of broth left. Strain and remove any grease. At this time, heat the breasts in their liquid, remove skin and bones and run the meat through a grinder. Heat a cup of rich milk and add the ground chicken to it. Force the whole thing with a wooden mallet through a fine sieve. Then add 3 cups of concentrated broth and 1 cup of warm cream. Beat the yolks of 5 eggs and add them gradually to the milk and chicken. Cook in a double boiler until thick, stirring constantly. Salt and pepper to taste, and just before serving, add a cup of old Marsala wine.

POTAGE DE CURÉ (*for twelve*):

It seems that in Brittany there lived a curé, and every Friday night he had this soup for dinner. I was told this by my little Brittany cook — I hope the curé doesn't mind.

Cut up 8 ripe tomatoes, cover with cold water, add the well-washed tops of 2 bunches of celery and 4 leeks. Boil slowly for an hour. In the meantime, peel and shred 5 or 6 big carrots. Wash and cut up fine the white part of 12 leeks, and the white part of 2 bunches of celery, from which you have removed as many strings as possible. Peel and dice 4 ripe tomatoes. When the first tomatoes have cooked an hour, put them through a fine sieve, getting as much of the pulp as possible. Add this liquid to the prepared vegetables and boil for an hour or so, until the vegetables are quite tender. Salt and pepper to taste, and when ready to serve, add a pint of thin cream, which you have heated in a double boiler.

LOBSTER CHOWDER (*for eight*):

Plunge two 2-pound lobsters into boiling salted water and cook twenty minutes. Remove from the water and cool. Then remove all the meat from the body and claws in the usual way, but save the green part and any roe there may be. Throw away the stomach and remove the intestines carefully. Then put the shells into a big enamel pan, crush them as fine as possible with a mallet, and cover with the water in which the lobsters were cooked. Put on the fire and simmer gently until there is only a cup left of the concentrated liquid. Put all the meat of the lobsters through your biggest meat-grinder, and place in the refrigerator for future reference.

Now cream a quarter of a pound of butter and, when soft,

incorporate it with the roe and green part from the lobsters. Also crush to a powder 2 large pilot wafers. Add these to the butter and make a thick paste. Now put 1 or 2 small white onions, left whole, in a pan with a quart of milk. Heat to boiling point. Place the mixture of butter, crackers, and lobster roe in an enamel double boiler, and add gradually the hot milk; then add the concentrated lobster water, and continue to cook for fifteen minutes. Then fish out the onions and add the lobster meat. Heat well until scalding hot, then add a cup of cream, which has been heated separately, and salt and pepper to taste. (Use freshly ground black pepper.) Add a dash of paprika, and serve in a soup tureen at once. Pass heated pilot wafers first, each person putting one in the bottom of his or her soup plate; then pass the soup tureen with a ladle in it, each person helping himself.

MARIE'S POTATO SOUP (*for eight*):

Peel and slice very thin 8 medium-sized yellow onions and cook them in 4 tablespoons of butter slowly, until they are a delicate brown. This takes almost an hour. Don't try to fry the onions; the result is not the same. When they are cooked, add 8 medium-sized ripe tomatoes, sliced but not peeled, a good pinch of dried chervil, salt and pepper, and 2 teaspoons of sugar. Simmer gently twenty minutes, then add 8 medium-sized potatoes cut up fine, and 6 cups of boiling water. Continue simmering until the potatoes are quite cooked — about one hour. Put the whole through a fine sieve. Taste, and add more salt and pepper and sugar if necessary, heat to scalding point and stir in a cup of cream. Serve in a soup tureen.

SALMON AND SHRIMP SOUP (*for eight*):

Wash 1 pound of fresh shrimps in cold water, plunge them into salted water, and cook ten minutes. Remove shells and intestines, which run from head to tail along the back of shrimps. Be sure they are perfectly clean. Reserve 6 of them and put the rest through your medium grinder.

Now open a small can of good salmon, pour off the oil, and put it through the grinder too, keeping it separate, however, from the shrimps. Put 3 tablespoons of butter in an enamel double boiler and add to it 2 small white onions chopped fine, some freshly ground pepper, and the ground shrimps. Cook a few minutes, then add gradually 1 quart of milk, stirring constantly. Cook for half an hour. Now, in another double boiler, heat 2 cups of thin cream and, when scalded, add 3 tablespoons of the salmon and remove from the fire at once. Slice the 6 whole shrimps lengthwise in three parts and put them into a small enamel pan with a quarter of a cup of dry sherry and heat slightly. Now add the salmon in cream to the shrimp soup, season to taste with salt, pepper, and a dash of cayenne, and, last of all, stir in the sherry and shrimps. Serve at once in a soup tureen with toasted pilot wafers.

POTAGE MAIGRE CANADIEN (*for eight*):

Peel and cut into small squares 1 small summer squash. Shred some Boston lettuce until you have 3 cups of it. Peel and cut in small pieces 2 tender small cucumbers, from which you have removed the seeds. Peel and chop fine 3 small white onions. Shell enough peas to make 1½ cups of small tender peas and 2 cups of older ones, sorting them as you shell them. Now put almost a quarter of a pound of butter into a large enamel pot and add the shredded lettuce, some salt, some freshly ground black pepper, and a dash of cayenne. Then add the cucumbers and squash, the onions, 2 leaves of fresh mint, a sprig of parsley, and, last of all, the tender peas. Cover and simmer for one hour.

In the meantime, heat 6 cups of water and, when boiling, add the older peas and a tiny pinch of soda. When half-cooked, add a little salt. When tender, rub them through a fine sieve, saving carefully the water in which they were cooked. Now add the pulp and water to the other vegetables and continue to simmer for another hour. When ready to serve, stir in a small lump of butter.

NEW ENGLAND FISH CHOWDER (*for eight*):

Cut 2 ounces of salt pork into little squares. Peel 8 onions and slice very fine. Place a little butter in a pan and try out the salt pork until tender, but not very brown. Peel and parboil about 8 potatoes. Slice them and put a layer of them in the bottom of an enamel pot which has had the bottom buttered. Then add a little of the salt pork and some of the onions and a layer of fresh haddock or cod, cut in half-inch slices, the skin and bones removed. Sprinkle with salt and freshly ground black pepper, then repeat the process using in all about 4 pounds of fish and all the potatoes. Pour over this 2½ cups of cold water. Cover closely, bring to a boil, then simmer gently three quarters of an hour or until the fish is quite opaque and tender. Now heat in a double boiler a pint of thin cream. Pour over the fish, taste, and add more salt if necessary. Tie a napkin around the pot and serve it in soup plates accompanied by toasted pilot wafers.

BOULA SOUP (*for eight*):

One afternoon when I was very sleepy, a very talkative man in a very checked suit — having been told that I was a food expert and that he must talk to me — described this soup in detail. I am dreadfully afraid I wasn't paying attention, for I let two years go by without trying it. At the same exclusive meal where I learned to like smoked salmon, the salmon was followed by Boula. As I finished the last drop of it, I suddenly had a vision of the man in the checked suit — one afternoon when I was very sleepy. From now on I am going to keep wide awake.

Shell 3 pounds of green peas and cook them until tender in boiling water with a tiny pinch of salt and soda. Drain and put through a fine sieve. Add a quart of green turtle soup, which can be purchased, if you have the where-withal, at food specialty shops. Heat to boiling point, then add half a cup of good sherry. Season to taste with salt and freshly ground pepper. Place the soup in 8 little earthenware individual casseroles, being sure that each one gets a piece or two of the turtle meat. Whip plenty of cream and put it on each casserole so as completely to cover the soup. Work quickly so that the soup doesn't cool off and the cream doesn't entirely melt. Place these casseroles under a hot broiler and watch carefully. As soon as the cream browns all over, send to the table at once.

III. FISH

Probably the most important thing about fish is to have it fresh. If you don't happen to know how to tell whether it is fresh or not, here are a few helpful clues. The eyes of fish should be clear, the gills should be red, the scales moist and not easily removed, and the flesh should be firm to the touch, showing no indentations when pressed with the finger. Laying fish in a big pan of cold water is another good way of judging condition. It should sink to the bottom; if it does not, it probably is decomposing.

Canned fish should be emptied out of the can as soon as opened. Lobsters should be alive when plunged into boiling water or before being split in two for boiling alive. A small heavy lobster is to be preferred to a large light one. The male is best for boiling, but if you are making a sauce with the lobster, the female is best on account of the coral. Clams should close up tight when removed from water. If they don't, they are not fresh. Oysters should do the same, or move when poked with a fork when opened, and the juice in them should be clear.

In boiling fish, always boil it in a court bouillon. This will add tremendously to its flavor and be very little more work. A simple court bouillon consists of enough water completely to cover the fish, 1 teaspoon of salt, 2 carrots,

3 onions sliced, some parsley, a bay leaf, a dozen whole
peppers, a tablespoon of vinegar — and sometimes white
wine. If wine is used, an enamel pan is preferable. The
fish should be put in when the water is hot, but not boiling.
It should then be allowed to come just to a boil, skimmed,
and put on the back of the stove barely to simmer until
done, allowing from ten to fifteen minutes to each pound
of fish.

If you are going to serve a boiled fish cold, it should be
allowed to cool in its own liquid, remembering, however,
to give it a little less time to cook, as it will continue cooking while the water is cooling.

In frying fish, it is better to clarify the butter before
using it.

FISH IN ASPIC WITH WATERCRESS SAUCE (*for twelve*):

Was I impressed when I had this for the first time at a
certain very famous streamline designer's house?

The aspic must be made the day before you plan to serve
this dish. Also the lobsters and shrimps and crab meat
should be ordered the day before, so that the butcher can
deliver them early on the morning of the day you are serving the dish.

Put in the bottom of a soup pot one-eighth of a pound of
chopped onion and a small bunch of soup greens consisting
of parsley, chervil, tarragon, thyme, and bay leaf. Add
1 ½ pounds of the shin of beef and 1 ½ pounds of the knuckle
of veal cut in pieces. Put this on a moderate fire and sear
lightly, wet with a wineglass of cognac and a bottle of dry
white wine and let simmer gently for a while, then add 3
quarts of water and a calf's foot which has been washed and
cracked and brought to a boil in a separate pot of water,

and a half-pound of ham which has also been brought to a boil separately. Before the liquid actually boils, skim very carefully, and when it does boil, cover and put it on the back of the stove on a small light and let simmer for five hours, never having it really boil. The next operation is to strain through a fine sieve and let it get perfectly cold so that the fat may be removed. Now pound 2 chicken giblets and 1½ pounds of lean beef cut in squares. Put into a big pot, then pour in the stock, previously strained through cheesecloth. This done, set it on the fire and stir constantly with a beater until the stock boils. Put it on the back of the stove and let it simmer almost imperceptibly for twenty-five minutes or so. At the end of this time pass through a clean, wet linen napkin. If it is then not clear enough, clear in this manner: For each pint of stock use one egg-white. Beat the whites slightly until broken up or foamy, add a wineglass of sherry or dry white wine. Pour all this into the cool stock, place on the stove again and bring very slowly to a boil, stirring all the time with an egg whip. Then put on the back of the stove to simmer for ten or fifteen minutes. Pour once more through a wet piece of linen. In other words, make a perfectly clear aspic.

The fish part is easier. Order 1 pound of crab meat, 2 lobsters of about 2½ pounds each, and 3 dozen shrimps. The lobsters should be washed and plunged into boiling water containing a tablespoon of salt, then boiled gently twenty minutes. The shrimps are washed and plunged into boiling water and cooked for twelve minutes. The crab meat is purchased already cooked and supposedly picked over by the fish man. It must be carefully picked over again, however, so that no particles of shell or grit will be left. When the shrimps are cooked, wash them in cold water, pull the heads off and remove the shells, and take out the intestines, which are found along the middle of the back.

When the lobsters are cooked, wash them in cold water and let them get cold. Then chop off the claws, split the lobster lengthwise, remove and throw away the stomach and the intestines, which run from the base of the tail to the stomach. Crack the claws and remove the meat. Take out the meat from the body and slice it in thin slices with a silver knife. Have ready to use a bowl of lobster meat, 36 clean shrimps, the crab meat, and the stiffly jellied aspic. Now take 2 molds shaped like a fish. Put the stock on just enough fire to melt it. Put a peppercorn in each eye of the fish mold, and split the shrimps lengthwise with a silver knife. Place them in the bottom of the molds to imitate the scales of the fish and then pack in, alternatingly, the crab meat and the lobster meat and the rest of the shrimps, until the molds are more or less filled. Then taste the aspic and season to taste with salt and pepper. Pour it into the molds until they overflow. Set them in the refrigerator until ready to serve.

The sauce to be served with this fish aspic is just a delicious tart French dressing which has been poured over a bowl of very finely chopped watercress.

SHAD ROE MOUSSE (*for twelve*):

We once went to a grand party at Voisins and had a delectable fish course — and for years after talked about it, and wished we knew what it was made of. Then one glorious day our new and very expensive jolly Scotch cook produced a fish dish, and it proved to be, if not identical, at least a first cousin to that delectably famous fish course at Voisins.

It was unlike any fish mousse we had had in Europe, the

secret being the shad roe which, of course, doesn't exist in France.

Remove the flesh only from 2 pounds of fresh halibut and put the bones, odd bits, and skin into an enamel saucepan with a small lump of butter, onion chopped fine, a little bouquet of parsley, a bay leaf, a tiny pinch of thyme, a few peppercorns, 3 cups of water, and 1 of white wine. Put on the fire to simmer. This liquid is to use later in making the sauce. Put the raw fish through the meat-grinder, add the unbeaten whites of 6 eggs, and mash the whole thing through a very fine sieve. Add some salt and pepper and stir well until it thickens up a bit, then gradually add 1 pint of cream. In the meantime, cook for about twenty minutes 3 pairs of shad roe slowly in a frying pan with plenty of butter. Carefully remove the skin and veins. Mash the roe lightly and add it to the fish paste. Mix well, add another cup of cream, and then season to taste.

Butter 2 medium-sized fish-shaped molds and decorate the bottoms with strips of red pimento. Fill the molds with the mousse, packing it well to get down into all the crevices. Set the molds in the refrigerator and keep there until forty minutes before you will be ready to serve. At that time place the molds in a pan of hot water, cover with a piece of buttered white paper, and set in a moderate oven (about 400 degrees) to cook.

In the meantime, make the foundation for your sauce by putting a half-cup of butter into an enamel pan to melt. Stir in three quarters of a cup of flour and cook a minute or two without browning. Add gradually the strained fish stock, of which there should be about 3 cups. Continue to cook in a double boiler until ready to serve. Then add the yolks of 2 eggs which have been beaten up with three-quarters of a cup of thick cream, stirring continuously and making sure it doesn't cook any more. At the last moment add a little paprika and stir in 1 cup of good sherry and the juice of 1 lemon. Pour around the mousses, which have first been very carefully emptied from their molds onto warm platters. Garnish and serve at once.

SOFT–SHELLED CRABS AMANDINE (*for eight*):

Order 16 small soft-shelled crabs cleaned ready for frying. Blanch and dry well one half a pound of good almonds and cut in slivers with a sharp knife. Clarify 1 cup of butter. Put a small lump of butter into a frying-pan, add the almonds and sauté them until a light brown. Drain and keep warm in the oven. Wash the crabs and dry them well on a cloth. Roll lightly in flour and sauté them in the very hot clarified butter. When done and of a fine color, put them on a hot platter. To the butter in which they were cooked, add the juice of half a lemon. Strain this butter over the crabs and sprinkle with the slivered almonds. Garnish with lemon and parsley and serve at once.

LOBSTER MOUSSE SURPRISE (*for eight*):

Feeling very nifty in my new Agnès hat, I learned to make this complicated dish, believe it or not, on the Rue Saint-Honoré in Paris. It was the eleventh of a series of private lessons with a very delightful French chef — with a very white hat and a ravishing smile. We solemnly concocted it together, and then, instead of sitting down together to eat our concoction as in the previous ten lessons, I announced that I was taking it home for lunch. I have never seen anyone look quite so disappointed. When I came back for the twelfth lesson, I was very sad to find that my smiling chef was replaced by another, equally white-hatted, but not nearly as agreeable, chef.

Remove the skin and bones from 4 pounds of fresh halibut and keep them. Put the flesh through a meat-chopper, add the whites of 12 raw eggs, and put through a very fine sieve. Mix well with a wooden spoon until quite thick, then salt and pepper and gradually add 1 pint of cream. Place this in the refrigerator for future use.

Put the fish skins and bones into a little enamel pan and add 2 carrots cut up fine, a little parsley, thyme, bay leaf, 2 onions, 4 cups of water, and let simmer gently.

Cut up two 3-pound lobsters while still alive. This is done by inserting a sharp knife in their backs between the body and tail shells, severing the spinal cords. Then with a hammer and strong knife chop off the claws and split lengthwise. When this is accomplished, remove the stomachs and intestinal canals. Put a large lump of butter into a large iron frying-pan and pour in 1 cup of olive oil. When it is hot, put in the lobsters and their claws and cook until they turn red all over. Then add 2 onions chopped fine, 2 wineglasses of cognac, 2 of white wine, 2 soupspoons of tomato paste, 2 cups of the liquid from the fish bones and skins, a fresh pinch of thyme, another bay leaf, a sprig of parsley, and a little salt and pepper. Simmer for about eighteen or twenty minutes. In the meantime, peel 2 dozen mushrooms, wash well and slice fine. Put 2 pieces of butter the size of an egg into an enamel pan and add a little lemon juice, a little water and cook the mushrooms in this for three minutes. Drain the juice into the lobsters and save the mushrooms.

When the lobsters are done, carefully pick out all the meat and slice it in fairly large pieces. Take all the shells of the lobsters, pound in a mortar until well crushed, put in the sauce, and continue to simmer while you start the finished sauce. Melt 2 tablespoons of butter, add the same

quantity of flour and then the strained lobster sauce.
Simmer until quite thick, then add the lobster meat and the
mushrooms.   Now butter well a 2-quart nickel mold and
with a spatula knife carefully line the bottom and sides
of the mold with an inch thickness of the halibut paste
which you have removed from the refrigerator. Keep out
enough of the paste to cover the top of the mold with an
inch thickness also. Now carefully fill the center of the
mold with the lobster and enough of the juice to fill the
mold within an inch of the top. Take the rest of the paste
and carefully spread it so as completely to enclose the
lobsters. Now place the mold in a baking-pan of cold
water and put it on the stove to heat. When it boils, place
in a hot oven for twenty-five to thirty minutes to set.
Empty it out carefully onto a hot platter and pour around
it any of the sauce which you may have left over. Garnish
with sprigs of parsley and serve at once.

FILLET OF FLOUNDER (*for eight*):

Have the fish man remove the fillets of 4 flounders, but
take the bones and skins as well. Butter plentifully a
large enamel baking-pan and sprinkle it with salt and
pepper. Chop fine 3 shallots and sprinkle the bottom of
the pan with them. Wash the bones and skins well and
put them on the bottom of the pan. Lay the fillets on them
carefully. Pour over them 6 tablespoons of white Bur-
gundy wine and salt and pepper them lightly. Add 6
tablespoons of water. Be sure that you have a hot oven,
then set the pan on the stove. When the liquid boils, put
the pan into the hot oven and let the fish cook for about
seven or eight minutes.

In the meantime, cook 2 dozen little shrimps by plunging
them into a boiling court bouillon consisting of half a

cup of white wine, 2 cups of water, and the usual chopped onion, carrot, parsley, bay leaf, and pinch of thyme. Cook for ten minutes. Drain and remove heads, shells, and intestines.

Now peel 16 little white mushrooms. Reserve 6 or 8 of them and chop the rest. Put the whole ones and the chopped ones into an enamel pan with 3 tablespoons of butter, the juice of 1½ lemons, some salt and pepper, and a cup of water. Then let simmer for five or six minutes.

For a sauce, melt 2 level tablespoons of butter, add the same quantity of flour and let cook without browning for a minute. Now add enough strained juice from the pan in which the fillets were cooked, and from the mushrooms, to make a fairly thick sauce. Let it simmer while you arrange the fillets carefully on an oblong glass cooking-dish. Place the whole mushrooms on top of the fish and the shrimps around the edge. Add 3 tablespoons of thick cream to the sauce, and more mushroom juice if too thick, salt it if it needs it, and stir in a small lump of butter. Pour this sauce over the fish and place the dish in a hot oven or under the grill to brown. Boil 3 truffles for three minutes in white wine. Slice and decorate the fish with them, also garnish with a sprig of parsley and serve at once.

SKATE WINGS WITH BEURRE NOISETTE AND CAPERS (*for eight*):

Make a court bouillon consisting of water, 1 onion, 1 carrot, chopped fine, a bouquet of parsley, a pinch of thyme, a bay leaf, some peppercorns, a little rock salt, and about a wineglass of vinegar. Let the bouillon cook for half an hour, then plunge in 8 pounds of skate fish which you have washed carefully. Let it boil up once, then put on the back of the stove and cook so slowly that the water will not even ripple. Skim carefully while cooking. In about half an hour it should be done. Take it out of the liquid and gently scrape off all the skin. Keep warm while you make the sauce by melting some butter slowly and letting it simmer until it browns. Salt and pepper it and add a tablespoon of chopped parsley, some lemon juice and vinegar to taste, and three quarters of a cup of capers. Pour over the fish and serve at once, garnished with fried parsley.

CANNED SALMON CURRY (*for twelve*):

Brown lightly 4 tablespoons of chopped onions in 4 tablespoons of butter. Add 1 pound of raw rice and cook a minute or two, stirring well. Moisten with 5 cups of chicken or veal broth (canned will do). Cover and put into a moderate oven for twenty minutes. In the meantime, put 12 fresh eggs to hard-boil gently. Also open 2 large cans of choice salmon. Drain off the juice and put it into a double boiler to heat with 2 small pieces of butter.

Make a béchamel sauce in the following manner: Chop 4 onions and put them in 6 cups of milk to heat with a tiny pinch of thyme, a pinch of mignonette, and a dash of nutmeg. Put on the back of the stove to simmer for ten minutes. Then melt 4 tablespoons of butter and stir into it 4 level tablespoons of flour in which you have mixed 2 good teaspoons or more of curry powder. Cook for a minute or so, then gradually add the hot strained milk and keep on the back of the stove to simmer gently until you are ready for it. When the rice is done, take it out of the oven and stir into it 4 more tablespoons of butter broken in little bits, put it into a plain border mold and place back in the oven for several minutes. Peel and slice the hard-boiled eggs and add them to the creamed curry sauce.

Empty the rice into a round vegetable dish, and pile the hot salmon in the center. Pour the sauce over the rice, garnish with parsley, and serve at once.

SALT COD BÉNÉDICTINE (*for eight*):

Soak 2 pounds of salt cod in cold water for twenty-four hours, changing the water three times. Then boil gently for twenty-five minutes. Drain well and pick it over carefully, throwing out all skin and bones. Peel 4 big potatoes and boil them until well done, then mash with the cod with a wooden masher until well mixed. Little by little add 8 tablespoons of olive oil and 2 cups of milk. Season to taste with salt and white pepper, and then with a spoon fold in 1 cup of thick cream, beaten stiff. Put the mixture carefully in a buttered, flat baking-dish and smooth the top of it. Pour a little melted, clarified butter over the top and put into a hot oven to brown.

SALT COD WITH DRIED BEANS (*for eight*):

Soak 1 pound of white dried beans overnight. Also soak 1 ½ pounds of salt cod for twenty-four hours, changing the water three times. The next morning, boil the beans in salted water to which you have added 2 leeks, 2 carrots, 1 onion, and a bouquet of parsley, a pinch of thyme, and 1 bay leaf. When the beans are done, drain and keep the water. Put the beans where they will keep warm. In the meantime, boil the cod for twenty-five minutes. Drain well and pick it over carefully. Now put 2 tablespoons of butter into a pan and heat in it, without browning them, 1 clove of garlic and 2 onions left whole. Moisten with 2 cups of bean water and salt and pepper to taste. Let simmer awhile. Then add half a cup of the beans and mash through a sieve, first having removed the garlic. Arrange the beans in alternate layers with the drained fish in a baking-dish. Beat into the sauce 2 tablespoons of butter and 3 tablespoons of whipped cream. Taste and, if necessary, add more salt and pepper. Heat again and pour over the beans and fish. Place in the oven until ready to serve. Sprinkle with a little chopped parsley and serve at once.

BOILED DEEP–SEA STRIPED BASS (*for twelve*):

Buy two 5-pound striped bass, wash and clean well. Lay on the rack of your fish boiler and cover entirely with a court bouillon, half water and half dry white wine, 6 little white onions, 3 carrots, peeled and sliced, 2 branches of celery, 1 clove of garlic, 1 sprig of thyme, 1 bay leaf, some parsley, 4 cloves, rock salt, and whole peppers. Put the kettle on a good fire and bring to a boil; skim carefully and put on the back of the stove barely to simmer for three quarters of an hour. Remove as much skin as possible, garnish with little potato balls, boiled, and plenty of crisp green parsley. Serve from damask napkins placed on two silver platters. Serve with the following butter sauce:

Chop very fine 8 shallots, add 3 teaspoons of vinegar, salt and pepper, and put all into an enamel saucepan with 1 pound of sweet butter. Place pan on a very low fire and stir constantly until butter is creamy and almost melted, then pour it into a sauce boat and serve with the bass.

TRUITE SAUMONÉE BRAISÉE (*for twelve*):

Buy 2 salmon trout and have the fish man clean them well. Wipe clean with a wet cloth. Wrap slices of bacon around them, tying it on with flat white tape. Brown several slices of onion and carrots in butter and add to them 2 cups of dry white wine, one quarter of a cup of fine cognac, and a bouquet of parsley, thyme, and bay leaf.

Put the fish in a fish roasting pan and pour this juice in the bottom. Cover the fish with well-buttered papers and put on the lid of the roasting pan to seal hermetically. Set in the oven to cook. Baste frequently, removing and replacing the paper each time. Cook about thirty-five minutes. Place the fish on hot platters and keep in warm place. Reduce the juice and then add, little by little, a half-pound of butter. Pour some of this over the fish. Decorate with lemon and parsley and send to the table with the rest of the sauce in a separate bowl and a dish of little potato balls, plain boiled.

BOILED SALMON, CREAM, EGG, HERB, SAUCE (*for twelve*):

Buy a 6-pound slice of fresh salmon, preferably from the tail end, and place it on a rack in an enamel fish boiler. Cover completely with a warm, not hot, court bouillon made of water, 1 cup of white wine, 1 teaspoon of salt, 2 carrots, some parsley, 1 tablespoon of vinegar, and 3 white onions sliced. Place on a gentle fire and bring slowly to the simmering point and simmer for one hour. Drain carefully, so as not to break the fish, and place on a warm platter. Garnish with tiny boiled potato balls and parsley. Serve with the following sauce:

Chop fine 4 shallots, plenty of chervil, some parsley, and 4 dozen tarragon leaves. Add the grated rind of 2 lemons. Now add 2 teaspoons of tarragon mustard, mix well, and add 2 cups of slightly beaten cream and the beaten yolks of 4 eggs. Put into a double boiler over a very slow fire and add 2 lumps of butter the size of eggs. Stir incessantly and don't let it boil. When thickened, add salt and pepper to taste and the juice of 1 lemon. Serve at once.

BAKED SHAD ROE (*for eight*):

Wash and dry 4 pairs of shad roes. Butter an oblong enamelware baking-dish and sprinkle the bottom of it with 3 white onions and 1 shallot, and a sprig of parsley chopped very fine. Lay the roes on this. Wash and peel a dozen mushrooms and slice them fine. Sauté them lightly in a tablespoon of butter. Add them with their juice to the roes. Salt and pepper the dish and pour 2 cups of dry white wine over all. Dot well with butter. Bring to a boil on top of the stove and then place the dish in the oven and cook for twenty minutes, basting frequently. Remove from oven and drain off the juice. Melt a tablespoon of butter in an enamel saucepan and stir into it 2 teaspoons of flour and the fish juice. Cook a minute or so and pour back over the roes. Sprinkle some very fine bread crumbs over them, dot well with butter, and bake in a hot oven for ten minutes, or until a golden brown. Squeeze some lemon juice over all, and a little very finely chopped parsley. Garnish with slices of lemon and serve at once.

TROUT WITH BACON (*for eight*):

Clean 8 trout. Dip them in milk, season with salt and pepper, and roll lightly in flour. Fry them in olive oil till brown on both sides. Split them carefully and remove the backbone, replacing it with a strip of bacon fried crisp. Pour a little melted butter mixed with lemon juice over them and serve at once.

TRUITES AUX AMANDES (*for eight*):

Speaking of trout, I once made the mistake of publishing a statement that trout were procurable in April, May, June, July, and August. I had an indignant letter in the next mail from the managers of a certain fish hatchery, who wanted to know on what possible grounds I had made that statement, and to prove to me (it then being September) that trout were procurable the year around, they would take great pleasure in sending me a complimentary case of trout if I would be gracious enough to tell them when to send it. I replied immediately that I was very sorry that I had been misinformed on the subject and would eagerly await the arrival of my trout, October 7, if this was convenient to them. I immediately planned a party for October 7. October 6 I received a letter saying that my trout had been mailed and would arrive on the morning of the seventh. Over a year has passed — I regret to say — and I'm still waiting for the trout to arrive with the morning mail.

Blanch three quarters of a cup of almonds, chopped very fine. Salt and pepper 8 small trout which have been properly cleaned. Roll them lightly in flour. Make an incision in the thickest part of the fillet. Heat plenty of butter in a frying-pan over a moderate fire, and lay the trout carefully in the pan. Brown them well on both sides. Put them on a platter, being careful not to break them, place the platter in the oven to heat, and add the almonds to the butter in the pan, and add a little more melted butter. Cook slowly until the butter and nuts brown slightly. Add the juice of half a lemon, and pour over the fish. Sprinkle with parsley. Serve at once.

SCALLOPS AMANDINE (*for eight*):

Blanch, sliver, and dry three quarters of a cup of shelled almonds. Brown them lightly in butter, but don't salt them. Wash 3 quarts of choice scallops and dry them well on a teacloth. Cut several slices of lean bacon in tiny squares and brown them in a little butter in a large frying-pan. Salt and pepper the scallops and roll them lightly in flour. Add plenty of butter to the bacon in the frying-pan and cook the scallops very quickly, turning them over and over until a light brown. Two or three minutes should be enough. Put them on a hot platter, bacon and all, and pour over them a little browned butter in which you have put a few drops of lemon juice and the almonds. Garnish with quartered lemons and crisp parsley.

LOBSTER AND SALMON PIE (*for eight*):

First make the paste for the pie. Sift 1½ cups of pastry flour with half a teaspoon of salt. Work in with the finger-tips three quarters of a cup of butter, which has been previously worked in cold water to the consistency of putty and squeezed dry in a piece of linen. Moisten the flour and butter with tepid water, kneading lightly and putting the moistened part aside until all is mixed. Roll into a ball, place in a bowl, cover with waxed paper and a saucer, and chill thoroughly five or six hours. In the meantime, pre-pare a court bouillon of water, half a cup of vinegar, 1 onion, 1 carrot, a bay leaf, a pinch of thyme, and some parsley. When boiling, plunge a 2½-pound lively lobster into the water and simmer for twenty minutes. Remove from the fire and cool in the court bouillon. When cold, re-move the meat from the claws and body, saving carefully the lobster coral. Place in the refrigerator. Now make a court bouillon, in an enamel pan, of 1 cup of dry white wine and 2 cups of water, a bouquet of parsley, thyme, and bay leaf, a teaspoon of salt, and some peppercorns. When boil-ing, place in this a 2½-pound piece of fresh salmon, prefer-ably from the middle of the fish, and place on a low flame barely to simmer for forty minutes. Remove from the fire and cool in its juice. Now make the following sauce: Peel and chop fine 1 onion, 1 good-sized shallot, 1 small carrot, a little parsley. Cook for a minute or two without browning in a tablespoon of butter, then add a teaspoon of flour, stir and add a cup of stock from the salmon and the pulp only of 3 tomatoes, a pinch of cayenne, a dash of paprika, freshly ground pepper, salt, and a pinch of nutmeg. Simmer gently.

Now cream 2 tablespoons of butter with the lobster coral and put it through a fine sieve. When the sauce has reduced to about 1¾ cups, strain it through a sieve and stir into it the lobster butter. You are now ready to assemble the pie. Butter a pyrex or earthenware baking-dish suitable for making a deep-dish pie, which will hold about 3 pints of liquid. Lay in the center the salmon from which you have carefully removed skin and bones, and place around this the lobster meat which you have sliced with a silver knife. Pour over all the sauce. Now flour a board and the rolling-pin and take a little piece of the paste. Roll it into a long inch-wide strip, enough to go around the edge of the baking-dish. Paint the outer edge of the dish with a little slightly beaten egg-yolk and press the paste securely around the edge. Paint the strip with more egg. Roll the rest of the paste and cover the pie. Trim the paste so that it hangs over the edge about an inch. Press it carefully to the narrow strip, then, with your fingers dipped in flour, crimp the edges. Work quickly. Brush the top with more egg and make a small hole in the center of the crust. Lay around this small diamond-shaped pieces of paste to form a decoration. Make small incisions around the edge of the pie and place in an oven of about 450 degrees. After ten minutes reduce the heat to 350 degrees and continue to cook slowly for about thirty or forty minutes. Serve at once.

HOT BOILED LOBSTER, BUTTER SAUCE:

There is probably nothing much better in the world than just plain but boiled lobster with melted butter. It retains all its juice if opened and eaten immediately. Male lobsters are considered best for boiling. A small heavy lobster for each person is ideal, but larger ones split in two will do for two people. Be sure they are alive and kicking when you plunge them into the actively boiling court bouillon consisting of water, a tablespoon of salt, a tablespoon of vinegar, 3 sliced onions, 2 carrots, a bouquet garni, and 12 peppercorns. Cover the kettle and keep it boiling for twenty minutes. Remove the lobsters from the water and place them on a chopping-board. Chop off the claws and split the lobsters lengthwise with a sharp, heavy knife. Remove the intestines and stomach. Place the bodies on a hot platter surrounded by the claws and send to the table at once with a nutcracker for each person. Clarify a half-pound of butter and add a few drops of lemon juice, and serve hot with the lobster. Also serve hot popovers with them if possible. The claws are cracked by each person individually and held right side up so that the juice may be drunk from them. Be sure to have a good supply of finger-bowls ready with a bit of rose geranium and lemon in each one, as this is a very messy dish — but oh, so good!

POPOVERS

Sift together 1¼ cups of flour, 1 teaspoon of sugar, and a quarter of a teaspoon of salt. Beat 2 eggs well and add 1 cup of milk. Add gradually to the flour and beat very well. Have ready some well-greased, very hot, iron muffin pans. Fill them half full of the batter and place in a hot oven — 450 degrees for twenty minutes. Reduce the heat then to 350 degrees and bake fifteen to twenty minutes more.

IV. EGGS

THE fundamentals of egg-cooking lie in mastering the art of frying, coddling, hard-boiling, baking, poaching, and scrambling eggs, and making a plain omelet that rolls up neatly and doesn't stick to the pan. All egg recipes are simply elaborations of one of these standards. How many times have you heard someone say, 'I can't even boil an egg'? They are probably being more truthful than they know, so please forgive me if the first seven of these recipes appear to be a little too simple. Of course you know the standard way of testing eggs for freshness is to put them in cold water. If they sink and lie on their sides, they are fresh; if the larger ends come up, they are not.

FRIED EGGS (*any number*):

Melt a tablespoon of butter for each egg in a frying-pan, and when it begins to hiss, slip in the eggs which have been broken one at a time into a saucer. Salt and pepper the whites only. Ladle a little of the butter over the yolks and cook slowly until the whites are set.

POACHED EGGS ON TOAST (*any number*):

Put 3 quarts of boiling water into a frying-pan. Salt it slightly. Break an egg into a saucer and slip it gently into the water. Repeat until the desired number of eggs are in, then remove the pan to a warm place and with a spoon gently ladle the water over the yolks for about three minutes, then with a skimmer or a perforated ladle slip them onto thin pieces of buttered toast.

CODDLED EGGS À LA COQUE (*any number*):

Heat in a deep pan enough water completely to cover the number of eggs to be cooked. Wash the eggs in cold water and when the cooking-water boils, carefully put in the eggs with a spoon. When they are all in, remove from the fire, cover and keep in a warm place for from five to eight minutes. Serve in warmed egg-cups with hot buttered toast cut in half-inch strips.

SCRAMBLED EGGS (*any number*):

If you are married, please don't let another day go by without finding out if by any chance your husband really likes *scrambled* eggs, or if he is still wishing wistfully that they would appear just once *squiggled*. After thirteen years of scrambling eggs with infinite care, my sister just discovered the other day that her husband likes them *squiggled* — which is quite another thing.

For each egg place a teaspoon of butter in a frying-pan. Beat the eggs very well with a fork and add a tablespoon of cream for each. When the butter is hot and melted but not at all browned, add the eggs and stir continuously with a silver spoon over a slow fire until the desired consistency is reached. Above all, do not overcook. They should be creamy and lumpy. When cooked, salt and pepper to taste, put on a warm, not hot, platter, garnish and serve at once.

HARD–BOILED EGGS (*any number*):

Wash the required number of eggs, plunge into boiling water carefully. A good way is to have all the eggs in a sieve and slip the sieve into the water, of which there must be plenty. Turn down the flame and let the eggs simmer for fifteen minutes — no longer. Remove from the fire and plunge into cold water to cool for at least fifteen minutes before peeling.

EGGS ON THE PLATE (*any number*):

Butter individual egg dishes with sweet butter. Break 2 eggs carefully into each dish without breaking the yolks. Salt and pepper the whites only. Set the dishes on a thick cold baking-sheet and put it into the top part of the oven so that they will cook more from the top than from the bottom. They will be done in about ten minutes.

PLAIN OMELET (*for eight*):

The three important rules for making a good plain omelet are: (1) Have a perfectly clean smooth pan; (2) don't try to make too big an omelet in too small a pan; and (3) but not least, be sure that the butter and the eggs used are of the very best quality. The pan should be slightly heated and then rubbed with fine kitchen salt and a coarse towel. Break 12 eggs into a bowl, add salt and pepper and 4 tablespoons of thick cream. Beat with a fork for about one minute. Strain through a sieve to remove the white strings so disagreeable. Melt 4 tablespoons of butter in the frying-pan on a brisk fire and tilt the pan so that the whole surface will be well buttered. In about two minutes the butter should have stopped foaming, and at this moment put in the eggs all at once. In about half a minute the bottom of the omelet will have set. Poke it here and there with a knife and let the liquid part run under, if possible. With a knife fold over and turn out onto a warm platter. Above all, do not overcook. If the omelet is to have a stuffing, it should be added hot just before folding.

POACHED EGGS WITH PATÉ DE FOIE GRAS (*any number*):

Cut stale bread in three-quarter-inch slices. With a sharp knife, trim to 3½-inch squares. Insert the point of a sharp knife a half-inch from the edge, and cut around the edge running down to within three eighths of an inch of the bottom. Then insert the knife horizontally through one side of the slice three eighths of an inch from the bottom. Cut out and remove the center. Melt plenty of butter and dip each box in the butter, then put into the oven to brown. Remove from the oven and put a generous spoonful of purée de foie gras into each hole. Poach as many eggs as you have pieces of toast and lay one carefully on each piece. Salt lightly and serve at once.

FRIED EGGS WITH CAPERS AU BEURRE NOIR (*for eight*):

Fry 8 eggs. Place them carefully on a platter in a warm place while you add a few drops of tarragon vinegar and a small handful of capers to the butter in which they were fried. Pour over the eggs, sprinkle with chopped parsley, and serve at once.

EGGS À LA TRIPE (*for eight*):

Peel and slice 8 little white onions. Cook without browning in 2 big tablespoons of butter. Sprinkle with 1 tablespoon of flour. Cook a minute or two, then add 2 cups of

thick hot cream. Salt and pepper to taste and add a scant
teaspoon of powdered sugar. Add to this 8 hard-boiled
eggs, sliced. Heat in a double boiler and serve at once with
dry toast.

SPANISH EGGS (*for eight*):

Chop 2 onions fine with 1 small clove of garlic. Brown
lightly in 3 tablespoons of olive oil. Peel 3 fine tomatoes,
remove the seeds, and cut in cubes. Also peel and cut up 2
small French or Italian squash and remove the seeds from 3
large green sweet peppers and cut up fine. Add the peppers,
squash, and tomatoes to the onions and olive oil. Season to
taste with salt and pepper. Cook very slowly for three
quarters of an hour and cool slightly. Break 10 eggs into a
bowl. Beat well with a fork, add the vegetables, and put
all into a double boiler containing 2 tablespoons of melted
butter. Cook as you do scrambled eggs. Serve at once.

EGGS IN TOMATOES (*for eight*):

Cut 4 big juicy tomatoes in half and scoop out the centers.
Fry carefully in olive oil without letting them lose shape.
Place them in a buttered baking-dish side by side. Sprinkle
with salt and pepper and finely chopped shallots and parsley. Break an egg into each half tomato. Sprinkle with
buttered crumbs and Parmesan cheese, mixed. Pour several
tablespoons of olive oil over these and bake in the oven
about ten minutes, or until the whites are set.

VEAL KIDNEY OMELET (*for eight*):

Pour a glass of red wine into a pan and add to it a teaspoon of beef extract. Reduce one half by simmering.
Slice up 1 veal kidney fine, being sure not to include any of
the white stringy part. Chop 1 onion fine. Peel, wash, and

slice 6 mushrooms. Prepare 1 teaspoon of chopped parsley. Brown the onion lightly in a tablespoon of butter. Skim the pieces out and put them into the wine. In the same butter, brown 6 little squares of salt pork. Fish them out and throw them away, then brown the mushrooms lightly in the remaining butter. Sprinkle a teaspoon of flour over them and add the wine. Let this simmer gently. Salt and pepper the kidneys well. In a clean frying-pan put a lump of butter, and, when sizzling hot, brown the kidneys, tossing them around. If they cook too long, they will be tough. Pour a teaspoon of cognac over them and light it. Pour the wine sauce over them and let them barely simmer while you make a 10-egg omelet. Just before flopping over the omelet, add a small lump of butter to the kidneys and the parsley and stuff the omelet with the kidneys and their sauce. Serve on a warm platter garnished with parsley.

EGG TIMBALES WITH TOMATO SAUCE (*for eight*):

First make a tomato sauce as follows: Peel 2 pounds of ripe tomatoes, cut in little pieces, put into an enamel saucepan with 2 white onions, sliced, 1 bouquet of parsley, 1 bay leaf, a pinch of thyme, 2 cloves, and 1 cup of dry white wine. Simmer for an hour, then pass through a fine sieve. Now melt 1 heaping tablespoon of butter and add 1 teaspoon of flour. Cook together without browning for several minutes, then add the tomato sauce. Salt and pepper to taste and add 1 teaspoon of beef extract dissolved in a little hot water. Continue to simmer gently until the right consistency. Then remove from the fire and add 1 level tablespoon of butter. Stir until melted.

For the timbales, beat 12 eggs well with 2 teaspoons of salt and a little pepper, add 1 teaspoon of onion juice and 3 cups of cream. Turn into buttered timbale cups. Place these in hot water and bake in a moderate oven until they are firm in the centers. Turn out on a hot platter and then pour tomato sauce over them. Garnish with parsley and serve at once.

EGGS IN SPINACH (*for eight*):

Wash, pick over, and stem 4 pounds of spinach. Cook in boiling salted water. Drain well and press dry. Run through a fine meat-grinder. Melt in an enamel pan one eighth of a pound of butter, add 1 tablespoon of flour, and cook together without browning for a minute or two, then add the spinach, cup of hot milk, and a pinch of granulated sugar. Cook well, stirring all the while. Salt and pepper to taste and add a pinch of nutmeg, if you like it. Remove from the fire and stir in 1 cup of heavy cream in which you have beaten 4 egg-yolks. In the meantime, hard-boil 8 eggs. When ready to serve, heat the spinach carefully in a double boiler, pour it into a dish, and garnish with the eggs which have been peeled and cut in half.

EGGS BAKED IN CREAM WITH BACON (*any number*):

Cook some choice bacon until crisp, but not burnt. Break into little pieces with a fork. Heat and butter individual egg plates and sprinkle well with the bacon. Break 2 eggs carefully into each dish, salt and pepper the whites and pour a little heavy cream around the eggs. Place in a slow oven for about ten minutes or until the whites are set.

SCRAMBLED EGGS WITH SHRIMPS (*for eight*):

Chop fine 1 small carrot, 1 onion, a little parsley, half a bay leaf, and a pinch of thyme. Cook these for three minutes in 3 tablespoons of butter. Add to this 18 shrimps.

Cover and cook for five or six minutes, then add a fourth of a cup of cognac and light it, then add three quarters of a cup of white wine and cook for five minutes longer. Remove the shrimps, peel them, and remove the intestines, which are to be found running along the back. Save out 8 of the shrimps, and run the rest through the fine meat-grinder. Add to these 2 tablespoons of thick cream. Now break 8 eggs into a bowl, beat well with a fork, add the shrimps and cream, place a large lump of butter in the top part of a double boiler, and when it has melted add the eggs and cook slowly, stirring all the while until cooked, adding from time to time, little by little, 2 tablespoons of butter. Just before the eggs are cooked, salt and pepper to taste. Pile in the center of a warm dish and decorate with the whole shrimps. Serve buttered asparagus or green peas with this dish.

STUFFED EGGS, BAKED (*for eight*):

Hard-boil 12 eggs. Make a cream sauce by melting 4 tablespoons of butter. Stir into this 4 level tablespoons of flour. Cook for a minute or two without browning, then add gradually 1 quart of hot thin cream. Cook in a double boiler for at least twenty minutes. Salt and pepper to taste when cooked. In the meantime, cut the eggs in half lengthwise, and carefully remove the yolks. Chop very fine 12 fresh peeled and washed mushrooms, 3 small white onions, and 3 peeled truffles which have been boiled in white wine for three minutes. Cook the onions in 2 tablespoons of butter, add the mushrooms and simmer for fifteen minutes, then add the truffles. Mash the egg-yolks in a bowl; add mushrooms, onions, and truffles. Salt and pepper to taste and add enough cream sauce to bind well. Fill the whites with the mixture. Now add 4 ounces of grated Swiss cheese to the cream sauce and continue cooking until the cheese is melted. Cover the bottom of a baking-dish with some of the sauce. Put two halves of the eggs together and lay them in this bed. Cover with the rest of the sauce, sprinkle with bread crumbs and more grated cheese. Pour a little melted butter over the top and brown in the oven. Serve at once.

CURRIED EGGS IN BROWN RICE (*for eight*):

Hard-boil 8 eggs. Peel and slice 3 white onions. Cook 2 cups of brown rice in plenty of boiling, salted water. Cook the onions without browning in 2 tablespoons of butter. Sprinkle with 1 teaspoon of flour mixed with 1 tablespoon of curry powder and add 2 cups of good chicken stock. Salt and pepper to taste. Cook until the onions are well done, then add 1 cup of hot thick cream and the eggs, which have been peeled and quartered. Heat well, but do not boil. Make a nest of the rice and pour the curry into the center. Serve chutney with this.

SOUFFLÉ OF CHICKEN AND CHEESE (*for eight*):

Chop fine 1 carrot, 1 onion, and 1 stalk of celery, and brown lightly in 2 tablespoons of butter, then add 2 tablespoons of flour. Cook together for five minutes and gradually add 3 cups of hot milk. Continue to cook for several minutes. Remove from the fire and mash through a fine sieve. Now add 1½ cups of finely minced chicken, a teaspoon of onion juice, and salt and pepper. Put back on the stove and heat well, then remove from the fire and add 1 cup of grated Swiss or Parmesan cheese and the yolks of 6 eggs, well beaten. When cold, fold in the whites of 8 eggs beaten very stiff. Turn into a buttered dish and bake in a slow oven for about thirty-five or forty minutes. Serve at once.

CHICKEN LIVER OMELET (*for eight*):

Take 5 or 6 chicken livers. Sauté them in plenty of butter, with 2 shallots chopped fine, until a golden brown. Pour 2 tablespoons of good cognac over them and light it. Remove from the pan and chop. Put back in the pan and add half a cup of boiling water in which has been dissolved 2 teaspoons of beef extract. Salt and pepper to taste and simmer for a few minutes. Make up a 10-egg omelet in the usual way, and, just before folding it over, pour in the chicken livers and their juice.

OMELETTE DE CURÉ (*for eight*):

Brillat-Savarin, in his *Physiology of Taste*, describes how his cousin Madame R——, wishing to consult M. le curé on some charitable subject, called on him at five o'clock and was surprised to find him already at table. Some crayfish soup had just been removed and a salmon trout, an omelet, and a salad were placed before him. Apparently Madame R—— was not invited to partake of the meal, for she later described to Brillat-Savarin how her mouth watered when the curé first put his spoon into the omelet and there ran out a thick juice, that tickled at the same time sight and smell.

That night at dinner, Brillat-Savarin dined with Madame R—— and it seems that throughout the whole meal, she spoke of nothing else but the curé's dinner and above all of his funny omelet.

Later, Brillat-Savarin took the trouble to find out just what the omelet consisted of, the recipe for which you may find on page 291 in the aforementioned book.

One day in France, in a little *auberge* near Paris, we had an omelet which, although it didn't contain the two carp roes as Savarin's recipe did, was so nearly the same and so delicious that I, too, took the trouble to find out how it was made, and here it is.

Open a big can of tuna fish, pour off the juice and put the fish in the top part of a double boiler to heat, breaking it up gently with a fork. In a separate pan melt 2 heaping teaspoons of butter and stir into it 2 heaping teaspoons of flour. Cook a minute or two and add 1½ cups of hot thin cream. Cook until thick, then remove from the fire, add salt and pepper and stir in 4 tablespoons of grated Parmesan cheese. Pour this sauce on the fish, mix well, and keep warm in a double boiler.

In the meantime, prepare 2 tablespoons of chopped tender chives. Clarify 4 tablespoons of butter, add to this the juice of 1 lemon and the grated rind of half a lemon.

Now make the omelet. First put your serving platter to warm. Then break 10 fresh eggs in a bowl, salt and pepper them, add a dash of cold water, and beat with a fork. Put a piece of butter in a good, smooth frying-pan and heat the pan until really hot. Dump the eggs into the pan all at once. Put them on a slow fire and let them set a minute. Then, with a fork, lift up the cooked part so that the raw part runs under. Be sure not to cook too fast. When the eggs are all slightly thickened, spread the tuna over half of the omelet and put the blaze on a little stronger under the omelet to brown it slightly. Then flop the plain half over onto the other half and turn the omelet upside down on the warm platter. Pour the melted butter sauce over it and sprinkle with the chopped chives. Serve at once.

BAKED EGGS CECILIA (*for twelve*):

Hard-boil 12 eggs gently for thirty minutes. Plunge into cold water and remove the shells. Wash and dry thoroughly

2 dozen large mushrooms. Remove and slice the stems and put them to boil slowly in a covered enamel pan in a little water to extract their juice. Make a sauce Mornay in the following manner: Melt 2 tablespoons of butter, add 2 tablespoons of flour, mix. Add 3 cups of hot milk and the juice of the mushrooms' stems. Boil for ten minutes, stirring continually. Add little by little 5 tablespoons of thick cream. Pass through a fine sieve and continue to cook for half an hour or more in a double boiler. Take from the fire and add 2 tablespoons of grated Parmesan cheese and 2 tablespoons of grated Swiss cheese. Stir well and add, little by little, 2 tablespoons of butter, salt and pepper to taste, and a little dash of nutmeg. Butter a small oblong pyrex dish and put into it 12 of the mushrooms stem-side up. Chop the other 12 mushrooms and fry them in a little butter in a hot frying-pan. Cut the eggs in half crosswise and remove the yolks. Squash the yolks up fine. Add the cooked mushrooms, their juice, and enough of the sauce Mornay to make a soft purée. Place a little of this paste in each half of the eggs and stick them together again. Put dabs of butter on whole mushrooms, salt and pepper them, and broil. When done, put a little of the egg paste into each one and carefully stand the eggs which have been stuffed in them. Cover all this with the sauce Mornay and sprinkle with Parmesan cheese. Pour a little melted butter over each egg and put the dish into a hot oven to brown, quickly.

EGGS IN ASPIC (*for twelve*):

Hard-boil 12 eggs. Cut lengthwise and remove the yolks. Press the yolks through a fine sieve. Also press through a fine sieve a medium-sized jar of pâté de foie gras. Mix the yolks and foie gras together, add salt and pepper to taste, and a few drops of cream. Fill the centers of the eggs with this, and put the halves together again, being careful to wipe off any excess stuffing, so that the whites are immaculate. In the meantime, make the following aspic: Heat 2 cans of White Rose Madrilène and add to it one third of a cup of cognac and two thirds of a cup of dry white wine. Soak 3 level tablespoons of gelatine in half a cup of cold water fifteen minutes. Stir into the boiling Madrilène. Strain and cool.

Decorate the bottoms of 12 individual molds with a few leaves of tarragon dipped in the cold jelly. Then pour in enough gelatine to make a half-inch coating. Lay an egg in each one when the gelatine has set, and pour the rest of the gelatine over them to fill the molds. Place on ice to set and thoroughly chill. Turn out on a platter and decorate with shredded lettuce. Serve French bread with these.

TABASCO EGGS (*for eight*):

Heat in a chafing-dish to boiling point half a pint of thick cream, half a cup of milk, half a teaspoon of salt, a pinch of cayenne, some freshly ground pepper, and Tabasco sauce as you like it. Remember, it is very hot. When milk is ready to boil, add 8 very fresh eggs one at a time, but as quickly as possible, and with a small ladle dip the cream over the eggs. When they begin to set, sprinkle them with half a cup of toasted bread crumbs mixed with an equal quantity of grated American cheese. Keep dipping the sauce over the eggs until the eggs are firmly set and the cheese and crumbs are well mixed with the cream. Serve each egg on a square of hot buttered toast with some of the sauce.

SQUIGGLED EGGS (*any number*):

Break 2 eggs for each person into a bowl. Melt plenty of butter in a frying-pan and empty all the eggs in at once.

With a large fork keep stirring the eggs over a low fire breaking the yolks and mixing all well together. When the eggs are almost set, sprinkle with salt and pepper, and serve on a warm platter.

V. FOWL

At the mere mention of guests, chicken is likely to pop up in one's mind as the best company dish — and it probably is. The trouble is, however, that in this country we almost always encounter it either broiled or roasted — which gets to be a bit of a bore. There are almost as many ways of cooking chicken as there are recipes for eggs, so there is no excuse for not being a bit more imaginative.

Next in popularity are the barnyard cousins, the duck, the turkey, and squabs. It is almost impossible to do anything unusual about turkeys except to discover a new stuffing. They are certainly very handsome, roasted to a golden brown, and ideal for a big party. The recipe I have given for a boiled turkey doesn't succeed in making it look at its best, but is very good. The duck has four — or is it five — inseparable affinities — applesauce, oranges, peas, turnips, and olives. I will give a recipe for cooking them with each of these. The squab has one great asset, it is about always procurable and requires no carving — an important item in a small *ménage*. Game birds are more complicated. There is always the question of how long they should hang; they are dreadfully expensive; they are never in market when you want them; somebody is always sending them to you as a present when you have a date for every day in the week; and we Americans know very little about cooking them, anyway. However, I still have to discover anything better than pheasants in cream, the recipe for which I have included in this chapter.

PHEASANTS IN CREAM (*for eight*):

Clean well 2 plump pheasants, cover their breasts with strips of bacon, and tie them up. Brown carefully in an iron cocotte with 3 or 4 tablespoons of butter and 8 shallots. Pour over them a little cognac and light it. Salt and pepper them and add 2 cups of veal or chicken broth and cook in the oven for half an hour, basting frequently with the juice. Then add 1 quart of thick cream and one quarter of a cup of pickled grated horseradish. Let all this cook for another twenty minutes, continuing to baste with the sauce. Season to taste. Place the birds on a platter, serve, and then pour the juice over them.

CANARDS AUX OLIVES (*for eight*):

Clean 2 ducks well, inside and out, with a damp cloth and stuff with a dressing made as follows:

Sauté the livers slightly, in a little butter, to a golden brown, then pour over them some cognac and light it. Let it burn out. Next remove the pits from two 8¼-ounce cans of large ripe olives and chop them very fine. Also chop the livers very fine and add them with their juice to the olives. Then add to this 1 pound of the fillet of raw veal put through the grinder twice and 3 shallots chopped or grated very fine. Salt and pepper to taste, mix lightly together, stuff the ducks, and sew them up.

Place the ducks in a large roasting-pan for which you have an airtight cover, but don't put the cover on. Place the pan in a hot oven and roast until the ducks become a golden brown. In the meantime, peel and slice thin 10 little carrots, an equal quantity of small white onions left whole, and 2 shallots. When the ducks are brown, remove from the pan, pour off all grease, and wash the pan. Now put a fresh lump of butter into the pan and 2 thin slices of salt pork cut in little squares, and then the onions and shallots. Set on the fire and brown the onions carefully. Then add the carrots and a little cheesecloth bag containing 2 cloves of garlic, a small bit of fennel tops, 2 small bay leaves, half a level teaspoon of thyme, and a little parsley. Lay the ducks on this bed, salt and pepper them, sprinkle with a dash of nutmeg, and pour over all 2 cups of hot chicken broth.

Cover and simmer very gently on the back of the stove for one and a half hours, adding more bouillon if necessary. Watch carefully, so that the carrots shall not burn. Half an hour before serving, add several teaspoons of good cognac and a 6-ounce glass of green pitted olives. Put into a moderate oven, without the cover, and continue to cook for another half-hour. Drain off almost all of the juice and remove as much grease as possible from it. Add to it a heaping teaspoon of beef extract and reduce almost to a glaze. Put the ducks on a hot platter, pour the glaze over them, carve them, and put the carrots and olives around the edge. Decorate with parsley and serve at once.

BOILED TURKEY, BUTTER SAUCE (*for eight*):

Choose a hen turkey weighing not more than 10 pounds. Have the butcher draw the sinews from the legs. Clean the bird well and tie securely so it will not fall apart while boiling. Place in a large pot, add 4 carrots peeled and cut up, 3 small white onions, 6 stalks of celery, 2 white leeks, some parsley, a pinch of thyme, half a bay leaf, and a small slice of good salt pork. Cover with warm (not hot) water and let come to a boil slowly. Skim carefully and let simmer about two and a half hours, or until quite tender but not falling apart. Remove the bird carefully to a platter. Strain the juice and remove all the grease, but work quickly, as the turkey shouldn't be out of the juice long enough to dry. Put into a clean pot and pour the broth back on it.

When ready to serve the turkey, put it on the fire to heat in its broth. When it is boiling hot, put the turkey on a large platter, remove as much of the skin as possible, and then decorate with large bunches of parsley. Pour a spoonful or so of broth over it and send it to the table to be carved. Pour the rest of the hot bouillon into cups and serve it to be sipped while eating the turkey. Serve the following sauce with the turkey:

Clarify a half-pound of butter by melting slowly. Skim any foam that rises to the surface, let stand a minute, then pour off the clear part, being careful not to take in any of the milky sediment. Put the clarified butter into a saucepan and add the grated rind of 2 lemons, a dash of nutmeg, salt and pepper, and a pinch of flour. Heat, and, when ready to serve, add 2 tablespoons of chopped chives.

ROAST STUFFED TURKEY (*for eight*):

Have the butcher remove the sinews from the legs of a fine 10- or 12-pound turkey. Clean carefully inside and out and fill with the following stuffing:

Sauté in butter to a golden brown the liver of the turkey and 3 extra chicken livers, which you will have to persuade the butcher to give you. When brown, pour over them a little cognac and light it. Grate 3 cups of white bread and pour a half cup of melted butter over it and dry it in the oven. Chop fine 3 hearts of celery, and prepare a tablespoon of finely chopped parsley. Grate 3 white onions. Wash and peel 2 pounds of mushrooms, chop them fine and sauté in 4 tablespoons of butter until almost dry. Boil 10 truffles in white wine with salt and pepper for twenty minutes, then peel and chop them very fine. Chop the sautéed livers, add to them the mushrooms and their juice. Add 1 pound of Deerfoot sausage meat, and stir well. Then add the bread crumbs, the truffles, the onion, the parsley, the celery, a dash of nutmeg, the grated rind of 2 lemons, a pinch of thyme, salt and pepper to taste, and a tablespoon of cognac or brandy. Stuff the bird with this dressing, sew up and tie for roasting.

Dredge the turkey with salt and pepper and put it into a roasting-pan on a bed of sliced carrots, 1 thin slice of salt pork, 1 little onion, and a very little hot water. Place it in a hot oven for half an hour, then reduce the heat and continue to roast for two and a half to three hours, basting carefully and frequently adding a little water, if necessary, and keeping the bird breast side down, if possible. Fifteen minutes before serving, rub the turkey well all over with butter. When cooked, pour off the gravy and remove as much grease as possible. Serve on a large platter and pass the gravy separately.

CANARDS AUX NAVETS (*for eight*):

Clean 2 fine ducks well, inside and out. Brown them in butter in a big iron pan on top of the stove. When brown, draw off the fat and pour over them a glass of dry white wine and let them simmer gently.

In the meantime, peel 3 dozen tender little white turnips and 1 dozen little white onions and brown them in butter in a big frying-pan on top of the stove; when they begin to brown, sprinkle them with a tablespoon of sugar to caramelize them. Now, have 2 separate iron cocottes, and put into each a good lump of butter. Place a duck in each one, salt and pepper them and smother with the turnips and onions. Add a little bouquet of parsley, half a bay leaf, and 1 carrot to each bird.

Melt 2 good tablespoons of beef extract in half a cup of boiling water and put it into the pan in which the ducks were browned. Bring to a boil and strain half over each bird. Cover tightly and place the casseroles in a medium oven to cook slowly for an hour and a half or more.

When thoroughly cooked, place the ducks on a large hot platter, cover them, and surround them with the turnips and onions. Remove any excess grease from the juice, and then pour the gravy over all. Garnish with parsley and serve at once.

POULET EN CONSOMMÉ (*for eight*):

Clean and tie up 2 good-sized fowls. Put them into a pot and cover with 3 quarts of boiling water and 3 quarts of chicken consommé. Add to this 12 whole carrots, 4 little white turnips, 4 leeks, 8 white onions, and 2 pieces of celery, salt and pepper, and 1 small cabbage, from which the core has been removed. Simmer gently until the chickens are ready to fall apart. Remove them from the juice, take off the skin, put on a hot platter. Sprinkle with rock white table salt. Arrange the vegetables around the chicken and decorate with parsley. Remove all grease from the consommé. It should be served piping hot in cups, at the same time as the chickens.

CHICKEN STEW (*for eight*):

Heat 2 quarts of water and 1 teaspoon of salt to boiling point in a large enamel pan which can be tightly covered.

When boiling, add to this one fourth of a pound of salt pork
cut in tiny squares, 2 small chickens, cut up as for fricassee,
2 carrots peeled and cut in little dice, 6 little white onions
peeled and cut in two, 1 cup of fresh lima beans, 2 cups of
corn cut from the cob (or a large can of corn), a pinch of
cayenne pepper, plenty of freshly ground black pepper, and
a little sprig of parsley. Cover tightly, bring slowly to a
boil, skim well, and continue to cook very slowly for two
hours, being sure to stir frequently. In the meantime, wash
and dice 1 bunch of celery. Parboil it in very little salt
water. Also dice in inch squares 3 or 4 potatoes and peel and
remove pits from 3 or 4 tomatoes and cut them up. When
the chickens have cooked for two hours, add the potatoes
and the tomatoes. A small can of tomatoes may be substituted for the fresh ones. Add a teaspoon of sugar, cover
closely, and continue to simmer for another hour. Ten
minutes before serving, add the parboiled celery. When
ready to serve, add half a pint of thick cream. Heat to
boiling point and serve in a large soup tureen. This is
eaten in soup plates, accompanied by hot crisp toast, or
crisp French bread.

GARBURE OF SQUABS (*for eight*):

Place half a pound of raw ham in a frying-pan. Cover
it with cold water. Bring it to a boil slowly and drain.
Cut it in inch squares and place it in the bottom of a soup
pot. Then add a quarter of a pound of salt pork cut in
tiny squares, also scalded in the above manner. Now add
to the pot the inevitable bouquet garni of thyme, bay leaf,
and parsley, 3 or 4 little white onions, 5 or 6 carrots cut
in quarters, 2 cloves, several stalks of celery cut into 2-inch
lengths, 1½ cups of fresh lima beans, or 1½ cups of white
beans soaked overnight, and last of all, a tender young

cabbage which you have cut in 6 sections and parboiled in salted water, having, of course, removed the tough core. Pour over this enough beef stock to cover. Place on a low fire and simmer very gently two or three hours. Half an hour before serving, place in a roasting-pan 8 little squabs, which have been thoroughly cleaned and dressed. Place a tiny white onion inside each one. Rub them with salt and pepper and soft butter, and roast them for about half an hour, being careful to baste them well. When done, remove the strings or skewers and put them into the soup pot whole. Let them cook two or three minutes to impart their flavor to the garbure. Place them back in their roasting-pan to keep warm, and draw off the juice from the vegetables. Pile the vegetables attractively on a big platter and perch the squabs on top. Garnish the platter with diamond-shaped croutons and serve at once. The broth is served in cups with the garbure.

BAKED CHICKEN CUSTARD (for eight):

Place 2 small roasting chickens, cut up as for fricassee, in a pan, add 2 onions, 2 carrots, 2 pieces of celery, salt and pepper, a lump of butter, and just enough warm water barely to cover. Place on the fire, bring slowly to a boil, skim and simmer gently until very tender and until the meat falls away from the bones. Remove from the fire and cool in the broth.

In the meantime, peel and slice very thin 8 little white onions. Cook them without browning until tender in a tablespoon of butter and a tablespoon of water. When the broth is cool, strain it from the chicken through a piece of muslin. Remove the skin from the chickens and pick it from the bones in as large pieces as possible.

Butter a baking-dish, put the dark meat in the bottom,

then the onions, and then the white meat. Beat the yolks of 7 eggs lightly and beat them into 3 whole eggs. Add 2½ cups of the broth, a cup of cream, taste, and season with more salt and a pinch of cayenne. Strain over the chicken. Place the baking-dish in a pan of hot water sufficient to reach to half its height. Set on the fire and bring to a boil; then place in a moderate oven to set. When firm to the touch, sprinkle the top copiously with buttered toasted bread crumbs. Garnish with parsley and serve at once.

ROAST PHEASANTS BASTED WITH GIN AND JUNIPER BERRIES (*for eight*):

We were discussing one day, with a sculptor in Paris, different ways of cooking pheasants. He told us that it is a well-known fact that pheasants found in parts of the country abounding in juniper berries have a particularly delicate flavor. Living in a part of the country once where there were no juniper berries to be had except in drugstores, he decided to make an experiment. If juniper berries were what flavored gin, why not baste the pheasant with gin? He tried it, and found it especially good. We tried it, and agree.

For eight people you really should have 3 pheasants, but perhaps 2 plump ones could be made to do. To roast, they must be young and tender. I prefer them not too-too high. It seems that if they are young, their feet are gray and their beaks are flexible, but the most infallible way of telling is by the last big feather in their wings. If it is pointed, they are young; if it is rounded, they are old. Anyway, ask the butcher to lard them carefully with a little fat salt pork and truss them nicely. Line the bottom of your roasting-pan with a few strips of bacon, some fresh butter, and salt and pepper. Wipe the birds, inside and out, with a damp cloth. Place 2 or 3 juniper berries inside each bird, salt and pepper them lightly, and rub them over with a little soft butter. Put the roasting-pan in a hot oven (500 degrees) for fifteen minutes, then pour over them a small wineglass of gin, mixed with a little hot water. Baste frequently, reducing the heat to 350 degrees. Cook for another three quarters of an hour, or until nice and brown all over. Serve on a hot platter, carve, and pour the juice, which you have strained, over them. Serve the following sauce with them:

Empty a small glass of red currant jelly into a bowl and break it up well with a silver fork. Add the grated rind of 1 orange, a pinch of salt, and a dash of cayenne. Then add the juice of 2 oranges, in which you have dissolved a table-spoon of good prepared mustard.

POULET BONNE FEMME (*for eight*):

Put half a pound of butter into a large iron frying-pan. When melted, add 4 carrots and 8 white onions, peeled and sliced fine in thin circles. Cook together for ten minutes, stirring the while. Now add 2 chickens cut up as for fricassee and brown lightly all over, turning the pieces over from time to time. Salt and pepper and sprinkle with 2 table-spoons of flour; then add 1 quart of good hot chicken broth and 4 small, peeled, and cut-up tomatoes. Bring slowly to a boil, stirring well, then simmer for twenty or thirty minutes. Add 1 pound of washed, dried, peeled, and quartered mushrooms and 2 teaspoons of chopped parsley. Continue to simmer until the chickens are quite tender, then add 1½ cups of red wine and simmer awhile longer. Season again to taste, and serve, if possible, in a hot earthenware casserole.

BONED SQUAB CHICKEN EN CASSEROLE (*for eight*):

Ask the butcher to bone for you 8 baby milk-fed squab broilers. Wash 2 cups of wild rice in four or five different waters until thoroughly clean; throw away all the rice that floats to the top. Cook the rice in plenty of salted boiling water until tender, but not mushy. Drain well and add 4 hearts of celery washed and chopped fine and 4 white onions peeled and chopped fine, salt and pepper, and 8 tablespoons of melted butter. Mix lightly together and stuff the birds with this and tie and sew them up securely, giving them as much shape as possible.

Melt 4 tablespoons of butter in a large iron cocotte big enough to hold all the birds or an aluminum roasting-pan which has a cover. Add 4 carrots and 4 onions sliced fine and brown them, carefully rolling them over and over. When delicately browned, add 4 teaspoons of Savita or beef extract dissolved in a cup of hot water, salt and pepper and seal hermetically. Cook slowly in the oven for about half an hour. Remove juice and pour over the birds one third of a cup of cognac and light it. Reduce the juice by simmering very slowly on top of the stove. Serve the chickens on a hot platter garnished with watercress which has been tossed in a little olive oil and lemon juice. Pour the reduced juice over the birds and serve at once.

POULET A L'ESPAGNOLE (*for eight*):

Put a tablespoon each of lard and olive oil into a deep iron frying-pan. Add half a pound of lean smoked ham cut in little squares and 2 small chickens cut up as for fricassee. Season with salt and pepper and fry for about a half-hour until golden brown all over. In the meantime, cook 2 pounds of green peas in a quart of veal broth until tender.

Also cook half a pound of well-washed rice in plenty of boiling salted water so that each grain is separate. Chop fine 2 green peppers from which you have removed the seeds, and peel and remove seeds from 3 tomatoes. When the chickens are cooked, remove them and the ham and place in a warm place while you add to the fat in which the chickens were fried 1 big Spanish onion chopped fine with half a clove of garlic, the peppers, the rice, the tomatoes cut up, the peas and the broth in which they were cooked, the ham, and last of all, the chickens. Season with a dash of cognac and salt and pepper. Cover tightly and simmer gently for half an hour. Arrange on a hot platter, decorate with parsley, and you are ready for serving.

CURRY OF CHICKEN (*for eight*):

Eating in a garden, in a little restaurant near Chantilly, we had chicken curry. We had had chicken curry many times before and had always liked it, but this chicken curry was very special. The chef was a retired English army officer who had lived in India, then retired to live in France, and had opened a restaurant. He had learned to make this dish in India, and all the rest of the fifty-seven varieties of accompaniments to the dish which he assured us should be brought in by fifty-seven Indian servants, each one bearing a separate one. He had had to cut the number down to a dozen or so. I in turn have chosen the six I liked the best. The recipe for the curried chicken part of the dish he wouldn't disclose, so I went home and worked it out this way. I hope you like it.

Put 2 small roasting chickens, cut up as for fricassee, into a saucepan with 2 carrots and 2 stalks of celery and a little salt. Add just enough water barely to cover the chicken.

Simmer until tender, keeping the pan carefully covered. Remove from the fire, take out the chicken, and pour the broth into a bowl. Chop 4 onions fine and put them in a frying-pan with half a pound of butter and fry them until a golden brown. Then skim out the onion and fry the pieces of chicken in the same fat for 3 or 4 minutes until slightly browned. Then sprinkle over it from 2 to 4 tablespoons of good curry powder (depending on how much you like curry) and some salt. Then pour over this the chicken broth and simmer for five or ten minutes. Beat the yolks of 4 eggs and add to them a half-pint of cream. Put into a double boiler and add the chicken broth. Cook until thick, stirring all the while. Pile the chicken in a bowl and pour over it the curry sauce. Serve with this dish a big bowl of hot flaky rice and a tray of as many different accessories as you like, such as shredded coconut, pine nuts, pickled onions, spiced currant, chutney, ginger preserves, and poppadums, which come packed in tin boxes with dried leaves between the wafers..

COLD BOILED CHICKEN, YORKSHIRE STYLE (*for eight*):

When I was seven years old, we lived with a charming English family in Yorkshire. My sister and I ate, of course, in the nursery with the other children, and consequently never had the pleasure of eating this delicious dish; but I used to watch the cook making it in the kitchen on Sunday mornings.

Clean two 5-pound roasting chickens, inside and out, carefully. Tie up for roasting; then put them into a big deep pot and barely cover with warm water. Add a dozen peeled whole carrots, 3 stalks of celery, 6 little white onions, and a little parsley. Boil gently until quite tender, but not falling apart. Remove from the fire and allow the chickens to remain in their broth until quite cold.

When cold, remove from the broth, place on a deep platter, and be sure that all the juice is drained out of them. Then carefully remove as much of their skin as you possibly can without spoiling the form of the chicken. Also remove all the strings.

Now make a thick cream sauce in the usual manner. Melt three quarters of a cup of butter and cook in it for three minutes without browning the same amount of flour. Add to this 1 cup of hot strained chicken broth and 4 cups of thin cream in which you have put the thin peel of half a lemon and which you have heated to boiling point. Stir well until perfectly smooth; then continue to cook in a double boiler for at least ten minutes. In the meantime, soak for ten minutes 3 level tablespoons of gelatine in half a cup of cold water. Add to the cooked cream sauce and stir until well dissolved. Salt to taste and add a dash of mace and the juice of half a lemon. When slightly cooled, pour it carefully over the cold chickens little by little with a spoon, until you have completely coated the chickens and the bottom of the platter. Decorate the platter with the whole carrots from the broth and place in the refrigerator to get very cold. Just before serving, fry a dozen slices of lean bacon until crisp and serve them around the chickens and sprinkle a little paprika on the breast of the chickens.

CHICKEN POLENTA (*for eight*):

Clean and prepare 2 small chickens cut up as for fricassee. Procure some good ham fat and chop it in little pieces. Place about a cup of it in a big iron frying-pan. Add 2 small carrots sliced fine, and a little chopped celery. Add the chicken, sprinkle with a pinch of allspice and salt and freshly ground pepper. Cover the pan and cook slowly until the chicken is tender, basting and occasionally turning the chicken over to brown lightly all over. When brown, add two thirds of a glass of red or white wine. When the wine has been absorbed, add 2 tablespoons of tomato paste dissolved in 2 cups of hot water or, better still, 2 cups of not too thick tomato sauce. (*Note:* Recipe for tomato sauce is given below.) Cover and continue to simmer until the chicken is thoroughly cooked.

In the meantime, make the polenta by heating 1 quart of milk to boiling point and adding to it, little by little, three quarters of a cup of yellow corn meal, stirring furiously. Cook in a double boiler for fifteen or twenty minutes, and just before serving, salt to taste. Dish it by spoonfuls around the chicken which has been put on a deep platter. Serve at once.

TOMATO SAUCE:

Peel 2 pounds of ripe tomatoes, cut in little pieces, place in an enamel saucepan with 2 white onions sliced, 1 bouquet of parsley, 1 bay leaf, 1 pinch of thyme, 2 cloves, and 1 cup of dry white wine. Simmer for an hour, then pass through a fine sieve.

Now melt 1 heaping tablespoon of butter and add 1 teaspoon of flour. Cook together without browning for several minutes, then add the tomato sauce. Salt and pepper to taste and add 1 teaspoon of beef extract dissolved in a little hot water. Continue to simmer gently until the right consistency. Then remove from the fire and add 1 level tablespoon of butter. Stir until melted.

CHICKEN EN COCOTTE À LA BONNE À TOUT FAIRE
(for eight):

Clean and tie up as for roasting 2 small tender roasting chickens weighing about 3 pounds each. Place 1 onion chopped fine and a tablespoon of butter in each chicken and sprinkle them inside with salt and pepper. Brown them in butter in an iron frying-pan on top of the stove, until a delicate brown all over. Place a big lump of butter in an earthenware casserole and add to it one quarter of a pound of salt pork cut in tiny squares. Place in the oven and, when the butter has melted and the casserole is hot, add the chickens. Salt and pepper lightly. Cover them with a big piece of buttered paper. Fit the lid of the casserole on tight and place in the oven to cook slowly for half an hour.

In the meantime, brown lightly in butter, in a separate frying-pan, a dozen little white onions and a dozen little peeled carrots. Now remove the chickens from the casserole for an instant and remove the strings. Pour the juice in the cocotte through a fine sieve and replace the birds and the strained juice. Add the browned carrots and onions. Pour over it 3 tablespoons of dry white wine, a wineglass of Madeira wine, and a tablespoon of beef extract dissolved in a little hot water. Taste and season, cover and place back in the oven for another half-hour, to cook slowly.

In the meantime, scoop about 20 little potato balls out of some big potatoes, wash and dry them carefully. Put them into a frying-pan with some hot olive oil and fry to a delicate brown and until they are thoroughly cooked. When ready to serve the chicken, add the potatoes, garnish with parsley, and serve at once. To be carved at table in the casserole.

ROAST CHICKEN, PRUNES AND BACON (*for eight*):

Put into the bottom of a roasting-pan 1 cup of melted butter, 2 or 3 small white onions cut up fine, and 3 small carrots cut in tiny pieces, also 2 slices of lean bacon cut up fine. On this bed place either 2 whole roasting chickens or 8 individual baby squab broilers left whole. Salt and pepper them and place in a moderate oven to roast slowly. Baste very frequently. About fifteen minutes before they are ready to serve, increase the heat so that they will brown well. Serve hot with large prunes prepared in the following manner as a garnish to the dish:

Soak in warm water for two hours extra large prunes, which have been carefully washed. Drain and dry them carefully and remove the pits; wrap each one with a strip of lean bacon. Put into a shallow tin and broil in the oven, turning them constantly until the bacon is crisp.

Another good accompaniment to broiled or roast chicken is a can of halved apricots drained of their juice and slightly sautéed in butter until a golden brown. At this point, sprinkle lightly with granulated sugar and pour over all a few tablespoons of the apricot juice. Simmer for a minute and garnish the platter of chicken with these.

MEXICAN CHICKEN STEW (*for eight*):

Clean and fry in lard to a deep golden brown 2 good-sized roasting chickens cut up for frying. Remove the pieces from the frying-pan and place them in a deep iron cocotte. In the lard in which the chickens were fried, fry 2 large onions whole and 2 pieces of garlic chopped fine, add 1 tablespoon of flour, and, as soon as the flour is browned, add 2 tablespoons of tomato paste or sauce and 1 cup of water. Mix thoroughly, boil, and pour over the chickens. Add 3 or 4 cloves, 1 tablespoon of vinegar, and 1 cup of sherry, salt and pepper to taste and add 1 large green pepper sliced in two. Cover the cocotte and simmer the contents until the chicken is tender. About fifteen minutes before serving, add 1½ dozen pitted olives and a handful of seeded raisins. Serve in the cocotte or in a deep hot platter.

POULET PATRON (*for twelve*):

This dish was the specialty of a little restaurant on the banks of the river Seine, a little way outside of Paris, near Sèvres. It was a charming place until M. Citroën decided to build a factory on the island opposite the restaurant. We had what was almost a tragic experience here once. It being the first of the month and our check from America having been delayed, we found ourselves with practically no money left at all, but with a terrible longing to go on a spree. We robbed the baby's bank and searched through all our pocketbooks, and finally unearthed the large sum of a hundred and fifty-three francs.

My family living in France at the time had a real genius for discovering those marvelous little restaurants full of charm and sawdust — and, oh, so cheap — and had for several weeks been urging us to try their last find. They had not been able to try it themselves, but had seen it while on an excursion on the Seine in a little boat.

We figured it all out and decided that, even if we took a taxi out and back, we could certainly manage it, so off we went. It was after eight, which is very important as you will see. We stepped gaily into a taxi, explained where to go, and the taxi-man knew all about the restaurant. We made a bargain and he promised to take us out and back for eighty francs, *pourboire* included. Everything was just as

the family had said: the place was charming, there were
just enough people — not too many — we were able to
get a table right next to the railing on the balcony. It
all looked very simple. The menu was presented to us. To
our horror, we discovered that the family were all wrong
— the cover charge was ten francs each, and everything in
proportion. There was only one way out. We pretended
we were bored and not hungry. We ordered soup for two
— one order of patty, a salad, and two black coffees. Being good mathematicians, we calculated that even with the
ten per cent tip we should have enough to get home, with
three francs to spare — which we should give to the taxi-
man as an extra *pourboire*. We settled back and leisurely
ate every bit of everything in sight, and had a very roman-
tic and pleasant evening. The time came to go home — we
asked for the check — and I can see Joe's face now. The
bill was twelve francs more than we had calculated. I
glared at it quickly and saw that there had been a mistake.
This had included one order of choufleur which we hadn't
had. The waiter was called and we showed him his mistake — but no, we were the mistaken ones; it didn't say
choufleur — it said chauffeur. That villain of a chauffeur
had had himself a grand meal and charged it to us. I have
always had a secret feeling that the waiter knew that we
couldn't pay that extra twelve francs, and being a kindly
soul, he saved the situation gracefully by informing us
that if we had taken the taxi-man after eight o'clock, we
were not responsible for his dinner, and that if we wished,
he would be glad to inform the taxi-man for us. We accepted his kind offer, but expected fully to be murdered on
the way home — by our taxi-man. To our amazement he
couldn't have been sweeter. We gave him our last three
francs, which he accepted gracefully, rang the bell, waited

the usual interminable time for the Concierge to press the opener, crept in quietly and up the six pitch-black flights of winding stairs — and to bed. Fortunately, the check arrived the next morning.

Take 4 broilers or 4 very young roasting chickens cut up as for frying. Use only the legs, second joints, and breasts. Put the other parts on to boil in cold water with a few soup greens. You will need this stock later.

Other ingredients: 1 pound of fresh mushrooms, 2 or 3 shallots or white onions, 1 pint of cream, 4 egg-yolks, 6 truffles, parsley and chervil, 1 glass of sherry or white wine, 1 liqueur glass of cognac, salt and pepper, olive oil and butter.

Season the pieces of chicken with salt and pepper. Fry them to a golden brown in a little hot olive oil. Take them out of the pan and pour off any oil that may remain. Replace the oil with a good big piece of butter and put the chicken back into the pan. Pour over this a glass of sherry and a liqueur glass of cognac and let it simmer. In a separate frying-pan, place a lump of butter to heat, and brown in it very lightly the onions chopped fine. Add the mushrooms, which have been peeled, washed, dried, and chopped very fine. Pour over this a cup of chicken broth and let simmer ten or fifteen minutes. In the meantime, boil the truffles in white wine for five minutes and chop them also very fine.

The chickens should be tender and thoroughly cooked, but not allowed to cook until the meat falls off the bones. When you think it is done, pour the juice off into an enamel saucepan, add a lump of butter to the chickens, and keep them hot in the oven. Now pour the mushrooms and their juice into the chicken juice and pour into this a pint of cream. Let it simmer a few minutes, but don't boil it.

Season to taste, remove to a corner of the stove, add the
finely chopped parsley and chervil and the truffles. Beat
the egg-yolks in a bowl and thin them with a little cream.
Pour into the hot sauce slowly and stir furiously to thicken
the sauce. Place the chicken — dark meat on the bottom,
white meat on top — in deep meat platters and pour the
sauce over all. Decorate with parsley and serve at once on
hot plates.

TWO PIGEON PIES (*for twelve*):

For these you will need 2 earthenware deep-dish pie casseroles measuring about 9 inches in diameter and 4 inches
deep. First make the puff paste. Put 1 pound of sweet
butter into a bowl and work it with the hands until it is
the consistency of putty, soft and pliable, squeezing it to
extract any water there may be in it. Now put 4 cups or
1 pound of flour in a bowl with 1 teaspoon of salt. With
the finger-tips work into this lightly 2 tablespoons of the
butter and then add gradually 1½ cups of ice-water, still
using your hands to mix it. Knead it lightly until it makes
a smooth ball. Toss onto a lightly floured table and roll
it out to about three eighths of an inch thick in a rectan-
gular shape about 15 by 20 inches. Place the dough horizontally in front of you, shape the butter into a slab about
6 by 12 inches, lay it prependicularly in front of you on
the center of the dough. Fold the flap of dough on the left
to cover the butter, then fold the right-hand flap over to
the left. The butter is now completely covered and out of
sight, and the whole secret of puff paste is to see to it that
the butter never breaks through to the surface. Roll the
paste away from you to make a longer rectangle. Now
give it a turn, which means to turn it so that it is horizontally before you. Now fold the dough so as to form a

square, flopping the left-hand third to the right and the right-hand third to the left. Press lightly with the rolling pin and place in the refrigerator to rest for twenty minutes. Then take it out and be sure to place it before you the way it was before. Roll away from you as before until you have a rectangle three times as long as its width. Be careful not to roll it too thin the first two or three times. Place it horizontally before you and fold from left to right and from right to left as before to form a square. Let it rest again for ten minutes and repeat the process until you have rolled and folded it eight times. Cover with wax paper and put on the ice until ready for use.

Now prepare 12 squabs, which should be plump and white. Wash them inside and out and dry well. Cut off their wings close to the body, also their necks and tails. Put these with the livers and gizzards into a pan and cover them well with cold water, add some celery tops, 2 carrots, and 1 white onion. Simmer gently for several hours to make a good stock.

Put 2 good tablespoons of butter into a big iron frying-pan, and when it has melted, add 3 onions chopped fine; brown the squabs in this to a golden brown, but don't cook too long. Salt and pepper them and put them on a platter to keep warm while you prepare the rest of the ingredients. Put 3 cups of the stock you have made into the frying-pan in which you browned the birds, and let it reduce by simmering until half its original quantity. Wash, peel, and cut in fours 1 pound of mushrooms. Sauté them in a tablespoon of butter on a slow fire for about ten minutes. Salt and pepper them. Chop fine 1 onion, 4 carrots, and 1 bunch of celery, and parboil them in a little of the stock. Hard-boil 6 eggs. If you find that you haven't enough stock, cover the squab bones again with water and make a second extraction from them. Now cut a pound of boiled ham in inch squares and brown them lightly in butter. You are now ready to assemble the pies.

Line the bottom of both pie dishes with raw top of the round steaks cut about half an inch thick. Lay on these 5 squabs and then 1 more in the middle, on top. Tuck here and there around the birds the ham, mushrooms, eggs cut in half, and the other vegetables, and any juice these ingredients may have formed. Strain the rest of the stock into the reduced stock and pour it over the birds. Taste, and add more salt and pepper if necessary. Now here comes the fun. Roll the pastry out once more into a piece about 12 by 24 inches, and three eighths of an inch thick. Cut in equal parts. Beat an egg in a teacup, and with a pastry brush paint the outside rims of both dishes. Then cut a strip of pastry about an inch wide and lay around the edge of each dish, and paint this with egg. Now carefully lift the pastry and lay over the top. With scissors trim so that about an inch hangs over. Press so that it adheres to the under strip. With the scissors cut a little hole in the center of the pies to let the steam escape. When both pies are covered, cut a dozen diamond-shaped pieces of dough from the left-over crust. Paint the tops of the pies with egg, and lay these leaves on the center of the pies, growing out of the center like the petals of a flower. Now fashion two roses out of scraps. Sticking out of the center of each, place 3 pigeon feet which you have carefully saved and skinned (by boiling in water for a second the tough outer skins fall off easily). Stick the roses in the center of the pies and paint with egg.

Put into a rather hot oven for about twenty minutes, then reduce the heat and cook slowly for an hour and a half more, watching it very carefully so as not to burn the crust. Serve hot.

FRIED CHICKEN (*for eight*):

Order 2 young chickens weighing not more than 3 pounds. Have them cut up as for frying. In a big thick frying-pan, fry half a pound of bacon carefully so as not to burn it. Remove the bacon and add a half-pound of butter or more to the bacon fat. Wipe the chicken with a wet cloth, dry, dip in milk, and then roll in flour which has been well seasoned with salt and pepper. Fry the chicken quickly to a golden brown, turning it on all sides, being careful not to knock off the crust. Cover the pan partly with a cover and continue to cook more slowly until a fork inserted shows that the chicken is tender and cooked through — about twenty-five minutes in all. Remove the pieces carefully and place them on white paper to absorb all extra fat.

ROAST STUFFED CAPONS (*for eight*):

Ask the butcher to bone 2 good capons, or, if you prefer, 2 good roasting chickens. Ask him not to cut them down the back. Also buy 2 chickens cut up as for fricassee, not boned. Boil these until tender in water containing celery, carrots, a little parsley, and several small onions. Cook in their juice. Then pick off all the meat, discarding all skin and gristle. Save out the breast and put the rest through the fine meat grinder. Also put through the grinder a pound of tender lean boiled ham. Add to this 1 tablespoon of onion juice, a cup and a half of bread soaked in milk and squeezed dry, 1 tablespoon each of chopped parsley and chopped celery, a handful of pistachio nuts if obtainable, and salt and pepper to taste. Moisten with stock. Stuff the 2 capons nice and full with this, inserting the boiled breasts in the center. Sew the capons up and shape them as nearly as possible into their original shape, tying them with white string so that they will keep their form. Brown lightly in butter in a good roasting-pan 2 carrots and 2 onions chopped fine, and lay the birds on this bed. Rub them with salt and pepper and soft butter, and roast to a golden brown in a good oven. When brown, reduce the heat and cook slowly about an hour and a quarter more, basting frequently with their own juice, adding butter and chicken stock as necessary. Watch very carefully so as not to burn. Remove from oven. Lay on platter. Pour the juice — from which you have removed the fat — over all and serve at once.

COLD CHICKEN IN A BLANKET (*for twelve*):

Choose two 5-pound roasting chickens. Wash and tie them up. Place them in a pan and cover with hot chicken broth — water will do, but will not be so good. Add 6 whole carrots, a little celery, and 4 onions. Simmer gently until quite tender. Remove from the fire and cool in their own juice. Remove from the water and skin them. Remove all the meat in as large pieces as possible, arranging it on a platter, the white in the center and the dark around the edges. Make a cream sauce by heating a pint of cream in a double boiler with the peel of 1 lemon. Melt 4 level tablespoons of butter and stir into it 4 level tablespoons of flour. Cook together without browning for five minutes, then add the hot cream gradually. Continue to cook in a double boiler for fifteen or twenty minutes, adding a little strained chicken broth if too thick. Salt and pepper to taste and add the juice of 1 small lemon and half a teaspoon of powdered mace. Pour over the chicken carefully, so as to coat it evenly. Place in the refrigerator to chill thoroughly. When ready to serve, decorate with the whole carrots from the stock and crisp hot bacon curls and parsley.

CURRIED DUCK WITH APRICOT AND DATE CHUT-
    NEY (*for eight*):

Have the butcher clean 2 fat, tender ducks and cut them up to about six pieces. Grate 2 fresh coconuts, and pour over them enough boiling water barely to cover them. Let them stand for fifteen minutes, then mash well with a spoon or a wooden mallet. Now place all this in a piece of linen and squeeze out all the milk. More hot water should be added to the coconut to make a second extraction, but let the coconut stand an hour the second time, and keep the second extraction separate. Place in the refrigerator until ready to use. The fat part of the milk will rise to the top and form a cake. Both the hard part and the liquid part are used.

Now peel and chop fine 6 little white onions. Wash the white part of 4 leeks and cut in one-inch pieces. Cut up fine 2 green peppers and a big piece of preserved ginger. Brown the onions in 4 tablespoons of butter, then brown the duck in the butter, being careful not to burn the onions. Then sprinkle the duck with 2 or 3 tablespoons of good curry powder, salt and pepper, add the leeks and the peppers, also the ginger, and moisten with the second extraction of the coconut milk. Cover tightly and simmer gently for fifteen minutes, then add the first extraction of coconut milk. Cover again and continue to cook until the duck is quite tender — at least an hour and a half. Remove as much fat as possible with a spoon, then add the juice of 1 lime and place the meat on a platter. Pour some of the juice over it and serve the rest in a gravy boat. Serve at once with fresh lima beans and a bowl of brown rice —

which, by the way, takes a long time to cook, at least an hour and a quarter. Serve the following apricot and date chutney with this:

APRICOT AND DATE CHUTNEY:

This makes 6 small jars.   Stone, weigh, and chop up 1 pound each of dates and fresh apricots.   Dried apricots may be used, but should be soaked for an hour first.   Grind 2 small cloves of garlic with 3 tablespoons of preserved ginger.   Place half a pound of white seedless raisins in a big enamel pan, add the apricots and dates, ginger and garlic, half a pound of light brown sugar and a scant half-cup of salt.   Then add enough cider vinegar to cover well and simmer for one and a half hours, adding more vinegar if too dry.   Cool and put in sterile jars and seal tight.

SQUABS STUFFED WITH PISTACHIO NUTS (*for eight*):

Ask the butcher to bone 8 little squabs without cutting them down the back.   Place the bones in a pan and cover with cold water.   Add 2 carrots and 1 onion.   Simmer gently for five or six hours to make a very concentrated broth. Put 1 pound of boiled ham through the meat-grinder. Soak in milk 12 slices of bread, from which you have removed the crust, and squeeze dry.   Add it to the ham. Cook the squab livers in butter until a golden brown.   Salt and pepper, chop them fine, and add to the ham.   Then add 2 cups of shelled pistachio nuts left whole, and 2 table-spoons of grated onion.   Mix together lightly and stuff the birds nice and full.   Sew them up.   Melt plenty of butter in a roasting-pan and sprinkle on the bottom 2 carrots chopped fine and 1 onion.   Salt and pepper the birds and spread a little butter on the breasts.   Put them in the roasting-pan and place in a hot oven to roast to a golden brown, basting carefully with the concentrated stock. When brown, turn down heat and let them cook slowly for half an hour. Drain off all the juice in the pan, strain and reduce to a glaze by simmering. Pour over the birds and decorate them with watercress, which has been lightly mixed at the last minute with a little olive oil, salt and pepper, and lemon juice.

COLD ROAST DUCK (*for eight*):

Roast 2 ducks in the usual manner. When cold, remove the skin and slice the breasts in 4 pieces. Also remove the dark meat in as large pieces as possible. Take a medium-sized jar of pâté de foie gras and rub it to a paste with a little cream until smooth enough to spread evenly on the different pieces of cold duck. Make a good meat aspic. The powdered gelatine aspic will do. When it is very cold and almost ready to set, dip each piece of duck in the aspic and lay it on a plate on ice to set. Repeat the process several times, so as to glaze the meat well. Lay on an attractive platter. Make some more aspic and put it on a shallow platter to cool, so that you can cut it in little squares. Decorate the platter of duck with this, and with parsley and thin slices of orange. Serve very cold with a delicious, crisp green salad.

FONDUE DE POULET À LA CRÊME (*for eight*):

This recipe was brought back to me by some friends who had eaten a fondue de poulet à la crême in a restaurant in Chablis, and finding it so delicious, begged the headwaiter to beg the chef to divulge the secret of its delectability, with promises never to tell anyone else how it was made. Apparently the chef was a very foreseeing and absolutely generous-spirited soul, for he immediately sent out a lovely little pink slip, with the recipe already printed out.

Clean 2 tender roasting chickens cut as for fricassee. Place a quarter of a pound of butter in a big shallow iron frying-pan. Melt it, and add the chicken. Also add 3 or 4 small onions sliced very thin, and salt and pepper. Cover the pan tightly and let the chicken smother slowly for about twenty minutes, or until tender. Then add a little glass of cognac and half a teaspoon of curry powder, and 3 cups of thick cream. Simmer for five minutes longer. Remove the chicken and place on a hot platter. Pass the sauce through a fine sieve, pressing hard on the onions. Heat, without boiling, stir in a small lump of butter, and pour over the chicken. Serve at once.

ROAST CHICKEN STUFFED WITH NOODLES (*for eight*):

Singe and clean two 5-pound roasting chickens, inside and out. Wipe with a dry cloth. Stuff them with the following stuffing: Heat 2 quarts of chicken broth and, when boiling, add 2 packages of wide noodles broken in little pieces. Cook for about five minutes. (The noodles should be only about half-cooked.) In the meantime, wash, dry, peel, and chop fine 1 pound of fresh mushrooms. Sauté them in a quarter of a pound of butter, until cooked, but not browned. Grate 2 cups of Parmesan cheese. Drain the noodles well, add the mushrooms and their juice, salt and freshly ground pepper, a cup of the Parmesan cheese, and half a pint of thick cream. Mix well, and stuff the chickens with this. Sew them securely and truss for roasting. Place 2 carrots, cut up, and 2 onions, left whole, in a large roasting-pan, with a quarter of a pound of melted butter. Place the birds in the pan and roll them around in the butter until buttered all over. Place the pan in a very hot oven and baste frequently, until roasted to a golden brown, adding from time to time a little hot chicken broth. Turn the chickens breast down, being careful not to puncture them. Reduce the heat, baste frequently, and cook for about an hour. When almost done, salt and pepper lightly.

In the meantime, make the following sauce Mornay: Chop 1 peeled carrot, 2 little onions, and 1 heart of celery, very fine. Cook them in 4 tablespoons of butter until a golden brown, then sprinkle them with the same quantity of flour. Cook together for a minute or two, and add gradually a quart of hot milk and a bouquet garni of parsley, thyme, bay leaf. Cook in a double boiler, stirring from time to time, for at least half an hour. When ready to serve the chickens, put them on a hot platter, remove all strings, carve them, and pour over them the chicken gravy, from which you have removed all fat, and which you have strained through a fine sieve.

Add half a cup of thick cream to the sauce Mornay, remove the bouquet, and add the other cup of grated cheese. Salt and pepper to taste, and serve with the chickens.

ROAST TURKEY WITH RAY'S STUFFING (*for twelve*):

We were having a Thanksgiving party. Each guest was to contribute something to the meal. We were living in a very grand apartment on Park Avenue. Our friends lived on the top floor. To the complete disgust of the dignified elevator man, our friends from above called the elevator and got in, bearing a very large yellow bowl neatly covered with a big plate. Nothing so very unconventional had ever before happened in that respectable elevator — the bowl contained the dressing for the turkey. Here is how it was made.

First, with a sharp knife, make an incision in about 30

chestnuts, and plunge them into smoking fat for a few
seconds, then remove and cool. Peel off the outer and inner
shells. Boil them until quite tender in boiling salted water.
Drain, and break them up into quite small pieces.

Now peel 1 pound of washed and dried mushrooms, and
chop them very fine. Place a large lump of butter in a pan,
add the mushrooms, cover tightly, and simmer for fifteen
minutes. Then remove the lid and continue to cook until
almost dry. Take a large frying-pan and put into it a small
piece of butter, 4 peeled onions chopped fine, and a quarter
of a pound of fresh sausage meat. Cook together, stirring
with a fork, until slightly browned. Now mix the chestnuts, mushrooms, and sausage meat together. Add the
juice of 1 lemon, a few drops of tarragon vinegar, salt and
pepper, 1 sherry-glass of French vermouth and 1 of cognac, a
teaspoon of chopped parsley, and, last of all, half a pound of
grapenuts.

Clean a fine 10- to 12-pound turkey. Stuff with the above
dressing, truss and sew up securely. Rub the turkey with
soft butter. Place it in a roasting-pan, containing a lump of
butter, 2 carrots, sliced, and 1 whole onion. Put into a good
hot oven for half an hour, basting carefully, and adding,
from time to time, a little chicken broth or water, so that
the pan is never quite dry. Now reduce the heat, salt and
pepper the turkey lightly, and continue to roast for two
and a half hours, basting frequently and keeping the bird
breast down as much as possible, adding broth from time to
time. Pour off the juice, and remove as much grease as
possible. Serve on a large platter, remove strings, garnish,
and send to the table to be carved. Pass the strained gravy
separately.

DUCK STUFFED WITH GREEN PEAS (*for eight*):

First shell 8 pounds of green peas and cook them in the usual way in salted boiling water with a tiny pinch of soda. When cooked, drain well and pass through a fine sieve. In the meantime, peel and cook in butter and a little water 1 pound of tiny white onions until tender. Add these to the purée of peas and season well with salt, pepper, and a lump of butter. Clean 2 fine ducks with care, inside and out, wiping them with a clean damp cloth. Sprinkle the insides with plenty of salt and a little pepper, then stuff them with the peas and onions. Truss and roast in the usual way, placing in a very hot oven for fifteen minutes, then salt and pepper them, reduce the heat, rub them over with a little soft butter, and continue to roast for three quarters of an hour more, basting carefully every ten minutes. Pour off juice and remove all fat. Place ducks on a hot platter, carve, pour juice over them, and serve at once.

DUCK À L'ORANGE (*for eight*):

Clean with great care 2 fine ducks, inside and out, wiping them with a clean damp cloth. Sprinkle the insides with salt and pepper. With a sharp knife peel two oranges, removing all the white tough part, exposing the pulp. Cut between each section to remove the pulp. Place half in each duck, and truss for roasting. Place in a roasting-pan in a hot oven for fifteen minutes, then rub over with soft butter and sprinkle with salt and a little pepper, reduce the heat, and continue to roast, basting frequently, for about three quarters of an hour more. In the meantime, boil the orange skins in several waters until they may be easily pierced with a fork. With a spoon scrape out all the white bitter part and cut in thin strips. Place half of them in a mortar with the duck livers, and pound to a paste. Now heat a pint of strong veal broth. Cook together without browning 2 teaspoons of butter with 2 of flour, and add gradually the veal broth. Add a teaspoon of beef extract to the gravy and reduce by simmering. Into the livers stir a liqueur glass of curaçao and add the juice of 1 orange and add it all to the sauce. Also strain off the pan gravy and remove all the fat and add the rest to the sauce. Taste and season with salt and a little pepper. Cook together a minute or two, then pass through a fine sieve forcing all the liver through. Now add the rest of the orange peel, and heat gently, while you place the ducks on a hot platter and carve them. Garnish the platter with parsley and sliced oranges and serve at once, passing the sauce in a gravy boat.

BOILED CHICKEN WITH DUMPLINGS (*for eight*):

First prepare the dumplings. You will need for this a tablespoon of chicken fat and a tablespoon of beef drippings. These you will have saved from a previously cooked roast beef and boiled chicken. Stir the two fats together until creamy and add one by one 3 eggs, a pinch of salt, and a pinch of powdered sugar. Add a teaspoon of grated onion and enough cracker dust to make a stiff paste which will hold its shape. Put on the ice for an hour or two to chill thoroughly. Then shape it into little balls. Place back on the ice until ready to cook.

Now, put 2 chickens, cut up as for fricassee, into a pot with 4 carrots and 3 onions peeled and left whole, a piece of celery, and a small piece of salt pork. Barely cover with warm water, salt lightly, and place on the fire. Just before it boils, skim carefully, and reduce the heat. Simmer until quite tender, an hour and a half or two hours. In the meantime, cook separately, in boiling salted water with a tiny pinch of soda, 2 cups of green peas. Fifteen minutes before the chicken is cooked, add to the chicken a cup of fine noodles, broken up. When cooked, add the drained peas to the chicken, but keep their water, and add it to a can of chicken broth which you will put into a shallow enamel pan that can be tightly covered. Add a little of the broth from the chicken to this and heat it all to the boiling point. Now place the dumplings in this broth all at once and cover tightly, and boil for twenty minutes — and please do not take off the lid to see how they are getting along. Most people ruin dumplings by obeying that impulse. When the dumplings are cooked, serve the chicken, noodles and peas, and all the broth in a big earthenware pot. Add the dumplings, but not their juice, and serve at once to be eaten from soup plates — soup, chicken, and all. Serve coarse salt in a salt grinder with this.

VI. MEAT

I ONCE had a silly dream. I dreamt I was at a dinner party where the bright young hostess served a new meat. I don't mean an old stand-by cooked in a new way — I mean a brand-new animal I had never met before — not cow — not pig — not lamb — not fowl — not red meat — not white meat — just a perfectly nice barnyard animal I had never heard of. Shouldn't you know I should wake up just as I was asking what on earth it was — and what it looked like and where to buy it, and how to cook it ——

Oh, dear, oh, dear! It was only a dream, after all, and there really wasn't anything new on earth, and we are still faced with the same old problem, What shall we have for dinner?

Perhaps the following recipes will help to vary the monotony:

FILLET OF VENISON, MARINATED (*for twelve*):

Ask the butcher for enough tenderloin or fillet of venison for twelve. This has to be marinated for at least forty-eight hours, so order two days before the party. Have the butcher remove all the fat and dry skin, and lard well for you. Place in an earthen dish, with 2 or 3 glasses of vinegar, salt, pepper, 4 or 5 onions cut in thin slices, some parsley and a few scallions. Keep the dish covered with a cheesecloth so that no dust can get into it, but do not place in the refrigerator. Turn over from time to time so that all the meat is well saturated. When ready to cook, remove from the pickle. Wipe clean and put several slices of bacon in the bottom of a casserole. Lay the fillets on this, add 4 or 5 little carrots sliced, 6 onions, 4 cloves, 3 bay leaves, and a pinch of thyme. Cover with a buttered paper. Pour over this 3 glasses of dry white wine, 3 glasses of bouillon, and a little salt. Cook slowly in the oven for an hour, basting frequently. Pour off some of the juice, add a little beef extract, and reduce to a glaze by boiling. When ready to serve, place the fillets on a hot platter and glaze by pouring the reduced juice over them. Slice thin and serve at once with the rest of the juice in which they have been cooked, and to which you have added a little beef extract, 3 dessertspoons of vinegar, some salt and pepper, and which you have reduced by boiling to half its original quantity.

ROAST SUCKLING PIG WITH CHESTNUT STUFFING (*for eight*):

Clean thoroughly a young suckling pig; salt lightly and sprinkle the inside with 3 tablespoons of brandy. Stuff with the following dressing:

Wash and pick over a half-pound of barley. Melt 2 tablespoons of butter and brown lightly in it 4 small white onions chopped fine, then add the barley, stir well, and add 3 cups of veal, chicken or turkey broth. Season to taste with salt and pepper and cook in a slow oven for two hours. In the meantime, with a sharp knife make an incision in about 40 chestnuts and put them into some smoking fat for a few seconds, then remove and peel off the inner and outer shells. Now boil in some chicken, veal, or turkey broth until the chestnuts become quite tender.

Cut up the pig's liver and sauté it in butter. Then broil 1 pound of little Deerfoot sausages and break them up with a fork. When the barley is cooked, add to it the sautéed liver and 2 tablespoons of chopped herbs consisting of parsley, chives, and chervil. Then add the sausage and the chestnuts, and salt and pepper to taste.

Stuff the pig carefully, sew it up, prop its mouth open with a stone or a piece of wood, and roast in a fairly hot oven for two hours, basting very frequently with butter. When ready to serve, replace the stone in the pig's mouth with a small red apple or a lemon. Put it on a hot platter decorated with parsley and let the master of the house carve it at the table.

Serve this either with applesauce or horseradish sauce, which are made as follows:

APPLESAUCE:

Pare and quarter 2 large quinces. Put them to boil in 2 cups of cider. When tender, add 8 tart green apples pared and quartered, and more cider if necessary. Cook until done. Drain and put through a fine sieve. Sweeten to taste with light brown and white sugar and heat until the sugar melts, adding a little of the drained-off juice if too thick. Remove from the fire and stir in a lump of butter the size of a walnut.

HORSERADISH SAUCE:

Boil a half-cup of port wine, to which you have added dashes of nutmeg, cinnamon, and salt and pepper, until it has reduced one third. Then add 1 cup of red currant jelly which has been melted, and 2 tablespoons of grated horseradish.

POACHED LEG OF LAMB (*for eight*):

We were having a cooking party. Madame Pierre Brissaud offered to cook the lamb which I had expected to roast.
She promptly took a sharp knife and calmly proceeded to remove every vestige of outer skin and fat from my nice leg of
lamb. I was frankly worried. Next she wanted a piece of
cloth, a needle, some thread and a thimble. I brought her a
clean old pillowslip, wondering what on earth she wanted
it for. It seemed that the roast was to be sewn up in the
cloth. I was now bewildered but very interested. She
didn't like the pillow slip — it wasn't linen — it had to be
linen. I gave her one of my best linen napkins. She carefully boiled it and hung it on the oven door to dry, and then
she wrapped the leg of lamb ever so neatly and sewed it up
securely and said 'Voilà.' Next she wanted half a cup of
pepper, a tablespoon of salt, 12 juniper berries and 10 cloves
of garlic. I said a silent prayer and good-bye forever to my
lovely leg of lamb, and concentrated on my praliné soufflés,
but nevertheless keeping an eye on Madame Pierre Brissaud.
Next she heated a large pot of water, and asked for the
scales. She carefully weighed the lamb. When the water
boiled, she asked for a clock. I gave her the one my children hadn't taken apart. She then put all the pepper and
cloves and garlic in the pot and then the leg of lamb. She
then sat down to rest and watched me, the result being that
my dessert was a definite flop. I really didn't care, however, because I knew her lamb was going to be even more of
a definite flop. Ray was to make the Béarnaise sauce for the
lamb — everything was ready. He did it with perfect ease.
The potatoes had been cooking merrily and were pro-
nounced cooked — by Jean. Joe had set the table — the
plates were hot — we were ready. Mrs. Brissaud stopped

watching us and with incredible dexterity extracted her leg of lamb, carved it, and placed it on the table. The Béarnaise sauce didn't curdle, and never have I eaten anything as superbly delicate as Madame Brissaud's leg of lamb.

Carefully trim off all the fat and the dry skin with a sharp knife and then weigh the leg. Wrap it in a piece of old white linen and sew it so that it is completely bound up. Choose a pan large enough to contain the whole leg. Fill with water and when it boils add half a teacup of ground white pepper, 1 tablespoon of salt, 10 cloves of garlic, and 12 juniper berries. Put in the leg of lamb. For every pound allow to simmer gently for fifteen minutes and not one minute longer. When cooked, remove from the water, cut away the linen, and carve as you would a roast leg of lamb. Garnish the platter with parsley and serve at once with a large bowl of peeled, boiled new potatoes and plenty of Béarnaise sauce, which is made as follows:

BÉARNAISE SAUCE:

Put 1¾ cups of tarragon vinegar, 6 shallots (chopped fine), 10 freshly crushed whole black peppers, and half a teaspoon of salt into an enamel pan and boil until but half a cup is left. Remove from the fire and, when cold, add the slightly beaten yolks of 8 eggs and half a cup of butter. Set the pan in hot water and stir furiously with a wire whisk until thick. Remove from the fire and pass through a fine sieve. Put the mixture back into a double boiler, but remove from the fire and add, little by little, 2 more cups of melted butter. If by any chance this should curdle, add a lump of ice, stir furiously, and add another egg-yolk. Just before serving, stir in 3 branches of tarragon, chopped. Don't try to serve this sauce too hot — it just can't be done, as heat enough to make it hot curdles it. It must be made at the last minute, however.

BOILED ROASTED HAM, HOT (*for eight*):

Soak a ham overnight. Wash it thoroughly. Put into a large pan, and cover completely with equal parts of cold water and cider, a bouquet of parsley, 2 tablespoons of olive oil, a carrot, a bay leaf, and a few whole spices. Bring to a boil and simmer twenty minutes for each pound of ham. Let the ham cool in its liquid and then remove the skin carefully. With a sharp knife slightly lacerate the fat in half-inch squares and place a clove in each square. Sprinkle liberally with brown sugar and then place it in the oven to brown. Serve hot with a sauce, which is made as follows:

SAUCE FOR HAM:

With a sharp knife, remove the peel from half an orange and half a lemon, being careful not to get any of the white part. Cut in tiny slivers, put into cold water and bring to a boil, drain, and repeat the process three times. Melt 4 tablespoons of currant jelly, add a half-cup of port wine, the orange and lemon peels, the juice of an orange and half a lemon, a teaspoon of mustard, a tablespoon of brown sugar, a pinch of powdered ginger, and a tiny dash of cayenne. Bring to a boil. In the meantime, boil half a cup of Sultana raisins in port wine until plump. Blanch half a cup of almonds and slice them in tiny pieces. Add raisins and almonds to the sauce and serve.

CIVET DE LAPIN (*for eight or ten*):

We had been very rash and allowed ourselves to be inveigled into buying a great big *lapin sauvage* from a passing huntsman in Normandy. I prided myself on my cooking, but I had never encountered a wild rabbit and hadn't the slightest idea what to do with it. Madame Agnès, the farmer's wife, next door, came in to admire the *lapin*, having heard we had bought it. I thrust it into her arms and told her to take it, please — with my compliments. She did, but brought it back at dinner-time in a big iron pot for us to eat. Wasn't it sweet of her! This is the way she cooked it:

Ask the farmer to kill 2 rabbits, skin them and cut them up. Keep the blood, and place in the refrigerator. Take a half-pound of salt pork, cut in squares and brown in a hot iron casserole or a deep iron frying-pan, add a half-pound of butter and brown the pieces of rabbit in it. Then sprinkle with 2 tablespoons of flour and add 2 glasses of red wine and 2 glasses of stock, a little salt, freshly ground pepper, a bouquet of parsley, 2 bay leaves, a pinch of allspice, 2 carrots, several juniper berries, and 4 chopped shallots. Let simmer an hour and add a dozen and a half small white onions which have been browned in a little butter and caramelized by adding 2 teaspoons of sugar. Add a dozen and a half small mushrooms which have been peeled, cut in quarters, and browned in a very hot pan with a little butter. Let the rabbits cook another hour slowly. Just before serving, stir in the blood in which has been beaten 2 tablespoons of vinegar. Sprinkle with chopped parsley and serve at once. Serve Italian or French bread with this.

BŒUF À LA MODE (*for eight*):

Have the butcher lard a 5-pound pot roast. Put in a big bowl, salt and pepper it, and add a pinch of allspice. Pour over it 1¾ cups of white wine, sauternes if possible, and 1¾ cups of Madeira wine. Let this soak for twenty-four hours.

At the end of this time put it into a hot iron casserole with
2 tablespoons of beef drippings. Brown for twenty minutes,
carefully turning it over and over. Then pour one fourth
of a cup of cognac over it and set ablaze with a match.
Remove from the casserole and put a quarter-pound of
bacon rind in the bottom of the casserole, put the roast
back into the pan, add a calf's foot, 12 little peeled carrots,
8 little white onions, a bouquet of parsley, a bay leaf, a
pinch of thyme, and 3 whole cloves. Moisten with 3¼
cups of good stock, the juice in which the meat soaked overnight, a third of a cup of white wine, and a third of a cup
of Madeira. Salt and pepper lightly, cover and bring to a
boil, then let it simmer slowly for about five hours.

When cooked, remove the meat and carrots, strain the
juice and take off all the grease. Clarify the juice by adding
the slightly beaten whites and the crushed shells of 2 eggs.
Bring slowly to a boil, stirring meanwhile. Remove from
the fire and strain through a cloth wrung out in cold water.

Cut the beef in slices perpendicularly. Decorate the bottom of a suitable mold with some perfect rounds of carrots
which have been cooked separately. Pour over these a
few tablespoons of the meat juice and place in the refrigerator to jell. Then arrange the slices of beef alternately
with the carrots which were cooked with the meat, until
all the meat and the carrots have been used, ending up with
meat. Pour over this the meat juice until the mold is full.
Place in the refrigerator to jell. Unmold on a platter decorated with lettuce and slices of lemon. Cut as if you were
cutting a loaf of bread. Serve French mustard with this,
and a big bowl of salad dressed with French dressing.

BLANQUETTE DE VEAU (*for eight*):

Soak 3 pounds of solid breast of veal cut in inch squares in cold water for two hours. Melt half a cupful of butter, add 2 tablespoons of flour and 1 quart of hot veal broth. Add the meat, which has been thoroughly drained, a bunch of parsley, 2 level teaspoons of salt, some freshly ground pepper, 10 little onions, 2 carrots, and 1 bay leaf. Let cook gently for one and a half hours.

Remove the meat, strain the juice, and take off any grease there may be. Put the meat back into the pan, pour over it the strained juice, add a half-pound of mushrooms, and continue cooking for another twenty minutes. Bind the sauce with the yolks of 3 eggs which have been slightly beaten into one third of a cup of cream, but do not let boil. Add the juice of 1 lemon at the last moment.

In the meantime, cook 1 pound of rice in the usual way, so that each kernel is separate. Arrange a pile of it in the middle of a large, deep platter and pour the blanquette of veal around the rice. Garnish with a sprig of parsley and serve at once.

KIDNEY STEW (*for eight*):

Ingredients: 4 veal kidneys, 1 quart of milk, 4 table-spoons of butter, 4 tablespoons of flour, 2 bay leaves, half a lemon, 10 mushrooms. This quantity of ingredients is all right for eight.

Remove the fat and skin from the veal kidneys, split and cut out the hard white substances and fat from the centers. Wash well, cover with cold water and soak for four hours, changing the water as it gets cloudy. Then put the kidneys into an enamel pan, cover with cold water and heat slowly. When at the boiling point, pour off the water.

Repeat the process three times. Then simmer very gently for twenty minutes. Place in the refrigerator overnight. When ready to prepare for breakfast, separate all the cords and veins from the kidneys and cut them in small pieces. Place in an enamel pan, add 2 bay leaves, 2 cups of water, a thinly sliced half a lemon, and 10 peeled, washed, and sliced mushrooms. Simmer for twenty minutes. In the meantime, make the sauce by melting 4 tablespoons of butter, adding 2 onions chopped very fine, 4 tablespoons of flour, and 1 quart of hot milk. Cook for half an hour in a double boiler. Add the kidneys and mushrooms, but first remove the lemon. Sprinkle with chopped parsley and serve with small pieces of freshly made hot toast.

VEAL KIDNEYS IN MUSTARD (*made in a chafing-dish at table for eight*):

The very same bachelor who told me all about boula told me how to make this dish. It is a perfect dish to make in a chafing-dish, when you want to show off your culinary genius.

Skin and cut up 6 veal kidneys, being careful not to include any of the white membrane. Prepare a large tray containing the chafing-dish, salt-and-pepper-grinder, a pot of German mustard, three quarters of a cup of cognac, a half-pound of sweet butter, a heaping tablespoon of chopped chives, and 2 teaspoons of finely chopped parsley. The kidneys are sautéed in the kitchen and brought to the table in a hot dish with their juice in a cup. To sauté them, put 3 tablespoons of butter in a very hot frying-pan, and, when it is sizzling hot, add the kidneys and shake them around until lightly browned. They should cook very quickly or they will be tough. At table, put a quarter of a pound of butter in the chafing-dish, and when it has melted add the juice from the kidneys and 4 dessertspoons of mustard, and the cognac and some freshly ground pepper and salt. Light the cognac as soon as it begins to boil and let it burn until the flame starts to turn yellow and green. At this moment, put out the flame by putting on the cover. Now add the kidneys and chives and simmer a minute or two. Then stir in another good lump of butter and sprinkle the parsley over it all and pass at once.

VEAL COOKED IN CHABLIS (*for eight*):

Buy a rump of veal weighing about 6 pounds. Have the butcher bone and roll it. Brown it carefully in 2 tablespoons of butter with 4 peeled carrots and 4 white onions. Season with salt and pepper and place the roast in an iron cocotte, add a half-cup of water to the butter in which the roast was browned and add juice and vegetables to the cocotte. Add the bones from the roast, 3 tomatoes peeled and cut up, 1 bay leaf, and pour over all a cup and a half of Chablis wine. Cover and cook in a very slow oven for four hours. Baste it from time to time with its own juice. When cooked, pour off most of the juice and strain it. Remove as much fat as possible and reduce by simmering until quite thick. Slice the meat on a hot platter, add the vegetables in the bottom of the cocotte to the gravy and pour over all. Serve with this a purée of spinach

LAMB À L'ALSACE (*for eight*):

With a sharp knife carefully cut off every bit of fat from a 6-pound leg of lamb. Place it in an oblong enamel pan with 3 peeled carrots sliced, 3 onions, 1 bay leaf, 4 cloves, some freshly ground pepper, and some salt. Pour over it a bottle of white Alsatian wine. Soak the lamb in this for twelve hours, turning it over from time to time so that it will be well saturated with the wine. Remove the lamb and cover it completely with bacon sliced paper-thin and tie it on securely. Put the wine in which the lamb was soaked into an enamel pan and reduce it by simmering on a low fire. Put the lamb back into the roasting-pan with the vegetables, and place it in a hot oven for twenty minutes to roast, basting it from time to time with some of the wine. Reduce the heat and continue to roast, basting very frequently with more of the wine, for forty minutes. In the meantime, sauté, in plenty of butter, until a golden brown, some little potato balls, cut out of big potatoes with a scooper. Strain the juice from the roast and remove as much fat as possible, then pour it on the potatoes. Carve the roast cross-grain, garnish with the potatoes, and pour the juice over all. Serve at once.

COLD HAM (*for twelve*):

Wash a ham well and soak for at least twelve hours in cold water. Then cook it slowly for four hours in half water and half cider, if you have any, or half any white wine, with a few spices. Leave the ham in its water to cool off for about an hour. Then skin it carefully, removing as much of the black part as possible, but being careful not to remove the fat. With a knife, mark it in half-inch cuts, so as to make a crisscross pattern all over. In each square place a whole clove. Put the ham into a roasting-pan, add 1 glass of sherry, 1 glass of brandy, 1 glass of liquid from sweet pickles, and 3 tablespoons of light brown sugar and a little powdered cinnamon. Place in a moderate oven and cook slowly, basting frequently, for about three quarters of an hour. Serve cold.

A WAY OF SERVING COLD ROAST BEEF:

Cut the slices very thin, spread with tarragon mustard, and roll the pieces up. Place on a platter decorated with watercress or parsley.

CROWN ROAST OF LAMB WITH PINK APPLE BALLS, MINT SAUCE (*for eight*):

Order a crown roast of 16 chops, but ask the butcher not to fill the center with chopped meat, and ask him to send the little frills for the ends separately. Also order a thick slice of salt pork cut in cubes. Place one of these on the ends of each bone to prevent charring while roasting. Place the roast in a roasting-pan with a half-cup of water in which you have dissolved a teaspoon of salt. Set in a very hot oven (500 degrees) for fifteen minutes. Then reduce to 350 degrees. Baste frequently. Allow twenty minutes to each pound of meat. Replace bits of pork with paper frills. Fill the center of the roast with little potato balls scooped out of big potatoes and fried in plenty of butter in an iron cocotte until golden brown and tender through. Serve with this the following apple balls and mint sauce:

PINK APPLE BALLS:

Peel 8 large delicious apples and with a scooper make as many balls as possible, placing them immediately in water containing a little lemon juice. Put the peels and remains of the apples into a pan and add 2 cups of water. Cook until the skins are tender, then strain through a cloth. Boil the juice five minutes, then measure. Add two thirds as much sugar as you have juice and boil rapidly until it sheets from the side of the spoon. In the meantime, boil the apples gently in the water in which they were soaking and to which you have added a little sugar. When just tender and not falling apart, drain them, and to a little of their juice add a touch of red vegetable coloring. Dissolve well, then dip the balls rapidly in and out to give them a faint blush of red. Place on a glass dish and pour the jelly over them when cooled enough not to break the dish. Place in the refrigerator to chill.

MINT SAUCE:

Wash a bunch of fresh mint carefully. Remove the leaves and chop them very fine. Take 1 cup of vinegar, a quarter-cup of water, 1 cup of sugar, and half a teaspoon of salt. Boil in an enamel pan until syrupy. Put the very finely chopped mint in a bowl and pour the boiling syrup over it. Cover tightly until ready to serve.

TRIPE EN CASSEROLE (for eight):

Wash 2½ pounds of cleaned tripe in warm water and cut in 3 by 1 inch strips. Make 2 kitchen bouquets containing 3 leeks, 2 bay leaves, a little parsley, 2 stalks of celery, and a pinch of thyme. Also make 2 muslin bags containing each 6 onions, 2 cloves, and 6 peppercorns. Peel and slice 6 small carrots. Butter the bottom of an earthenware casserole or bean pot. Put half of the carrots in the bottom, then add one of the bags and one of the bouquets and a teaspoon of salt and half of the tripe. Now add, if procurable, a calf's foot, split in two lengthwise; otherwise half a dozen strips of bacon. Now add the rest of the carrots, the other bag and bouquet, more salt, a pinch of nutmeg, and the rest of the tripe. Pour over this 2 cups of cider containing no preservatives or half a bottle of sauterne, 2 tablespoons of cognac, and enough consommé barely to cover. Put the cover on and seal it with a thick paste made of flour and hot water, so that none of the aroma will escape while cooking. Put in a slow oven and cook for four or five hours at least — the longer the better. When ready to serve, remove the bags and bouquets.

BAKED CALF'S LIVER (*for eight*):

Buy a fine piece of calf's liver weighing about 3½ pounds. Ask the butcher to leave it whole, but ask him to lard it for you just as he would prepare a pot roast. Also buy one eighth of a pound of salt pork cut in tiny squares. Peel 8 young carrots and cut them in four pieces. Peel 8 little white onions and stick a clove in each one. Make a bouquet garni of parsley, a pinch of thyme, half a bay leaf, and half a clove of garlic. Brown the pieces of salt pork in a tablespoon of sweet butter, and place them in the bottom of an iron cocotte with a tablespoon of fresh butter. Add the carrots, onions, bouquet, and liver. Sprinkle with salt and freshly ground pepper and a dash of nutmeg if you like it, and pour over it a cup of meat stock, a small glass of dry white wine, and half a glass of Madeira. Top it all off with 3 thin slices of lemon from which you have removed seeds and rind. Cover and place on a slow fire. Bring gently to a simmer, then place the cocotte in a slow oven and continue to cook, basting frequently, for about two hours or until very tender. Remove the bouquet, pour off most of the juice, skim off as much of the fat as possible, strain and reduce by simmering until quite thick. Carve the liver in thin slices and place it back in the cocotte with the vegetables around the edge and pour over all the reduced juice into which you have stirred a teaspoon of butter. Fold two serviettes and tie them around the casserole, a knot at either handle, and send to the table piping hot. Mashed potatoes go well with this.

POUPIETTES OF BEEF (*for eight*):

Put through the meat-grinder a half-pound of bacon. Add to this 2 tablespoons of finely chopped shallots or onions and 4 tablespoons of chopped raw mushrooms. Add a teaspoon of butter, and cook all this for a few minutes; then add 2 tablespoons of chopped parsley, salt and pepper, a dash of Worcestershire sauce and a teaspoon of French mustard. Continue to cook a minute or two longer. This paste is spread on 8 individual very thin slices of the top round of beef which have been pounded with a wooden mallet and neatly trimmed. The pieces of meat are then rolled, as you would roll a blanket, and secured with string. Salt and pepper them and place them in a frying-pan with a good piece of butter and put on a hot fire. Roll them over and over to brown gently evenly all over. In the meantime, peel, wash, dry, and slice fine a dozen mushrooms. Sauté them in a little butter, add a tablespoon of tomato sauce or tomato ketchup and a teaspoon of beef extract dissolved in a little boiling water. Simmer awhile longer, then add the juice of one half a lemon and a good lump of butter, but don't let it boil. Place the poupiettes on a hot platter, remove the strings, pour the sauce over them, and serve at once.

BROILED STEAK AND BÉARNAISE SAUCE (*for eight*):

If you want good steaks, be sure you have a good butcher. They should be bright red, the tender cuts well mottled with fat. The suet should be dry, crumbly, and white. A steak is best cut about an inch and three quarters thick. I prefer a tea bone steak. Light the broiler well ahead of time. For eight people, you will need 2 steaks weighing at least 3 pounds each. Wipe the grill with a piece of suet before placing the steak on it. Place the grill as near the flame as possible and sear them quickly, then turn and sear the other side. Reduce the heat slightly and cook not more than eighteen minutes in all. The steaks should be turned frequently during the cooking and not salted and peppered until five minutes before they are cooked. Place on a hot platter, cut and serve at once with a bowl of Béarnaise sauce. (See recipe, POACHED LEG OF LAMB.)

CORNED BEEF AND CABBAGE (*for eight*):

Buy a choice brisket of corned beef weighing about 6 pounds. Peel 6 little white turnips, 6 carrots, and 6 parsnips, and leave them whole, also cut a fine white cabbage in quarters and remove the core; peel 6 or 8 potatoes. Soak the corned beef in cold water for an hour. Drain and cover again with cold water. Put on the fire and bring briskly to the boiling point, but skim carefully just before it boils. Reduce the heat and simmer gently for three or four hours. Add more boiling water if necessary to keep the meat covered. An hour before the meat is cooked, pour off enough water from the beef to cover the carrots, parsnips, and turnips, and cook them until tender. In a separate pan boil the potatoes in plain water and in still another pan cook the cabbage, which will only take fifteen or eighteen minutes to cook. It should be put into boiling water with a tiny pinch of soda and some salt and cooked until just tender through.

Fifteen minutes before serving, add a teaspoon of sugar to the corned beef. When ready to serve, place the meat on a large hot platter, and rub it over with a little butter. Slice thin and garnish the platter with the cabbage, potatoes, parsnips, carrots, and turnips.

Serve the following hot horseradish bread sauce with this dish:

Remove the crusts from 6 slices of white bread and cut into little squares. Place a small lump of butter in the bottom of the top part of a double boiler. Add the bread and pour over it half a cup of cold milk. Place on the fire and heat through, stirring lightly with a fork. Add half a cup of cream, and a little salt, and just before serving add 4 tablespoons of freshly grated horseradish.

BOILED TONGUE (*for eight*):

Wash carefully a smoked tongue and soak it overnight. Drain and cover with fresh cold water, and bring it slowly to a boil; put 2 cloves in the water and 1 carrot and simmer until quite tender — about two hours. Place on a hot platter and remove the skin very carefully, beginning at the tip and stripping it back. Cut off as much gristle and fat as possible from the root and slice very thin. Garnish the platter with a ring of plain boiled noodles which have been well drained and in which you have stirred a big lump of butter. Sprinkle over the noodles some buttered crumbs made by toasting little pieces of bread in the oven until a golden brown and crisp. Then roll them into fine crumbs. Melt some butter in a frying-pan and heat the crumbs in this.

Serve the following sauce with the tongue:

Cut 4 slices of bacon in tiny squares and cook until crisp in a small frying-pan. Pour off most of the grease and add three quarters of a cup of heavy cream, and heat very slowly. In the meantime, place the yolks of 2 raw eggs in a bowl with a pinch of salt and three quarters of a teaspoon of dry mustard and a dash of pepper. Stir well and add gradually a teaspoon of cider vinegar. Stir this into the hot cream and continue to cook slowly until thick. Serve at once.

POT–AU–FEU (*for six*):

Peel 6 carrots and 4 turnips. Peel 1 onion and stick 2 cloves in it. Cut the green part off of 4 leeks and split them down the middle and wash well. Make a bouquet garni of parsley, half a bay leaf, and a tiny pinch of thyme. Put 3 pounds of brisket of beef in a big pot and cover with 3 pints of cold water. Heat again to boiling point and skim carefully once more. Then add the vegetables and the bouquet, a large marrow bone, and a little rock salt. Simmer gently, partially covered, for six or seven hours. When cooled, pour off the juice and strain through a cheese-cloth. Reheat, season to taste, and serve in a soup tureen, accompanied by a plate of toast made from French bread, cut thin and toasted on both sides and buttered lightly.

The meat is then served on a hot platter, carved and garnished with the vegetables, and sprinkled with rock table salt, accompanied by a pot of mustard and any other relish you happen to like. As usual, boiled potatoes may be served with this.

BOILED LEG OF LAMB WITH CAPER SAUCE (*for eight*):

With a sharp knife trim a leg of lamb weighing 6 or 7 pounds, removing carefully all the dry skin. Wrap it carefully and tightly in a piece of clean linen and sew it securely. Peel 12 little white onions, 12 medium-sized carrots, and 12 tender small white turnips. Leave them all whole. Heat some water in a teakettle. Place the leg of lamb surrounded by the vegetables in a flat white enamel oblong pan, if possible, which has a cover. A vegetable container from the refrigerator is just the thing if big enough. When the water boils, pour in just enough of it barely to cover the lamb. Place on the fire and let it come to a boil, then skim it carefully and cover — and simmer for about two hours. Salt to taste an hour before it is cooked. When done, make the sauce, by melting 3 tablespoons of butter and cooking in it, without browning, for a minute or two, the same quantity of flour; then add gradually 3 cups of the hot lamb broth, carefully strained. When smooth, add a large bottle of capers and half of the liquid from the capers. Taste and season again with salt.

Now remove the cloth from the lamb and place it on a large platter. Carve and place the boiled vegetables attractively around the edge; garnish with parsley. Serve the sauce separately in a large gravy boat, but just before serving it stir in a lump of butter the size of an egg. Serve with the lamb a bowl of plain boiled potatoes which have been cooked separately, well drained, sprinkled with salt, and placed in the oven for a minute or two to dry out.

Another way of serving the same dish is to use the broth as a soup for the meal, and serving the following caper sauce instead of the thick one: Clarify a cup of butter and add to it 2 tablespoons of capers and 2 teaspoons of vinegar. Stir over the fire for a minute or two, then serve.

COLD BOILED BACON FOR BREAKFAST:

Please don't shudder. It's really quite good. Take a piece of Yorkshire bacon weighing about 2 pounds. It should be well streaked with lean. Put it into cold water and boil briskly for an hour and a half. Drain well, and tear off the rind, which should come off easily. In the meantime, dry some bread in the oven until crisp and brown and well toasted. Roll fine and sift. Dust the entire bacon with these crumbs. Serve cold, sliced very thin, with a pot of English mustard — for breakfast!

GIGOT BRAISÉ (for eight):

Put a quarter of a pound of butter in a roasting-pan and place on the fire to melt. Pare off all extra fat and skin from a leg of lamb weighing about 5 pounds. Stuff a clove of garlic at the small end of the roast between the bone and meat until well hidden. Now brown the roast in the pan on top of the stove, turning it over and over until brown on all sides, then salt and pepper it well and place a bouquet of 3 bay leaves and parsley at one end of the pan and sprinkle a scant teaspoon of thyme over the bottom of the pan. Put a big clove of garlic on a fork and rub the roast all over well with it. Then add half a cup of boiling water in which you have dissolved a good teaspoon of beef extract. Cover tightly so that no steam can escape and let it simmer very, very slowly on a low fire on top of the stove for at least three hours. Don't remove the cover while cooking if you can possibly help it. When almost cooked, pour off most of the juice into a little pan and reduce by simmering until almost a glaze. Scald two cups of pitted olives — drain well and add them to the lamb with a tablespoon of butter and let them simmer with the meat — rolling them over so that they are well coated with the remaining meat juice and butter. Remove all fat from the glaze. Carve the lamb on a hot platter, garnish with the olives, and pour the glaze over all. Serve a purée of lima beans and peas with this.

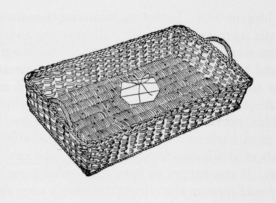

VII. ALMOST NO MEAT

THE idea of this chapter on meat dishes is to see just how little meat we can use and still have the audacity to call them meat dishes. Some of them are made with leftovers and some are made with honest-to-goodness meat straight from the butcher, but precious little of it. The usual fate of leftovers is to be made into a hash, which isn't a bad idea, provided they are made into good hash. The reason most hash isn't good is that it's generally full of hard bits of gristle and raw bits of onions and cold boiled potatoes. If you happen to have cold boiled potatoes and a bit of cold meat in the refrigerator, don't obey that impulse to join them together. Let the potatoes be made into a salad, but boil some nice fresh ones for the hash, and, while we are on the subject, either grate the onion or brown the chopped onion in the butter you are going to use, then fish the bits out and throw them away. The flavor will still be there, and the hash will be much more delicate. As several of the recipes call for a tomato sauce, I will first give directions for making it.

TOMATO SAUCE:

Peel 2 pounds of ripe tomatoes, cut in little pieces, place them in an enamel saucepan with 2 white onions, sliced, a bouquet of parsley, 1 bay leaf, a pinch of thyme, 2 cloves, and a cup of dry white wine. Simmer for one hour, then pass through a fine sieve.

Now melt a heaping tablespoon of butter and add a teaspoon of flour. Cook together without browning for several minutes, then add the tomato sauce. Salt and pepper to taste and add a teaspoon of beef extract dissolved in a little hot water. Continue to simmer gently until of the right consistency. Then remove from the fire and add a level tablespoon of butter and stir until melted.

SPINACH AND TONGUE IN HORSERADISH CREAM (for eight):

Remove the stems from 4 pounds of spinach, wash with meticulous care in ever so many waters. Boil in a little salted water for ten minutes. Drain well and run through a fine meat-chopper. Place 2 tablespoons of butter in a saucepan, add the spinach, and put on the fire. Stir continuously until hot. Salt and pepper to taste. Buy 18 slices of cold boiled tongue sliced thin from the big part of the tongue. Put a spoonful of spinach on each slice and roll and secure with a toothpick. Place in a buttered dish. Put 4 teaspoons of grated, fresh horseradish in half a pint of cream, mix well, and pour around the tongue rolls. Put immediately into a hot oven until well-heated through. Serve at once.

CABBAGE STUFFED WITH CORNED–BEEF HASH (for eight):

Parboil a large white cabbage, leaving it whole. Drain well, but save the cabbage water. Remove the core and scoop out enough of the cabbage to leave a good-sized hole. Open 1 large can of corned beef, break it apart and chop fine. Peel and boil 2 pounds of white potatoes, and when they are done drain and chop or cut into little squares. Place 2 tablespoons of butter in a frying-pan and add 2 grated onions. When the butter is hot, add the corned beef and a cup of cabbage water in which you have dissolved 2 tablespoons of tomato ketchup. Cover and simmer without browning for half an hour, adding more cabbage water if necessary. Now add the potatoes and half a cup of cream, and salt and pepper to taste. Remove from the fire and fill the hole in the cabbage with the hash. Cover the top with the scooped-out cabbage. Place in a well-buttered baking-dish. Dot with butter, moisten with cabbage juice, and cook in a slow oven until the cabbage is tender. Remove the cover, pour in a little more cream, and put under a hot blaze to brown lightly.

ANOTHER STUFFED CABBAGE (*for eight*):

Parboil a medium-sized white cabbage whole. Drain, and with a sharp knife cut out the core. Remove the leaves carefully, one by one, starting with the outside. Place them flat on the table in relation to the spot from which they were removed until the whole cabbage is laid out. Now reconstruct the cabbage, leaf by leaf, putting a little of the following stuffing on each leaf until it is back in its original form:

For the stuffing, mix 1 pound of ground veal with one eighth of a pound of salt pork ground fine, add a half-cup of fine bread crumbs, 1 grated onion, salt and pepper, a pinch of thyme, another of chopped parsley, and 2 raw eggs. Mix well together. When the cabbage is back in its original form, wrap the slices of bacon around it and tie it up securely. Place it in an iron cocotte containing some beef drippings, bacon grease or butter, and pour over it 3 cups of bouillon. Cover and bake slowly for three hours. A half-hour before serving, remove the cover and let the juice reduce. Remove the strings, pour hot tomato sauce over it, and serve at once. (See beginning of chapter for TOMATO SAUCE.)

ARTICHOKE HEARTS STUFFED WITH HAM AND MUSHROOMS WITH TOMATO SAUCE (*for eight*):

Cook 8 large artichokes in salted water. Take off the leaves and scrape the ends of each with a dull knife to remove the good part. Remove the thistle carefully and trim the hearts. Peel, wash, and chop fine a half-pound of mushrooms. Chop 3 little shallots and brown them lightly in a little olive oil and butter. Add the mushrooms and cook until almost dry. Put 3 thin slices of cold boiled ham through the meat-grinder. Mix the mushrooms and ham together, cool a bit, and add a little chopped parsley, the artichoke meat, and bind with the yolks of 2 eggs. Salt and pepper to taste. Fill the artichoke hearts with this mixture heaping full. Cover each one with a little circle of thinly sliced ham. Place these in a buttered baking-dish and put a little lump of butter on each one. Bake in a hot oven until the ham begins to brown. Serve with the tomato sauce given before.

PURÉE OF GREEN PEAS IN HAM CORNUCOPIAS (*for eight*):

Make a stiff purée by boiling, until quite tender, 4 pounds of green peas in salted boiling water with a tiny pinch of soda. Mash them through a fine sieve. Add a lump of butter, some salt and pepper and hot cream, and beat until smooth and of the consistency of mashed potatoes. Make 8 cornucopias of 8 thin slices of cold boiled ham and secure them with toothpicks. Fill with the mashed peas. Place in a buttered glass cooking-dish, pouring a little melted butter over them. Put the dish into a hot oven, and when heated through set under a hot blaze for a minute or two to brown the ham. Remove the toothpicks and serve at once.

STUFFED BERMUDA ONIONS (*for eight*):

Boil 8 Bermuda onions in their skins for one hour. Drain, peel, and cut out their centers. Chop fine a quarter of a pound of boiled ham, tongue, or chicken, or a little of each mixed. Soak for twenty minutes, in a cup of milk, a cup and a quarter of bread. Squeeze dry, mix with meat, add the onion that was removed from the centers, salt and pepper to taste, and fill the onions. Stick 2 cloves in each. Dab a lump of butter on each one. Place them in a buttered dish and sprinkle with bread crumbs. Pour 1 cup of cream in the dish and bake slowly for an hour.

BAKED POTATOES STUFFED WITH BEEF (*for eight*):

First make the tomato sauce, substituting, however, a half-cup of vinegar for the white wine. Reduce the sauce until only 1 cupful is left. Now bake 8 large potatoes carefully, and in the meantime prepare 2 cups of finely ground or chopped roast beef. Brown lightly 2 little white onions in a tablespoon of butter, remove the onion, add the meat, 1 teaspoon of chopped parsley, and a little beef stock or water. Bring to a boil, stirring all the while, then put on the back of the stove and simmer gently for a few minutes. When the potatoes are cooked, slice a piece off the side of each. Scoop out the potatoes, mash well with a fork with a large lump of butter, add the meat and stuff the potato shells. Pour as much tomato sauce over each one as it will absorb. Put a lump of butter on each, cover with the piece you sliced off, set in the oven to cook for about ten minutes, place on a folded napkin, and serve at once.

CABBAGE, POTATO, AND SAUSAGE (*for eight*):

Gabrielle was old and fat and cross, but she could make a cabbage, potato, and sausage dish that tasted like something straight from heaven; but she couldn't make cake, so I undertook to teach her how. I mixed the cake, put it in the oven which was just the right temperature, and went out in the garden to pick flowers. For some mysterious reason the cake was a dismal failure — all sunken in the middle. She looked suspiciously gleeful. The next day I made another cake — and this time I only pretended to pick flowers. In a little while I saw her come innocently to the door to see where I was, then I also saw her deliberately open the oven door wide with a diabolical smile on her face. We soon parted, but not before I learned how to make her cabbage dish.

Cut in quarters and remove the cores of 2 big green cabbages; soak in salted water for half an hour. Shred fine and boil in salted water for ten minutes. Drain well. Boil 16 or 18 new potatoes with their skins on. Peel them and cut in half-inch squares. Brown 2 pounds of Deerfoot sausages in a big iron frying-pan. Pour off the grease and cover with alternate layers of potato and cabbage. Salt and pepper to taste and simmer for thirty or forty minutes until well browned. Turn upside down on a hot plate and garnish with parsley.

PANCAKE DELICACIES (*for eight*)

These were a specialty of a friend of ours living in Paris. He was very generous-minded and gave me many good ideas and new recipes.

This dish consists of French pancakes stuffed with chicken and mushroom hash and rolled. They are then placed in an oblong glass cooking-dish, covered with cream sauce, sprinkled with Parmesan cheese, and baked in the oven until brown.

For the hash prepare 2 cups of finely ground chicken minus all gristle and skin. Peel, wash, and chop fine three quarters of a pound of mushrooms. Sauté in 3 tablespoons of butter until almost dry. Brown lightly 3 sliced white onions in 2 tablespoons of butter, then fish out the onions and throw them away. Sprinkle the chicken with 2 heaping teaspoons of flour and put it into the butter. Add the mushrooms. Cook gently a minute or two without browning and add 1¼ cups of hot cream. Salt and pepper to taste. Cook a minute or two longer.

In the meantime, make about 16 small thin French pancakes. The batter should be prepared two hours before cooking. Sift 2 cups of flour with half a teaspoon of salt and 1 teaspoon of sugar. Make a hole in the center and break into it 3 eggs. Add three quarters of a cup of milk and stir with a spoon until smooth, then add gradually 2 more cups of milk and 1 tablespoon of cognac.

Take a small, light-weight frying-pan. Heat well, then sprinkle liberally with salt. Scour with tissue paper and wipe clean with a towel. This will keep the crêpe from sticking. Put a little lump of butter into a hot pan, pour a small quantity of the batter in at once, and tilt the pan so as barely to cover the bottom. When the crêpe is a delicate brown, flip it over and brown the other side. When you have made enough, spread the hash on thin, roll up the pancakes, and place in a buttered glass cooking-dish. Cover with a cream sauce. Sprinkle with Parmesan cheese and bake until brown.

VIII. VEGETABLES

People are funny about vegetables. Children eat them because they jolly well have to, but grown-ups eat them because doctors tell them they contain alkaline salts and carbohydrates and vitamins and what not — to help their lovely complexions and make their hair curl. But precious few eat them because they really like them. Probably the real blame can be laid directly to those horrid, miserable blue-plate vegetable lunches with the cold poached egg in the center to lend a dash of color — they make me fairly shudder.

A great deal of patience, but fortunately not too much skill, is required in preparing vegetables properly. Each and every one of the fifty or more edible vegetables on the market is worthy of being served alone as a separate course, but of course some of them have their affinities — peas with lamb, spinach with veal, and so forth.

The following recipes are not very complicated — and I hope most of them are unknown to you:

NOODLES WITH BUTTERED CRUMBS (*for eight*):
Into 6 quarts of actively boiling salted water drop little by little 1 pound of fine noodles. Cook until tender, then drain well through a colander. Put a large lump of butter in the bottom of a pan, add the noodles, and stir with a fork

so that they are all well coated with butter. Place in a hot dish and sprinkle copiously with buttered toasted crumbs made by toasting bits of bread in the oven until a golden brown, then rolling them into a powder with a rolling-pin. Melt plenty of butter in a frying-pan and heat the crumbs in this.

STRING BEANS IN BUTTER (*for eight*):

With a sharp knife cut off both sides of 3 pounds of string beans, then cut down the center. Wash well. Put them little by little into furiously boiling water with a tiny pinch of soda and salt, and cook for not more than ten or fifteen minutes at the most. Melt a large lump of butter in a pan, add a tiny pinch of sugar, then the thoroughly drained beans, salt and pepper lightly, then shake the pan over the fire for a second or two, and serve at once.

ASPARAGUS, BROWNED BUTTER, AND CHEESE (*for eight*):

Scrape and wash 2 bunches of asparagus. Cut off the tough ends and tie the bunches top and bottom with white string. Place the asparagus, heads down, in cold water to soak until ready to cook. Plunge into boiling, salted water in which is a tiny pinch of soda. Cook until tender, but not floppy. In the meantime, brown some butter by placing it in an enamel saucepan to simmer. It will eventually brown. Put the asparagus on a hot platter; remove the strings, drain well, and pass with a bowl of grated Parmesan cheese and the browned butter.

PETITS POIS À LA FRANÇAISE (*for eight*):

Petits pois à la française require 4 pounds of peas, 8 little white onions, a head of lettuce, 2 lumps of sugar, three quarters of a cup of butter, grated nutmeg, and a little parsley. Put half the butter in the bottom of a pan. Shred the lettuce and the onions and add these, the parsley and the sugar, and one tablespoon of cold water, salt and pepper and a dash of nutmeg. Last of all, put in the peas. Set on the fire and cook quickly for about twenty minutes. Drain off the juice, when the peas are tender, and reduce it by letting it boil. Add the rest of the butter to the peas. Put in a hot dish and pour the juice over them. Serve at once.

POTATOES PANIER (*for eight*):

This was the specialty of a little bar in Chantilly where one stopped after the races for an *apéritif* and a bite of supper. The chef was rather evasive about it, but I think I managed to discover exactly how he made it.

Butter a shallow, round copper pan shaped like a pie tin. If you haven't such a thing, a glass cooking-dish will do, but is not quite so satisfactory. Peel 3 pounds of white Holland potatoes, wash carefully, and leave them soaking in cold water. Have ready a small bowlful of cold milk. Take 1 potato at a time and very carefully cut it in a manner to have little slivers of uniform size, 1 inch long by one eighth of an inch square, like match sticks. Put these immediately into the milk. This is to keep them from turning dark. When you have enough prepared, line the bottom of a buttered pan by placing the strips in a basket-weave pattern. The sides of the pan should also be covered. The rest of the potatoes are then cut up in the same way, but put in just as they come until the pan is full to the top. Now melt 1¾ cups of butter and add half a teaspoon of salt and a dash of pepper. Pour three quarters of it over the potatoes so as to cover all of them well. Cover with an inverted pie tin and put into a moderate oven. Bake for half an hour, then add a little more of the butter, and remove the cover. Increase the heat. Continue baking for another fifteen minutes. When ready to serve, empty them out onto a hot platter. They should be brown on the top and bottom and soft inside. Whip half a cup of cream and put on top of the potatoes. Sprinkle with salt, pepper, and chopped parsley; and serve at once.

ITALIAN ZUCCHINI, FAN–SHAPED (*any number*):

There was a certain restaurant on the Rond Point in Paris where I always ordered courgettes. They cooked them even better at the Café de Versailles, near the *gare* on the Boulevard Montparnasse. They don't grow courgettes here, but Italian zucchini are the next best thing to them and are delicious cooked in this way.

Buy Italian zucchini or French courgettes, one for each person. They should be not more than six inches long; peel as you would cucumbers, parboil in salted water, drain carefully, and dry on a teacloth. When cold, slice lengthwise within an inch of the end, then press gently with your hand to make them open like a fan. Sprinkle lightly with flour, salt and pepper, and fry to a delicate brown on both sides. Place carefully on a hot platter, pour over them the melted butter from the frying-pan, squeeze on a few drops of lemon juice, sprinkle with finely chopped parsley, and serve at once

PARSNIP FRITTERS (*for eight*):

Wash and boil 6 or 8 parsnips. When tender, take off the skin and mash them fine. Add 2 heaping teaspoons of flour, 2 beaten eggs, and a little salt and pepper. Have some good whole walnut meats ready and form the parsnip mixture into little balls with one walnut in each. Fry to a golden brown in butter in a frying-pan. Decorate with parsley and serve on a hot platter.

STRING BEANS, CREAM AND EGG SAUCE (*for eight*):

With a very sharp knife carefully cut off the ends and sides from 4 pounds of string beans. Wash carefully and tie in little individual bunches, as you would asparagus. Put the bunches into furiously boiling water with a tiny pinch of soda and a little salt; cook until tender, but not floppy. Place the bunches carefully on a hot platter, removing the strings, but still keeping in bunches. Pour over them a sauce made by heating 1½ cups of thick cream in a double boiler, and when it is very hot, pour it slowly onto the beaten yolks of 3 eggs. Salt and pepper to taste, place back in the double boiler and stir a few seconds until thickened, stir in a small lump of sweet butter, then pour over the beans and serve at once.

BAKED BEETS IN CREAM (*for eight*):

Wash thoroughly 20 beets of uniform size and put them into a hot oven. Bake for one hour, until they become soft, then peel and slice thin. Pour 1 cup of thick cream over them and heat the beets in it. Salt and pepper to taste, and, just before serving, add the juice of 1 lemon.

PROVINCIAL POTATOES (*for eight*):

Wash and boil in their skins 3 pounds of new potatoes. Put one eighth of a pound of butter in a saucepan. Cut it up and pour over it 3 dessertspoons of olive oil, and grate into this the rind of half a lemon. Add some chopped parsley and some chopped chives, a little freshly grated nutmeg, a pinch of flour, and some salt and pepper. When the potatoes are cooked, peel and cut into quarters or eighths and put

them into the butter mixture. Heat, but don't let the butter
boil. When ready to serve, add the juice of 1 lemon.

RED CABBAGE (*for eight*):

Wash and slice fine 2 tender red cabbages and put them to
soak in 2 tablespoons of vinegar and some water. Then
chop 1 onion fine and brown it in 2 tablespoons of bacon fat
and 2 tablespoons of butter in a frying-pan. Put in the cabbage, which has been drained well. Add 1 bay leaf, 3
cloves, 2 peppercorns, and 2 tart, juicy apples, sliced fine.
Cook slowly until tender, stirring frequently, as red cabbage burns easily. When done, melt 1 tablespoon of butter
in a saucepan, add 1 teaspoon of flour, stir and put in the
cabbage and its juice. Sprinkle with 1 teaspoon of sugar
and the juice of half a lemon. Simmer for a minute or two
and serve.

PURÉE OF MUSHROOMS WITH ENDIVES BRAISED
(*for eight*):

Wash and dry 1 pound of mushrooms. Peel and chop very
fine. Put a heaping tablespoon of butter in a frying-pan and
cook the mushrooms in it over a hot fire until all juice has
evaporated.

Make a Béchamel sauce by melting 1 heaping tablespoon
of butter in a saucepan. Add to it 1 small piece of celery, 1
small onion, and 1 small carrot, cut fine. Brown lightly,
then add 3 level tablespoons of flour. Cook without browning for five minutes and add slowly 1 pint of hot milk. Add
a bouquet of parsley and 1 little bay leaf. Reduce until
quite thick, then salt and pepper to taste and pass through a
fine sieve. Add the mushrooms, 1 heaping tablespoon of
grated Gruyère cheese, 1 heaping tablespoon of grated Parmesan, and one quarter of a cup of thick cream.

In the meantime, take the outer leaves off 18 endives, wash thoroughly and rapidly in cold water, dry and place them in a well-buttered enamel dish. Sprinkle a few drops of lemon juice on them, salt and pepper and dot with 4 tablespoons of butter. Add 1 cup of good meat stock, preferably veal or chicken. Cover with a buttered paper and put on a fire. Bring to a boil and then put in the oven to cook slowly for about an hour and a half. Put the purée of mushrooms in a long oblong glass cooking-dish and place the endives on top of it side by side. Pour the juice from the endives over all and serve at once.

ASPARAGUS TIPS COOKED À LA FRANÇAISE (*for eight*):

Wash thoroughly and soak, heads down, in cold water for one hour 2 bunches of tender green asparagus. Cut in uniform pieces the size of a pea. Put in boiling, salted water and let boil for just a few seconds, or until barely tender when crushed between the fingers. Drain and place in cold water. Fifteen minutes before serving, drain them well. Place 2 good tablespoons of butter in a saucepan, add the asparagus, salt and freshly ground pepper and warm in the butter. Sprinkle with 2 teaspoons of flour, half a cup of meat stock, and 1 teaspoon of sugar. Bring to a boil and simmer a minute or two, then bind the same with the yolks of 3 eggs. Serve with fried croutons.

CAULIFLOWER WITH CREAM SAUCE AND BUT-TERED CRUMBS (*for eight*):

Cut away the leaves and part of the thick stem of 2 small cauliflowers, and put them to soak, heads down, for twenty minutes in salted water. Plunge into rapidly boiling water and cook for fifteen or twenty minutes. Drain well and place them in a vegetable dish, heads up, and pour over them the following sauce: Melt 2 tablespoons of butter and cook in it without browning for three minutes 2 tablespoons of flour. Add gradually 2 cups of hot cream. Continue to cook in a double boiler for fifteen minutes. Salt to taste and pour over the cauliflower.

In the meantime, cut 8 slices of white bread in little squares and put them in the oven to brown and dry thoroughly. Roll them out fine. Melt a little more than an eighth of a pound of butter in a frying-pan and add the crumbs. Stir with a fork over the fire until hot and dry and well buttered. Place in a bowl and pass with the cauliflower.

CARROTS VICHY (*for eight*):

Peel and wash about 3 bunches of tender young carrots and cut them in tiny thin slices. Melt half a pound of butter in an enamel baking-dish and add some salt and a teaspoon of sugar. Mix well. Add the carrots and pour over all one third of a cup of cognac. Cover the dish and place in a moderate oven to cook for one hour. Do not stir, but watch carefully so that they don't cook too long and get hard or brown.

PURÉE OF WATERCRESS (*for eight*):

Wash and pick over carefully 10 bunches of watercress, removing the coarse stems. Do this the day before you wish to serve the dish. The next morning put them into salted boiling water and cook for twelve minutes. Drain and rinse in cold water and put through a sieve. Then leave in the refrigerator until night. When ready to use, pour off the juice which has formed. Melt 3 tablespoons of butter in a saucepan and add 1 tablespoon of flour. Cook for a minute without browning, then add the cress and 1 ¼ cups of cream. Salt and pepper to taste and heat slowly, stirring meanwhile. When hot and well mixed, serve garnished with fried croutons.

SAVOY CABBAGE (*for eight*):

Wash and soak 2 Savoy cabbages, cut in quarters, in cold salt water for a half-hour. Then cook in salted boiling water for ten minutes. Drain well and chop fine. Put 1 little onion (chopped fine) in a frying-pan with 2 table-spoons of butter. Brown until a light golden color. Sprinkle lightly with 1 tablespoon of flour. Add the chopped cabbage and half a cup of meat juice or a teaspoon of beef extract dissolved in a little water and thinned with a little of the cabbage juice. Add salt and pepper and a sprinkling of nutmeg. Cook for ten minutes and serve.

SQUASH IN CREAM (*for eight*):

Butter a deep glass baking-dish. Peel 4 white summer squash and remove the seeds. Slice the squash into the dish, sprinkle with salt and pepper, and add here and there 3 tablespoons of butter in little dabs. When the dish is full, place in a hot oven and cover with an inverted pie tin. As the squash becomes tender, add a half pint of cream and let cook without the cover until perfectly done. When slightly browned, sprinkle with parsley and serve in the cooking-dish.

GREEN PEPPERS IN OLIVE OIL (*for eight*):

Wash and remove seeds from 10 sweet green peppers. Parboil in salted water, drain well, and dry on a cloth. Put 1 clove of garlic in a frying-pan with half a cup of good olive oil. When hot, remove the garlic and add the peppers, which have been quartered, to the olive oil. Cook until the peppers begin to brown. Add salt and pepper to taste and serve with Italian bread.

PURÉE OF ONIONS (*for eight*):

Peel 2 pounds of little white onions. Wash and cut in thin slices. Melt half a pound of butter in a saucepan and add the onions. Cook very slowly for a half-hour without letting them brown. Put through a sieve. Put a tablespoon of butter in a pan, add 3 level tablespoons of flour, and make a roux of this. Add 1 ¼ cups of cream. Cook a minute or two and add the purée of onions. Salt and pepper to taste and add a few grains of sugar to the mixture. Serve with pork chops, if possible.

GLAZED TURNIPS (*for eight*):

Peel 2 dozen tender white turnips, wash well and boil in salted water until almost done. Then drain well and put in a frying-pan with some very hot butter. Brown them carefully and season with salt and pepper and granulated sugar. Drain off the butter and add a little meat extract dissolved in water. Let the turnips simmer until almost dry or until the juice is reduced to a glaze. Sprinkle lightly with chopped parsley and serve at once.

PURÉE OF LIMA BEANS AND PEAS (*for eight*):

Shell 3 pounds of green peas and 3 pounds of lima beans. Wash and cook together in boiling, salted water to which has been added a pinch of soda. Meanwhile, put 2 small onions cut up fine and half a cup of cream in a double boiler to heat. When peas and beans are done, drain well and put through a sieve. Place a lump of butter in a saucepan, add the purée, and beat in the hot cream from which the onions

have been removed. Salt and pepper to taste and serve with
thin slices of broiled ham.

SWEET POTATO PUDDING (*for eight*):

Peel 10 sweet potatoes and boil until perfectly tender.
Drain them well and mash them with one eighth of a
pound of butter, then add the grated rind of 1 lemon, salt
and very little pepper and a half-cup of some good brandy.
Gradually beat into this a half-pint of cream, and last of all
add another one eighth of a pound of sweet butter. Beat
until smooth and fluffy, then put the mixture into a glass
cooking-dish, decorate the top with fork marks, dot with
butter, and put the pudding into a hot oven to brown.

PURÉE OF MARRONS (*for twelve*):

Remove the outer skins from about 80 chestnuts. Place a
little butter in a frying-pan and sauté the chestnuts until
the second skin comes off. Take from the fire and remove all
the skins. Cook the chestnuts in some consommé for an
hour and a half. Pass them through a fine sieve with a
wooden mallet. Just before serving, heat and beat well
with a little cream, plenty of butter and a little salt.

PURÉE OF SPINACH (*for eight*):

Wash and pick off the leaves of 5 pounds of spinach.
Wash again and again until you are sure there is no sand
left, then soak in a big pan in cold water for several hours.
When ready to cook, lift them out of the water and cook
them in plenty of boiling salted water for not more than
fifteen minutes. Drain well and let some cold water run
over them. Press them to extract all the water and pass
them through a sieve. Put a quarter of a pound of butter
in an enamel pan, melt, and add the spinach. Stir well

and keep on a low fire for five minutes or so. Serve very hot.

VEGETABLE CURRY (*for eight*):

Peel 4 potatoes and cut in half-inch squares. Shell half a pound of green peas. String and cut in half-inch pieces a handful of string beans. Shell half a pound of baby lima beans. Peel, remove pits, and cut up 2 tomatoes. Peel a dozen white onions, and chop fine. Cut up 1 small cauliflower. Melt a quarter of a pound of butter in a big pan. Add half a tablespoon of curry powder and a little salt. Add all the vegetables and a cup of hot water. Simmer gently until all the vegetables are tender. Watch carefully so as not to burn them. Serve at once.

VEGETABLE PLATE (*for eight*):

A beautiful dish is a tender green cabbage, boiled whole in some water left from cooking corned beef, or, lacking that, a shank of ham boiled with the cabbage. Place on a big platter surrounded with little piles of baby carrots, long summer squash peeled and cooked whole, boiled onions, grilled tomatoes. Cut the top off a tender green cabbage and soak for two hours in salt water to remove any insects lurking inside. Boil as stated above in corned-beef water or ham water. Cook all the other vegetables carefully, butter lightly, and serve them attractively about the cabbage.

TOMATO SOUFFLÉ (*for eight*):

Soak in a cup of milk 4 thick slices of bread from which the crust has been removed. Mix it to a paste with a fork. Peel 10 small ripe tomatoes, remove the pits and cut up fine. Prepare 2 teaspoons of onion juice. Melt 3 tablespoons of butter. Add the tomatoes, onion juice, bread, salt and pepper, and a dash of paprika. Also add 3 tablespoons of grated Parmesan cheese. Then add the beaten yolks of 8 eggs. Beat the whites of the 8 eggs until stiff and fold in the tomato mixture. Put in a well-buttered, big, deep baking-dish. Sprinkle with Parmesan cheese and bake in a moderately hot oven for twenty minutes or until well risen and set. Serve at once on hot plates.

CUCUMBERS IN CREAM (*for eight*):

Peel 8 small tender cucumbers. Cook in boiling salted water until tender to the touch. Drain, pour cold water over them, and spread on a teacloth to drain. Make a cream sauce by melting 2 tablespoons of butter and adding to this 2 tablespoons of flour; then add 2 cups of thin scalded cream. Cook in a double boiler at least fifteen minutes longer. Salt and pepper to taste. Add the cucumbers and half a pint of thick cream.

SPINACH RING WITH MUSHROOMS (*for eight*):

Cook 5 pounds of spinach. Drain well and squeeze dry, then press through a sieve. Drain again. Then add to them a dessertspoon of grated onion and salt and pepper to taste. Beat the whites of 4 eggs stiff and fold them into the spinach. Fill the ring with this, place the ring in a shallow pan of hot water, cover the ring with a piece of paper buttered on both sides, and place the pan in an oven heated to about 400 degrees. Cook for ten minutes and reduce heat slightly; continue to cook for about half an hour. In the meantime, wash, dry, peel, and slice a pound of mushrooms in fairly thick slices. Also peel and boil in a little white wine 3 or 4 truffles for five minutes, then slice them as you have the mushrooms. Now put 3 good tablespoons of butter in a saucepan. Add the mushrooms and truffles and place on the fire. When the butter is melted, add the juice of 1 lemon, continue to cook a minute or two, then add salt and freshly ground pepper, a pinch of nutmeg, 4 tablespoons of tomato sauce, and a little beef stock or beef extract dissolved in hot water. When all this begins to boil again, add a little glass of sherry and continue to cook gently for twenty-five minutes. When the spinach ring is cooked, turn it out onto a hot platter and pour the mushrooms in the center. Serve at once.

FRENCH–FRIED POTATOES (*any number*):

Holland potatoes are best, but any good mealy potato will do. Peel and square them, then wash and cut them in regular pieces, long, and about one third of an inch square. Soak a few minutes in ice-water and then dry them well and quickly on a teacloth. Have 2 pans of fat on the fire. One should be moderately hot and the other smoking hot. Put some of the potatoes into the moderately hot fat and cook until they barely change in color, then fish them out and plunge them into the very hot fat until a golden brown. They should not take more than eight to ten minutes, in all, to cook. Drain on paper, salt, and serve at once.

MASHED POTATOES (*for eight*):

Peel 12 potatoes, wash well and cut in quarters. Place in an enamel pan with a lemon cut in two. Cover well with water. Salt lightly and boil until tender. Drain immediately and well. Remove lemon, and put the potatoes through a ricer. Add a good lump of butter and some salt and place the pan on a low flame and beat well with a wooden masher, adding little by little a cup or so of hot cream. Continue beating until light and fluffy.

BOILED POTATOES (*any number*):

Peel old potatoes, removing all eyes, wash well, soak awhile in cold water, put into boiling water containing a little salt, and cover. Cook gently until they may be easily pierced with a fork — about thirty minutes. Drain in a colander, shake over the fire a few minutes. Sprinkle very lightly with salt and cover with a cloth. Keep on the back of the stove for a minute or two, then serve on a folded napkin. Sprinkle lightly with very finely chopped parsley.

To serve new boiled potatoes, cook them with their skins on, just as above, but scrub them well first with a stiff brush so that they are perfectly clean. When cooked, drain well, and place them in a gay-colored napkin. Tie the opposite corners together, making two knots, and send to the table just like that. Of course not at a formal party.

BAKED POTATOES (*any number*):

Select smooth medium-sized potatoes. Scrub well with a stiff brush until you can almost see through the skin. Now rub them well all over with soft butter and sprinkle with salt. Place in a buttered pie tin and put in a very hot oven and bake until tender, from thirty to sixty minutes, depending on size. To test, squeeze them with the hand wrapped in a cloth. When soft, break open and serve at once. The skins may be eaten and taste as good as popovers.

IX. SALADS

W<small>HAT</small> are the most important requisites for a good salad? In my opinion, first, the greens must be thoroughly washed and freed from sand; second, they must be shaken completely dry in a wire basket made especially for that purpose, or wiped dry, very gently, on a teacloth; and third, they must be crisp and cold. As for French dressing, I might as well say, make it any way you like — for you will do so, anyhow. No two people agree on salad dressing, I find. My particular phobia is mayonnaise on lettuce.

The classic recipe for French dressing is: 1 teaspoonful of salt, a dash of freshly ground pepper, 3 tablespoons of olive oil to 1 tablespoon of vinegar. There are many ways of varying this, however. Some people like to add a pinch or two of sugar, or a dash of Worcestershire, or curry powder, or ketchup, or red wine, or a bit of meat juice, or pickle juice, or a little horseradish, or what-have-you.

And now about garlic, one should never be able to discover even a microscopic piece of it in the salad. The correct system is by use of a chapon — a dry heel of bread that is rubbed with a clove of garlic and placed in the bowl while the salad is being tossed. This is removed before serving. If you are really a good salad-maker, you will be sure that the bowl you use to toss and serve the salad in is ice-cold.

By the way, when I say to toss the salad, I don't mean to have a modified game of baseball with it — it's more of a folding process. In France they say, *fatiguer la salade*. I'm afraid some of us take that too literally. It should be tossed, but it should not be bruised or crushed. I know of a bachelor living in France who is famous for his lettuce salads. It seems that he paints each leaf with dressing with a broad camel's-hair brush so that every crevice of the lettuce is thoroughly coated — the advantage being that the leaves don't get bruised.

And now about the ever-so-important *fines herbes* — so intrinsically part of a supreme salad. It's all very well to say add a tablespoon of fresh chopped tarragon, chervil, chives, and so forth, but where may these illusive plants be found? Unless you can grow them yourself, the best bet is to find a good Italian greengrocer. He may possibly have enough imagination to carry them. He will certainly have the chives. If he hasn't the tarragon, don't worry — it fortunately can be purchased pickled in glasses in big specialty shops specializing in imported provisions. The chervil is the most difficult of all. There are many places in New York where it may be bought, but that doesn't help the rest of the people in the United States. A very good substitute for it is the use of the feathery tops of fennel, or finochio, a plant resembling celery, but which tastes like licorice and is a great favorite of the Italians. Chop it very fine and add it to the salad. It will at least give the illusion of *fines herbes* if nothing else. If you can't procure these herbs fresh, they do, however, exist dried, and are now sold in New York done up in neat little cellophane packages. Soaked in the vinegar awhile before making the salad, they help a lot.

Condiments for your salad shelf should include mustard

— French and English, salt, black pepper, white pepper, paprika, horseradish and Worcestershire sauce. Little pepper mills can be bought to grind the pepper freshly. This adds greatly to the success of a dressing.

There are many kinds of vinegar which may be used, tarragon, cider, red wine, or white wine. Lemon juice may be substituted for vinegar. French olive oil or Italian olive oil is most frequently used in making dressings.

And now about the greens themselves. We are likely to make the mistake of forgetting what a great variety of greens there are that may be eaten raw. Here is a list to refresh your memory: watercress, endive, field salad, dandelion, chicory, escarole, romaine, young spinach leaves, Chinese cabbage, red cabbage, green cabbage; and I'm sure there are others.

MIXED SALAD WITH FRENCH DRESSING (*any number*):

Wash escarole, chicory, lettuce, romaine, watercress, and endive, and use only the tenderest parts. Cut up with a silver knife and dry one way or another. Set in the vegetable part of the refrigerator until it is ready for tossing. Make your own idea of a French dressing, for no two people seem to agree on this subject, but I do thoroughly think that red wine vinegar, the kind they use in cheap Italian restaurants, is a great improvement. And if you don't frequent Italian restaurants, try adding a little red wine. You will undoubtedly make it the way you like it, but one thing that is essential is thoroughly to toss the salad in a big bowl and put in a lot of finely chopped fresh tarragon and chervil.

CELERY SALAD WITH MUSTARD DRESSING (*any number*):

Use a head of celery for each person. Remove all the tough outer stalks: use only tender stalks and take off as many strings as possible. Cut in 2-inch pieces and split each piece several times, almost to the end. Curl by putting in ice-water for several hours. Shake or wipe thoroughly dry. Then pile them in a cold bowl and treat with a dressing that is made up as follows: Put a small soup-spoonful of German mustard in a bowl, add some freshly ground pepper and salt to taste, and the juice of a small lemon. Stir well and then add three quarters of a cup of thin cream.

CAULIFLOWER SALAD WITH FRENCH DRESSING (*for eight*):

Boil 2 cauliflowers until tender but not too soft. Drain well. Pull apart in uniform bunches, then pile in a cold bowl and chill thoroughly. Sprinkle liberally with chopped chervil and finish off with French dressing.

CUCUMBER, TOMATO, AND RADISH SALAD (*for eight*):

Peel 2 cucumbers and slice fine. Soak in ice-water, but do not put salt in the water. Peel 8 ripe, juicy tomatoes and chill them thoroughly. Wash a dozen baby radishes and put them to soak in ice-water. Remove cucumbers and wipe dry on a linen cloth. Place them in a bowl containing French dressing and mix well. Remove and place in a shallow, cold dish. Slice the tomatoes in thin circles with a sharp knife and arrange them in a wreath around the cucumbers. Pour the dressing left from the cucumbers over all, then slice the radishes very thin and sprinkle these slices over the cucumbers and tomatoes. The radishes may be omitted and the tomatoes and cucumbers heavily sprinkled with chopped tarragon and chervil mixed.

POTATOES AND WATERCRESS SALAD (*for eight*):

Boil 3 pounds of little new Bermuda potatoes with skins on in salted water. Peel and slice while still hot. Put in a bowl and marinate them in a cup of dry white wine. Chill, and at the last moment add a bunch of watercress which has been carefully washed, dried, and picked over. Then treat with French dressing. Sprinkle the top with 2 hard-boiled eggs chopped fine and a little chopped chervil.

CHICORY AND ESCAROLE WITH CHICKEN LIVER DRESSING (*for eight*):

This was Maurice's specialty. Maurice was a business man, but definitely a gourmet. He offered to cook quail for me in the following manner: For six people, put 6 quail inside of 6 partridges. Put 6 partridges inside of 6 pheasants. Put 6 pheasants inside of 6 chickens. Put 6 chickens inside of 6 turkeys. Make a big deep hole in the sand in California, line it with rocks, build a roaring fire in the hole, and throw in the turkeys. Watch the fire carefully and keep it blazing furiously until the turkeys are completely burned away, until the chickens are completely burned away, until the pheasants are, too, until the partridges are well charred, then watch carefully. At just the right moment, just before the partridges are completely charred, remove them from the fire and extract the little quail, who will by then have acquired the full benefit of the juice from the turkeys, chickens, partridges, etc. Serve a vintage wine with these.

Wash a head of chicory and a head of escarole, pick over carefully, soak in cold water and dry thoroughly. Make up the following dressing: Wash 2 chicken livers and boil until tender with a carrot, an onion, a piece of celery, and a bunch of parsley. Remove from the juice. Hard-boil 2 eggs. Pass the livers through a very fine sieve. Do likewise with the yolks of the eggs. Place in a bowl together with a heaping teaspoon of French mustard. Mix to a paste; add freshly ground pepper and salt to taste and pour in, drop by drop, 2 tablespoons of olive oil, stirring always in the same direction. Now thin this by adding a teaspoon of red wine vinegar and a tablespoon of red wine. Sprinkle some chopped chervil over the escarole and chicory or chopped tarragon. Pour the liver dressing over all and toss well. Serve this salad very cold.

ROMAINE SALAD WITH HARD-BOILED EGG
    DRESSING (*for eight*):

Prepare salad in the usual manner. Hard-boil 3 eggs. Pass the yolks through a fine sieve and put them in the bottom of a cold salad bowl. Add a teaspoon of French mustard, freshly ground pepper, and salt. Then add 3 tablespoons of olive oil and then 1 tablespoon of tarragon vinegar. Add romaine, broken in small pieces, and sprinkle with a teaspoon of fresh-chopped tarragon. Mix well. Sprinkle the top with the whites of eggs which have been chopped up fine.

WILTED SALAD (*for eight*):

Strange as it may seem, wilted salad is good. Try it and see.

Lettuce or field salad or dandelion may be used for this. Prepare the greens in the usual way, but in this case put into a hot bowl and sprinkle with salt and freshly ground pepper, and use this dressing: Cut 6 slices of fat bacon in little squares and fry in a hot pan until crisp. Pour the hot grease and the bacon directly on the greens; put a teaspoon or so of vinegar into the hot pan and then pour it over the salad. Mix well and then eat at once. The salad will wilt slightly, but it is really supposed to, and it is quite delectable for a change.

HOT POTATO SALAD (*for eight*):

Boil 3 pounds of new potatoes. Peel and slice while hot. Sprinkle with chopped chives or shallots and finish with French dressing. Place in a bed of fresh lettuce and serve warm.

VEGETABLE SALAD (*for eight*):

Boil 2 pounds of new potatoes with their skins on. Cook separately 1 pound of green peas, a half-pound of string beans, 1 pound of lima beans, 6 beets, 6 carrots cut in little cubes, and the tips of 1 bunch of asparagus.

Make a boiled dressing for the potatoes in the following manner: Mix 2 tablespoons of sugar with 1 level tablespoon of flour, 1 level teaspoon of salt, and some freshly ground pepper. Add three quarters of a cup of vinegar and one quarter of a cup of water. Put this mixture in an enamel double boiler, add a lump of butter the size of an egg, and the yolks of 2 eggs well beaten. Place on the fire and stir constantly until thick. Remove from the fire and chill. When ready to use, add half a cup of thick cream to the dressing. Season again to taste and pour over the potatoes, which have been peeled and sliced thin while still hot, and which have been sprinkled with a teaspoon of chopped tender chives or chopped onion.

Marinate the rest of the vegetables separately, when they are thoroughly chilled, with French dressing for a half-hour. Arrange the potato salad in a pile on a bed of tender lettuce leaves and place the different vegetables in neat piles around the potato salad.

SPINACH SALAD (for eight):

Wash and pick over carefully 5 pounds of spinach leaves. Soak in cold water until all sand has been taken off. Place them in a pan with a little cold water and bring quickly to a boil. Drain well, and chill thoroughly.

Put into a salad bowl 1 teaspoon of French mustard, some salt, freshly ground pepper, 3 tablespoons of olive oil, and 1 of vinegar. Mix well, add the spinach and let it soak well, turning it over several times so as not to squash the leaves. Serve very cold. This is particularly good with cold roast veal.

LETTUCE SALAD (for eight):

Wash and dry well 2 heads of Boston lettuce, treat with a French dressing and some chopped chervil or a little chopped fennel tops. Toss well and serve.

CHICORY SALAD (for eight):

Wash and dry well the white part of 2 heads of chicory. Toss well in French dressing with some chopped chervil and 2 or 3 hard-boiled eggs sliced in it.

HARD–BOILED EGG SALAD (for eight):

Wash and dry well 2 heads of Boston lettuce. Wash, pick over, and chop very fine 1 bunch of watercress. Make a French dressing and hard-boil 8 eggs. Put the cress into the dressing. Pour over the lettuce and toss well. Slice the eggs lengthwise and arrange them on the bed of lettuce.

ASPARAGUS, EGG, AND WATERCRESS SALAD (*for eight*):

Scrape and wash thoroughly 2 bunches of fresh green asparagus. Cut off the tough part and tie in bunches. Soak them heads down in cold water for one hour. Cook in the usual way in salted boiling water with a tiny pinch of soda until tender, but not floppy. Drain carefully and arrange on a platter. Put in the refrigerator to chill thoroughly. Hard-boil 3 eggs. Wash and pick over carefully 2 bunches of fresh watercress. Pick off the leaves and chop very fine. Make a good tart French dressing, using red wine vinegar. When ready to serve the salad, chop the whites of the eggs and sprinkle them over the tips of the asparagus, and over this the yolks put through the potato-ricer. Put the chopped cress into the French dressing and pass it in a bowl with the salad.

BABY GARDEN–LETTUCE WITH HARD–BOILED EGG DRESSING (*for eight*):

Wash thoroughly and dry well a big bowl of baby lettuce leaves. Toss well in the following dressing: Hard-boil 3 eggs. Slice the whites and sprinkle them over the salad. Crush the yolks in a bowl, add salt and pepper and a teaspoon of sugar and a heaping teaspoon of tarragon mustard and 2 tablespoons of vinegar. Stir well and add gradually 6 or 8 tablespoons of olive oil.

STRING–BEAN SALAD (*for eight*):

With a string-bean cutter, sold especially for this purpose, cut the sides and ends from 3 pounds of string beans. This will be much easier if you soak the beans in very cold water for an hour before preparing them. Tie the beans in 8 or 10 bunches as you would asparagus. Boil them in plenty of furiously boiling salted water with a tiny pinch of soda. Cook until just tender, not floppy. Drain well. Arrange them neatly in a row on a pretty platter, remove the strings, and place in the refrigerator to chill thoroughly. Make some good tart French dressing, using red wine vinegar, and put in it 1 small white onion grated fine. Pour this over the beans fifteen minutes before serving.

POTATO AND TRUFFLE SALAD (for eight):

Wash and boil in salted water 3 pounds of new potatoes. Peel when cold and slice fine. In the meantime, boil as many truffles as you can afford in white wine for five minutes. Peel them carefully and slice in very thin slices. Sprinkle some finely chopped chervil over the potatoes, and pour over it all some good French dressing. Add the truffles and mix very lightly so as not to break the truffles or the potatoes. Place in the refrigerator. When ready to serve, make a nest of lettuce and pile the potato and truffle salad in the middle.

ROMAINE, ORANGE, AND ALMOND SALAD (for eight):

Mr. Newnham Davis, in his gourmet's guide to London, says that this is a specialty of the Ritz Hotel in London.

Take the hearts of 4 heads of romaine. Wash and soak in ice-water until crisp, then dry carefully leaf by leaf. Make a good French dressing (no garlic). Peel 6 small navel oranges, cutting off all the white skin with a sharp knife. Cut between the sections so as to remove the pulp in perfect whole pieces. Pour a little dressing over the oranges. Take the romaine leaf by leaf and dip in the rest of the dressing, arranging the leaves around the inside of your salad bowl. Pile the oranges in the center and serve. Blanched almonds split in two may be added to this salad.

X. FILLING AND FATTENING
FOODS

THE Italians certainly have the monopoly on doing wonderful things with fattening foods. What could be better than ravioli, polenta, gnocchi, and spaghetti? But France certainly contributed with her cassoulet; and the United States deserves one wreath of laurel, anyway, for baked beans. A recipe for each of these is included below.

GNOCCHI (*for eight*):

For years every so often I encountered a dish called gnocchi in Paris. I could never see what the French saw in it. Then one day I had it in New York cooked by a friend just back from a year in the Academy, at Rome. She had seen possibilities in it and worked on her recipe for it, evolving this version, which I wheedled out of her. It is now one of my specialties.

Melt half a cup of butter in the top part of the double boiler. Mix half a cup of cornstarch and half a cup of semolina and salt together. Add to melted butter. Stir well and add 4 cups of hot milk gradually. Put directly on the flame and stir furiously. It will get very thick. Remove from the fire and cook in the double boiler three minutes. Keep stirring. Add 1 cup of grated Parmesan cheese. Remove from the fire and add 4 well-beaten egg-yolks. Stir well and spread out to three quarters of an inch thickness in an oblong, buttered pyrex dish. Let it get thoroughly cold, then cut in equal-sized squares of about 2 inches. Butter a large oblong pyrex dish and cover the bottom with the squares, put neatly side by side, but not touching each other. Put a tiny dab of butter on each piece and sprinkle with grated Parmesan cheese. Put a second layer of gnocchi on top of the first and repeat the butter and cheese process. Place the dish in a very hot oven and cook about fifteen minutes, or until brown. Serve at once. (*Note.* Semolina may be bought at Italian grocers and is a fine wheat meal.) Farina may be used as a substitute.

POLENTA WITH SAUSAGES (*for eight*):

Into 6 cups of actively boiling salted water pour slowly, stirring all the while, 1½ cups of yellow corn meal. Cook in a double boiler half an hour, then pour out on a platter to about a half-inch thickness, and let it get cold. Now prick with a fork a half-pound or more of Deerfoot sausages and place them in a frying-pan to brown very delicately on all sides. Don't cook too long. Remove from the pan and slice in little pieces. Now butter an oblong earthenware or glass baking-dish. Cut the cold corn meal in squares. Put a layer of them into the dish, place a dab of butter on each piece, and sprinkle with grated Parmesan cheese. Next comes a layer of the sausages, then another layer of polenta, etc., until the dish is full, ending with a layer of corn meal. Pour over this 1½ cups of tomato sauce (see page 121). Sprinkle with cheese and bake in a hot oven until lightly browned. Serve at once.

SPAGHETTI (*for eight*):

Chop 6 onions fine, and fry them to a deep golden brown in 4 tablespoons of olive oil. Fry separately in butter half a cup each of finely chopped celery and carrots. Put these in with the olive oil, and add a quarter of a pound of Italian ham cut in little shoestring slices an inch long. Pour into this 3 cups of strong stock, to which you have added a teaspoon of beef extract. Simmer gently until reduced at least one third. If you happen to have any clear meat jelly in the house, by all means add it to this.

Now wash, dry, peel, and slice very fine half a pound of mushrooms. Put half a clove of garlic into a frying-pan with 3 or 4 tablespoons of olive oil and let it get quite hot. Then remove the garlic, and sauté the mushrooms in the olive oil until they begin to get brown, then add them to the reduced sauce. Salt and pepper to taste.

A pound or more of spaghetti should be put into a big pot of boiling water and boiled until just tender — not floppy. Drain and pour a little cold water over it. Put back into the pan and mix well with the sauce. Serve a big bowl of Parmesan cheese with this.

CASSOULET (*for eight*):

Salt and pepper 2¼ pounds of fresh fillet of pork the night before using. Take 2¼ pounds of fresh shoulder of lamb. Cut the lamb away from the bones and salt and pepper it; save the bones. Wash and carefully pick over 1 quart of dried baking beans, then put them in cold water and bring to a boil for ten minutes. Remove from the fire, cover and let cool. The good ones will sink to the bottom; those floating on the top should be thrown out. Now put them into 3 or 4 quarts of boiling water with half a pound of slightly salted pork rind or salt pork which has been rolled up and tied, the scalded shank of 1 ham, 5 little onions, and a bunch of parsley, thyme, and laurel. Skim carefully and boil for an hour and a half. Now add half a pound of Salsicietta or Luganica sausage and a bit of pepper; turn the flame down a little and let the beans cook slowly for another hour.

Brown 5 small onions with the lamb in an iron casserole. Pour off the grease and add the bones and a chopped clove of garlic. Cook in a slow oven for two hours. Half an hour before it is done, add a cup of tomato sauce. (Use the recipe for tomato sauce on page 121.)

In the meantime, roast the fillet of pork.

Remove the ham, the pork rind, and the sausage from the beans; pour off the water from the beans, but do not throw it away.

Slice in uniform pieces the ham, the pork rind, the sausage, the lamb, and the pork. Arrange these in alternate layers with the beans in an earthen baking-dish, reserving some of the sausage for the top layer. Pour over this the juice from the pork and the lamb which has had the grease carefully skimmed off. Moisten with the juice from the beans. Put back into a slow oven and cook for about an hour longer. Serve in the dish in which it was baked.

RAVIOLI (*for six*):

The simplest recipe for ravioli is to make yourself acquainted with a good Italian restaurant and catering establishment. Order the ravioli the day before they are needed. Failing that, take 3 eggs, beat them slightly, add to them as much flour (Gold Medal) as they will absorb, which will be at least 2 cupfuls, kneading the whole with the finger-tips into a stiff paste. Work 1 teaspoon of salt into this paste. When the paste is smooth, roll it with a rolling-pin as thin as possible into a sheet about 2 feet square, working quickly and keeping the paste as cool as possible. Now the paste is ready to be filled with the force-meat which you will have prepared beforehand. Dabs of this filling, about half a teaspoon for each, are arranged in a row, with an inch between each dab. Leave a lower margin of about an inch or a little more. This margin is folded over the force-meat. Then with your fingers press down tightly around each mound and then cut out each mound in a half-circle with a small biscuit-cutter. Repeat the process until the entire sheet of paste has been used up. It is important that the upper and lower surfaces of the paste are tightly pressed together so that no water will enter when the ravioli are boiled. The prongs of a fork can be used to make an ornamental edge to each piece of raviolo. When finished, they should be put aside in a cool place to dry out, but should be cooked within an hour or two of their being made. Boil in plenty of salted water until tender. This takes about twenty minutes, depending upon the thickness of the paste. The thinner the paste, the more successful the ravioli.

Force-meat:

Force-meat for ravioli may be made of a variety of ingredients: ground-up chicken livers seasoned with onion juice or according to taste; leftover cooked beef, lamb, or chicken properly minced and seasoned; fresh upper-round of steak, part of which may be used for the sauce. Take half a pound of round steak; pan-broil it and then turn down the flame so that it will cook slowly, drawing out the juices. When the steak is tender, run it through a meat-grinder, using the bread-crumber knives. A little flour on the steak, sprinkled as it is cooking, will give a slight thickness to the pan gravy. Add to this 1 teaspoon of chopped onion and a bit of chopped parsley and salt to taste. This pan gravy is used to moisten the ground-up steak.

SAUCE FOR RAVIOLI:

Lightly browned butter in which a piece of garlic was placed while browning is the simplest sauce for ravioli, but the following sauce is even better: Grind up half a pound of round steak (raw); brown it in a frying-pan with a little butter. Into another frying-pan put about a tablespoon of butter and cut into it 3 onions, 1 clove of garlic (paper-thin). Brown slightly. Add to this 4 large mushrooms, peeled and slivered. Also add half a can of Italian tomato paste and a tablespoon of olive oil, half a cup of water, a pinch of thyme, a pinch of marjoram, a pinch of celery salt (or a tablespoon of chopped celery). Add to this the browned meat. Set on a low flame to simmer for an hour. Add salt to taste. It may be necessary to add more water if it cooks down too much.

(*Note*. This sauce is capable of variation in many ways; chicken livers instead of beef makes a delicious sauce. There are as many fillings for ravioli as the cook has ingenuity for devising.)

BOSTON BAKED BEANS (*for twelve*):

By the way, speaking of baked beans, it seems that we are all wrong when we serve them right in the old brown pot. My Boston cook tells me that the best Bostonians serve them emptied out into a silver dish, pork on top (the master of the house usually helping himself to most of the pork). We should have them every Saturday night accompanied either by chops or small steaks and hot Boston brown bread, ending up with pie. She went on to say that to complete the ritual our waitress should be dressed in a long black alpaca dress with a very high stiffly starched standing collar with cuffs to match, a skirt apron with a stiff bow in the back and long streamers floating behind, and to complete the picture there should be a perk little organdy bow in her pompadour. Her name should be Kate, and she assured me that there are still many Kates in Boston.

Pick over, wash, and soak overnight 6 cups of dried pea beans. The next morning cover them with fresh water, heat slowly, and cook, keeping below the boiling point, until the skins burst when you take some on a spoon and blow on them. Don't overcook. When done, drain well and place the beans in a big earthenware bean-pot. Bury in the center of them 1 small white onion. Take 3 pieces of salt pork weighing a quarter of a pound each and scald them with boiling water. The outer rind should have been cut off first. Now cut through the top part of each piece in half-inch strips about a half-inch deep. Bury these, exposing them slightly. Now dissolve 1½ level teaspoons of dry mustard and 1½ teaspoons of salt in a little water and add 6 tablespoons of light New Orleans molasses or 4 of dark. The light is much better, but hard to find. Pour this over the beans and pour in enough boiling water completely to cover the beans. Bake in a moderate oven for eight hours. It is not necessary to cover the beans, but watch them carefully, and should they brown too fast, reduce the heat. Never stir the beans.

SOUTHERN BAKED BEANS (*for twelve*):

Far be it from me to take any justly deserved laurels away from the Boston baked beans, but this version from the South has much to be said for it. Try it and see.

Cut three quarters of a pound of salt pork into squares about 2 inches big. Wash 2 pounds of small navy beans, and scald the pork. Put the beans and the pork on to boil with sufficient water to allow for swelling of the beans. It is better to start the beans boiling with just enough water to cover, adding more boiling water as they swell and absorb the water. Cook the beans until the skins roll back when gently blown upon. Boil them the day before you want them. The next morning, place a layer of the beans in a deep earthenware bean pot, then cover with a layer of dark brown sugar. Repeat until the dish is full, using a pound of sugar and all the beans and their juice, and having the last layer a layer of sugar. Cover the top with another quarter of a pound of scalded pork cut in squares also. Cover and bake in a slow oven from eight to ten hours. The beans should absorb most of the liquid, but should not be cooked too dry. Add a very little more boiling water if necessary.

XI. CUSTARDS AND PUDDINGS

Nine times out of ten the fruit dessert is the correct dessert with which to end a meal, but just the same many of us wish it could be a pudding or a custard. Plain custards and simple puddings are good, but it's fun to dress them up a bit. A macaroon here or some praliné there may make all the difference. These little fancies are sometimes hard to produce on a moment's notice and I have found that a shelf in the pantry well stocked with trimmings, such as orange sugar and crystallized violets, will be well worth the trouble.

So, some day, when you are feeling energetic and domestic, go on a little marketing expedition. Buy a dozen and a half pint-sized glass jars with screw-on tops (fruit jars will do), a yard or so of gay oilcloth, some jelly labels, a box of thumb tacks, and, unless you already have one, a stone mortar and pestle. On the way home stop at the grocer's, and ask him to send over two or three whole vanilla beans, five pounds of granulated sugar, a package of white Sultana raisins, a package of black seeded raisins, six slicing oranges, six lemons, half a pound of shelled filberts, half a pound of shelled first-quality almonds, several tangerines, a pound of dry almond-paste macaroons, a package of pearl tapioca, a package of minute tapioca, three packages of gelatine, some white rice, some Baker's unsweetened chocolate, some first-quality triple vanilla sweet chocolate, some shredded coconut, cornstarch, farina, a large bottle of vanilla, almond extract, lemon, orange, rose, and coffee extracts, a bottle of orange-blossom water, and some Burnett's coloring for desserts, and silver balls.

This buying orgy is all so that you will be prepared when the spirit moves you some day to make a superlatively fancy dessert. When you get home, and the groceries have arrived, clear a shelf in the store closet and cover it with the gay oilcloth. Arrange the different bottled flavorings on the shelf, and empty the raisins, macaroons, tapiocas, and so forth into the different jars and label them. Now, if you follow these directions you will make vanilla sugar, lemon sugar, orange sugar, and tangerine sugar, and praliné, also to be put into jars, ready for future use.

These flavored sugars are to be used in making méringues, soufflés, and whips, where the use of liquid flavorings sometimes brings disaster.

To make vanilla sugar, cut the vanilla beans into small pieces and pound them well in the mortar with two cups of granulated sugar. Then sift the sugar carefully, put into the jar, and cover tightly. Also put away carefully the pieces of vanilla bean.

To make orange sugar, carefully remove the thin orange rind of the six oranges, being sure not to include any of the white part. Place it in the warming oven for a day or so until dry, then pound in the mortar with two cups of granulated sugar. Sift and put into the jar, and cover at once.

To make lemon and tangerine sugar, do the same as with the oranges.

To make the praliné, place just enough water in a pound of sugar to moisten it, then place in an aluminum pan, or, better still, a copper pan, and set on the fire to boil. Watch carefully until it has caramelized to a very light golden brown. Now put in the half-pound of filberts and the shelled almonds and pour immediately into a buttered platter or onto a marble slab. When cold, break and work through a fine meat-chopper, then pound it in the mortar with several pieces of vanilla bean. Keep in a dry covered glass jar.

You might also keep on hand some candied violets and rose petals. Your favorite confectioner probably can supply you. It's true they don't do much to improve the taste of anything, but they are fun to use for pure ornamentations. I have even heard of using a real rose or a pansy or two to decorate the dessert dish.

Now for some more practical hints. I wonder if you know how to catch liquid custard when it starts to curdle? Add a little cold milk, put the pan immediately into cold water and beat with an eggbeater. Never make liquid custard directly on the fire — always use a double boiler. Always add liquid flavoring to custard when it has cooled, and stir well. In making caramel custard or any pudding calling for a caramelized mold, try to make it at least ten hours ahead of time in order to give the caramel time to melt in the refrigerator, so you won't have to resort to putting it on the blaze to melt it before turning it out. Also whites of eggs for floating island are much better cooked in milk than in water. In making liquid custards, always keep stirring the same way, and don't stop stirring until the custard has been removed from the fire for at least a minute or two. Never put custard into the refrigerator until thoroughly cold — sudden change from hot to cold produces humidity which causes moisture to form on top of the custard. To test baked custard, insert the blade of a sharp knife in the center of the custard. If the knife comes out clean, the custard is done. Never melt chocolate directly over the fire. It should be melted in a double boiler. In boiling a pudding never let the water stop boiling in which it is cooking. Don't try to bake custard in too hot an oven — and it's much safer to place the custard in a pan of water while baking. Brown eggs make a more yellow custard.

Here are my favorite puddings, custards, and so forth.

PRALINÉ CUSTARD (*for twelve*):

Praliné custard has an exasperating way of not always turning out as it should, especially if it is being made for a party. Don't let it get the better of you, however, but just be prepared to make it over again. Have a large supply of eggs and milk and burnt, sugared almonds in the house, just to be sure.

Make the custard part early in the day and place it in the refrigerator so that it will be thoroughly chilled by night. Heat 3 pints of milk in a double boiler with 12 level table-spoons of granulated sugar. Separate yolks and whites of a dozen fresh eggs, being very careful not to let any of the yolks get into the whites. Put the whites away in the re-frigerator and concentrate on the custard part. Beat the yolks well, but not until they are foamy, and pour them gradually into the scalded milk, stirring all the time. Keep on stirring until the custard makes a thick coating on the spoon. Remove from the fire and keep stirring for a few minutes. Add vanilla flavoring when it is cold — into the refrigerator it goes.

To make the méringue, first caramelize two angel-cake tins. Light the oven, which has to be at a moderate temperature to bake the méringue. Pound a half-pound of burnt, sugared almonds until they are very fine. Now beat the egg-whites in a big bowl until quite stiff and add 24 level tablespoons of powdered sugar gradually, just as if you were making méringues. When this is done, add vanilla and very gently fold in the powdered almonds. Put the mixture gently into the caramelized molds and place the molds in a roasting-pan filled with hot water. Set in a moderate oven and bake for one hour. It then should have risen quite high out of the pan. Take the molds out of the pan of water and let the soufflés cool in the molds. They will fall a little bit. If they sink in a miserable heap, however, the only thing to do is to take it philosophically and repeat the whole process. It's bound to come out right the second time. Place them in the refrigerator right in their molds until about an hour before serving.

Turn them carefully out into deep bowls, having first placed them over a hot blaze for a second to loosen the caramel. Pour lots of custard around them. The islands will float on top.

CRÊPES SUZETTE (*for eight*):

I hesitate to include this recipe in my book because it seems that everybody in the world who is anybody at all already has the one and only original recipe. Anyway, I like mine best, and I'm just as sure as I'm sure of my name that the printed recipe sent to me personally by the chef on the S.S. *Paris*, by way of a certain charming officer of the boat, is the only copy in the world of the original recipe.

By the way, in France on the second of February, which is the feast of la Chandeleur or Purification, they always make crêpes. Holding a gold coin in the left hand, each person in turn undertakes to toss the crêpe he is making in such a manner that it falls neatly back into the pan, having turned over during the process cooked side up. If he or she is successful in doing this without dropping the crêpe on the floor or on the stove, it is a sure sign that he or she will have money the year around. I advise that you do a bit of practicing before trying out your luck.

Ingredients: 2 cups of sifted flour, 3 eggs, 2¼ cups of milk, a half-teaspoon of salt, 2 teaspoons of granulated sugar, 1 teaspoon of maraschino, 1 teaspoon of kirsch.

For the sauce: 6 lumps of sugar, 1 orange, 1 lemon, juice of half an orange, 3 tablespoons of sweet butter, a half-cup of granulated sugar, 1 liqueur glass of rum, 1 liqueur glass of Bénédictine, 1 liqueur glass of Cointreau, 2 liqueur glasses of Grand Marnier.

Make the crêpes mixture two hours before it is needed, proceeding as follows: Place the sifted flour in a bowl. Make a hole in the center and break the 3 eggs into it. Add the sugar, salt, and a little of the milk. Beat with a spoon until smooth and then pour in the rest of the milk gradually. Now add the maraschino and the kirsch.

Prepare in the meantime the ingredients for the sauce. Cream the butter. Rub 4 of the lumps of sugar carefully over the orange so as to saturate the sugar with the oil in the skin. Rub the other 2 lumps of sugar on the lemon. Squeeze the juice of half an orange and strain it onto the lumps of sugar. Crush until the sugar is melted. Mix this with the creamed butter. Measure the different liqueurs in a glass and mix them together. Measure out the granulated sugar. Put all these ingredients on a large silver tray, together with the chafing-dish, a tablespoon, a fork, and a box of matches, so that there will be no confusion when the time comes to make the sauce at the table.

To make the crêpes: Take a small light-weight frying-pan. The pan should be well heated and then sprinkled liberally with salt, scoured with tissue paper and wiped clean with a towel. This will keep the crêpes from sticking. Then put a small lump of butter into the hot pan, pour in at once a small quantity of the batter and tilt the pan so as barely to cover the bottom of the pan. When the crêpe is a delicate brown, flip it over, brown the other side, and put it on a hot plate in the warming oven. In this fashion make 16.

In the meantime, start the sauce by lighting the alcohol stove under the chafing-dish. Then place in it the prepared butter, to melt. The crêpes should now be brought to the table with hot dessert plates. One by one, put the crêpes into the melted hot butter, turn them over, and fold them in quarters. After this, sprinkle them liberally with the granulated sugar and pour over all the glass of liqueurs. When they have simmered down a few seconds, tilt the pan a little so that the flame will ignite the liqueurs, being careful not to be too near the flames. When they stop burning, serve 2 crêpes on each plate with a generous spoonful of juice over each.

THE QUEEN'S CUSTARD (for eight):

Beat the yolks of 8 eggs, add 3 cups of milk and 3 tablespoons of lemon or vanilla or orange sugar. Strain into a buttered pyrex dish, and cook in a slow oven until the custard is firm. Pour over this a liqueur glass of curaçao or kirsch. Let this soak in well. Then beat the whites of 5 eggs with 3 heaping tablespoons of lemon, orange, or vanilla sugar, and spread over the custard. Decorate the top by putting some of the méringue through a pastry bag. Put in a hot oven (325 degrees) until brown. Decorate with candied violets and then serve with cream.

SNOW PUDDING (*for eight*):

Mix 4 tablespoons of gelatine with 2 cups of sugar, add a cup of cold water, and a cup and a half of boiling water. Stir over the fire until thoroughly dissolved. Add a cup of grapefruit juice, a cup of lemon juice, and 3 cups of cold water. Strain and mix well. Set in the refrigerator to cool. When it begins to congeal, whip until frothy and fold in the well-beaten whites of 4 eggs. Pour into individual molds which have been rinsed out in cold water.

Make a liquid custard of 6 egg-yolks, 3 cups of milk, and 4 level tablespoons of sugar. Flavor when cool with 1 teaspoon of lemon extract, and serve poured around the gelatines which have been turned out on a deep dessert plate.

CHOCOLATE PUDDING (*for eight*):

Melt 3 squares of chocolate with several drops of water in a double boiler, and then add slowly a half-cup of sugar and a heaping tablespoon of flour after they have been mixed together. Next, pour in a half-cup of melted butter and 2 teaspoons of vanilla. Remove from the fire and add 4 well-beaten egg-yolks. Then beat the egg-whites stiff and fold carefully into the chocolate mixture. Put into a well-buttered mold and set this in a pan of hot water. Cook in a moderately hot oven for one hour. If necessary, cover with a piece of buttered paper to keep from burning on top.

Cool in the tin, and when quite cold turn out into a dessert dish and serve with Mocha cream made in the following manner: Beat 2 egg-yolks, add a quarter of a cup of sugar, a pinch of salt, and a half-cup of very strong coffee. Cook in a double boiler until thick. Cool, and when ready to serve fold in a cup of whipped cream.

PRALINÉ CREAM (*for eight*):

Moisten two thirds of a cup of sugar with a little cold water, and caramelize it to a golden brown. Then pour in a half-cup of boiling water and let the mixture boil until it becomes syrupy.

Scald a quart of milk and add to the syrup. Stir well. Beat the yolks of 8 eggs and gradually add to the hot milk. Cook over boiling water until thick, then put in 4 tablespoons of praliné. When cool, add 2 teaspoons of vanilla.

Make a méringue by beating the whites of 6 eggs and adding 3 tablespoons of vanilla sugar. Cook by spoonfuls in hot milk. Drain well and serve on the custard as desired.

TAPIOCA PUDDING, ZABAIONE SAUCE (*for eight*):

Heat 1 quart of milk, add two thirds of a cup of orange sugar, a pinch of salt, and a half-cup of butter. Add slowly to the boiling milk one and three quarters cups of minute tapioca. Cook in a double boiler fifteen minutes.

Put into a baking-dish and cook in a slow oven for twenty-five minutes. Remove from the fire and stir in 6 beaten egg-yolks and three eighths of a cup of butter, then fold in the stiffly beaten whites of 4 eggs.

Pour into a well-buttered mold and place the mold in a pan of hot water, then bake in the oven until it is elastic to the touch. Remove from the oven and in ten minutes remove from the mold. Serve hot with zabaione sauce.

ZABAIONE SAUCE:

Beat six egg-yolks with one and a third cups of granulated sugar until creamy, put into a double boiler and stir furiously until it gets ribbony, then add 1 cup of Marsala or Madeira wine. Beat on the side of the fire until thick and frothy, and serve at once.

BREAD PUDDING (*for eight*):

Cut white bread in half-inch slices. Remove the crusts and butter well. Cut in fours to make small squares. Arrange these neatly so as to line a shallow baking-dish. Sprinkle with white Sultana raisins or seeded black raisins which have been soaked in warm water until plump and then well dried; add another row of buttered bread and sprinkle with cinnamon. Heat 1 quart of milk with one and a third cups of sugar. Break 4 whole eggs and 2 extra yolks into a bowl. Beat with a fork and slowly add the hot milk. Strain through a fine sieve, flavor with lemon or vanilla extract and pour over the bread. Place in the oven and bake until the custard is set. Serve hot or cold.

CARAMEL RICE PUDDING (*for eight*):

Wash 6 tablespoons of rice thoroughly and put into a quart of milk. Cook in a double boiler until creamy. Add 2 tablespoons of butter and the yolks of 8 eggs beaten well, and 4 heaping tablespoons of sugar. Flavor with lemon rind and vanilla.

Caramelize an earthen dish and spread the rice in it evenly. Then over that sprinkle powdered sugar liberally and dot the top with bits of butter. Put under a hot flame until the sugar melts. Serve hot with cold custard sauce.

RICE PUDDING (*for eight*):

Wash two thirds of a cup of rice and put into a double boiler with a quart of milk and 4 tablespoons of butter. Cook until thoroughly creamy. Soak 2 tablespoons of gelatine in 2 tablespoons of cold water. Remove the rice from the fire and pass the mixture through a fine sieve and then add the gelatine. Whip a pint of cream and add that to the rice and gelatine, along with a cup of confectioners' sugar and some vanilla extract. Place in a mold and set in the refrigerator.

Make a sauce by melting a cup of light brown sugar in a cup of maple syrup. Add 2 tablespoons of butter. Bring to a boil for a minute or two. Cool and just before serving add a cup of cream to this and pour over the rice pudding.

FARINA OR CREAM OF WHEAT PUDDING (*for eight*):

Heat 2½ cups of milk with a half-cup of sugar and 2 tablespoons of butter. When it boils, slowly add a cup of farina or cream of wheat. Let it cook a minute or two in a double boiler. Then remove from the fire and let cool a little. When lukewarm, add 6 well-beaten egg-yolks and fold in the stiffly beaten whites. Two spoons of candied fruits or raisins cooked in brandy may be added if desired. Put into a caramelized mold and cook for half an hour in a moderate oven in a pan of hot water.

Serve with a caramel custard made by putting 2 tablespoons of sugar into an enamel pan with just a drop or two of water to melt it. Cook until it is light brown, then add a half-cup of boiling water. Let it cook down until syrupy. Heat 2 cups of milk with a third of a cup of sugar. Add the caramel to this. Beat the yolks of 4 eggs and add them to the milk. Cook in a double boiler until thick.

POT DE CRÊME VANILLA (*for eight*):

Heat 3 cups of cream with 3 tablespoons of vanilla sugar in a double boiler. Beat the yolks of 6 eggs. Pour hot cream on the eggs. Strain into little custard cups. Place the cups in a pan of warm water and bake in a slow oven.

POT DE CRÊME CHOCOLAT (*for eight*):

Melt 3 squares of Baker's unsweetened chocolate in a few drops of water, in a double boiler. Put 3 tablespoons of sugar into 3 cups of cream and heat in a double boiler. Pour on the melted chocolate and stir well. Beat the yolks of 6 eggs and add the chocolate cream slowly. Add a teaspoon of vanilla and strain into cups. Place these in a pan of warm water and put into a slow oven until set.

POT DE CRÊME CAFÉ (*for eight*):

Add three quarters of a cup of strong coffee to 3 cups of cream heated in a double boiler with 3 tablespoons of sugar. Pour onto the yolks of 6 eggs. Strain into custard cups and place these in a shallow pan of warm water. Bake in a slow oven until set.

CRÊME RENVERSÉE (*for eight*):

Caramelize a round mold. Beat together the yolks of 6 eggs and the whites of 5 eggs. Heat a quart of milk. Add 6 dessertspoons of sugar to the eggs and stir in the hot milk. Flavor with 2 teaspoons of vanilla extract. Strain into the caramelized mold. Place the mold in a pan of hot water and bake in a slow oven until an inserted knife comes out clean. Remove from the oven, and when cold set in the refrigerator for eight to ten hours. When ready to serve, turn out onto a round shallow glass dish. Set the dish on a slightly larger glass plate and place heads of pink roses or pansies on the bottom plate so as to form a wreath.

PUMPKIN PUDDING (*for twelve*):

Take 4 cups of steamed mashed pumpkin. Canned pumpkin is almost as good and more certain, as pumpkins vary so in texture. Add to the pumpkin 1 cup of light brown sugar, 2 tablespoons of molasses, and 1 cup of white sugar. Mix well and add 3 level teaspoons of ground cinnamon, 3 level teaspoons of ground ginger, a dash of nutmeg, 2 very scant teaspoons of salt, 2 tablespoons of melted butter, 2 tablespoons of good brandy, 6 well-beaten eggs, and, last of all, 4 cups of good thick cream. Caramelize 2 round glass cooking-dishes and pour the mixture into them. Place the molds in a pan of warm water and bake in a moderate oven until set — about fifty minutes. Remove from the oven, cool, and place in the refrigerator until ready for use. Turn out onto glass platters and serve with a small bottle of kirsch and a pitcher of cream, each person sprinkling on a few drops for himself.

RICH CHOCOLATE PUDDING WITH MOCHA
    SAUCE (*for eight*):

If you just adore caramels, you will just adore this richest of all rich desserts. It's so simple to make, but has been known to do very strange things, indeed, if you aren't very, very careful.

Put a half-pound of Maillard triple vanilla sweet chocolate into the top part of an enamel double boiler containing hot, not boiling, water. Place on a low fire until the chocolate has melted. Remove from the fire and add, little by little, half a pound of very fresh sweet butter, stirring it well with a silver tablespoon. Beat the yolks of 4 eggs and add to the mixture. When well mixed, put into a buttered mold, and place in the refrigerator overnight; to turn out, dip the mold in boiling water for a second. Serve with the following sauce:

Make a cup of very strong coffee. Add 3 cups of rich milk and 5 level tablespoons of granulated sugar. Heat in a double boiler to scalding point, then stir in the well-beaten yolks of 6 eggs. Cook until it coats the spoon, stirring all the while. Flavor with vanilla.

CHOCOLATE ICE CREAM, WITH COFFEE SAUCE (*for eight*):

Melt slowly in a double boiler a half-pound of unsweetened chocolate. Scald in a double boiler 5 cups of cream and 2 cups of milk, with 2 cups of sugar and a vanilla bean cut in two lengthwise. When scalded, add a little of it to the chocolate to make a smooth mixture, then add the chocolate gradually to the cream. Cool (not in the refrigerator), stirring from time to time. Freeze and pack in the usual way, removing, of course, the vanilla bean. Serve the following sauce with the ice cream:

COFFEE SAUCE:

Make half a cup of very strong black coffee, almost an essence. Cool. Beat the yolks of 2 eggs, with a heaping tablespoon of granulated sugar, until creamy, and add the coffee. Cook in a double boiler until thick. Chill thoroughly, add a few drops of vanilla and fold in three quarters of a cup of cream whipped stiff. Serve in a silver bowl with a small ladle.

ICED ZABAIONE:

Soak a tablespoon of gelatine in a quarter of a cup of cold water for fifteen minutes. Then add to it a tablespoon of boiling water and stir until liquid. Beat the yolks of 10 eggs with 2 level tablespoons of granulated sugar. When creamy, add 1½ cups of Marsala wine and a vanilla bean split in two. Place in a double boiler and beat with a spoon until hot. Remove the double boiler from the fire, remove the vanilla, add gelatine, and beat for two minutes, still over the hot water. Then stir in a tablespoon of good cognac and 1 of maraschino. Beat again for a second and pour into a glass bowl. Place the bowl in another bowl surrounded by chopped ice. Serve very cold.

MÉRINGUED RUM CAKE:

The Italians, I believe, invented this dish. They call it soupa inglese. Never, never make the mistake of serving it to anyone just back from Italy. They apparently have had it just once too often there.

Make 2 thin square layer cakes. Make a thick custard by cooking 2 cups of milk with 1½ tablespoons of cornstarch and 3 tablespoons of granulated sugar in a double boiler until quite thick and the raw taste has disappeared. Beat the yolks of 6 eggs, stir into the hot custard and cook a minute or two. In the meantime, beat the whites of 6 eggs until very stiff. Add a tablespoon of vanilla to the custard and pour it into a large bowl. Fold in the whites of the eggs carefully and place in the refrigerator when cool, to chill.

When the cakes are perfectly cold, split them through the center with a sharp knife so as to make four thin layers. Sprinkle these liberally with good rum. Place one layer, brown side down, on a large pyrex plate. Spread the layer with a thin coating of chopped, candied fruits which have been soaked in cognac. Now spread a generous layer of the custard over the fruit, and place the next layer of cake, cut surface up; and so on until all the custard, fruit, and cake have been used. Hold the layers in place while assembling by inserting a couple of long wire cake testers. Now make a méringue by beating the whites of 6 eggs very stiff and folding in 12 heaping tablespoons of powdered sugar. Flavor with vanilla and cover the cake, sides and top, with a thick layer of the méringue. Put the rest in a pastry bag and decorate the cake to please your fancy. Put into a medium oven to brown. Be sure to watch carefully.

BOILED FIG PUDDING (*for eight*):

You will need for this a porcelain pudding mold with a tight lid — two-quart size. First cut up in little pieces good flat figs until you have half a cup of them. Do the same with pitted dates until you have the same quantity. Grate the inside of a loaf of stale bread until you have a cup and a quarter of crumbs. Chop some good sweet beef kidney suet until fine and crumby. Sift twice, a cup of flour with a cup of sugar and 3 level tablespoons of baking powder and a quarter of a teaspoon of salt. Grate the rind of 1 orange and add it to the bread crumbs. Add the suet to the bread crumbs. Add the fruit and the sifted flour and sugar. Beat 2 whole eggs until light and add to them a quarter of a cup of milk, a teaspoon of vanilla, and a teaspoon of cognac. Add this to the rest of the pudding and mix well. Pour into the well-buttered mold, being sure to leave at least an inch of space for the pudding to rise. Put a piece of buttered floured cloth over the top and clamp on the cover. Place the mold in a pan of boiling water so that it is a little more than half-immersed in water. Boil four hours, adding more boiling water as needed. Serve with the following sauce:

Put the whites of 2 eggs into a bowl. Into another bowl put the yolks, and into a third larger bowl put three quarters of a cup of cream. Measure out 3 tablespoons of powdered sugar. First beat the whites of the eggs until stiff, then with the same beater beat the cream until stiff; last of all, the yolks. When they are creamy, add the sugar and a tablespoon of cognac and beat again. Add the yolks to the whites and fold them in, then fold in the cream. Serve at once, with the pudding, which has been turned out on a platter.

BOILED APPLE DUMPLINGS:

Peel and core 6 small juicy apples. Make a biscuit dough, by sifting 2 cups of flour with 1 teaspoon of salt and 4 teaspoons of baking powder. Work into this with the fingertips 3 good tablespoons of butter. Then moisten with about three quarters of a cup of milk or until of the right consistency to roll out. Prepare 6 pieces of old linen dipped in boiling water and well floured. Roll out the dough on a floured board to about an eighth of an inch thickness. Cut in squares large enough to cover the apples. Place an apple in the center of each square. Fill the center of the apple with some quince preserves, and sprinkle the apple with sugar. Wet the edges of the dough with milk and fold together the points, meeting on the top. Push the edges slightly together. Place each dumpling in a cloth and tie securely, but leave plenty of room for the dumpling to swell. Boil plenty of water in a big pot and put the dumplings in when boiling. Cover at once and continue to boil for three quarters of an hour without once removing the cover.

Remove the cloths and place dumplings on a hot platter. Serve with powdered sugar and cream, or a bowl of preserved quince and a pitcher of thin cream.

CRÊME BRÛLER (*for eight*):

Here again we have a recipe that is very exclusive, the trouble being that no one has really ever quite decided just how it should be made — nor just what it's called.

Heat a quart of cream in a double boiler until hot, but not scalding. Add 2 tablespoons of granulated sugar and stir

until dissolved, then add the well-beaten yolks of 8 eggs
and 2 teaspoons of vanilla. Mix well and pour into a shallow pyrex baking-dish of the right size so as to have the
custard about 1½ inches deep. Place the dish in hot water
and bake in a slow oven until set. Cool and place the dish
in the refrigerator for several hours to chill thoroughly.
Then remove from the refrigerator and cover the surface of
the custard with a quarter of an inch of soft light brown
sugar. Dark brown will not do. Place the dish under a
blazing hot broiler and watch very carefully. The top of
the sugar should melt leaving a shiny caramel top. As I
said before, watch very carefully or it will burn up. When
the entire surface is glazed, remove and cool. Place back in
the refrigerator to chill thoroughly. It must be served ice-
cold to be good. A light tap of the spoon breaks through
the glaze.

BLAZING BAKED ALASKA (*for eight*):

Cover a wooden board, that will fit in your oven with the
door shut, with a stiff white paper. Lay on this an oblong
thin sheet of sponge cake, an inch larger all around than a
two-quart brick of ice cream. If you have a really good
caterer, order a two-quart brick of your favorite ice cream
and ask to have it packed well so that it will be very stiff.
Light the oven well ahead of time so that it will be very hot
when you are ready to assemble the baked Alaska. Measure
out 6 tablespoons of granulated sugar. Separate the whites
from the yolks of 6 fresh eggs and place in the refrigerator
with the eggbeater. Save 2 halves of the eggshells, choosing
those that have no cracks in the bottom. Put a little good
kirsch in a small enamel pan. Now remove the whites
from the refrigerator and make the méringue by beating the
whites until stiff, then add sugar gradually while beating

constantly, also adding a few drops of vanilla. If you have sugar which has been previously flavored as per instruction in the introduction to this chapter, it is infinitely safer to use it, as vanilla in liquid form, unless added with great care, sometimes makes the méringue fall. I recommend also making the méringue in as cool a spot as possible. Unpack the ice cream and place the brick on the center of the sponge cake. Cover immediately with the méringue, spreading it with a knife so that every bit of cream and cake is well covered. Now place the eggshells, open side up, on top of the méringue and push them down in a little, and pop the board right into a very hot oven, shutting the door. The méringue will brown quickly, so watch carefully, but don't open the oven wide to peek at it. When brown, remove from the oven and pour a little of the kirsch into each eggshell, having previously heated the kirsch slightly. Light the kirsch and send blazing to the table.

XII. FRUIT DESSERTS

It just happens that I should rather eat fruit than anything in the world, so you must forgive me if I'm a little excited about writing this chapter.

Fruit appeals to at least four of the senses; and it is always tempting, always a perfect ending to any meal.

Perhaps because of the very fact that it is so good, served just raw or possibly stewed, we neglect some of the more glamorous and exciting ways of serving it. In any event, let's not be guilty of serving sliced peaches and cream five days in succession, just because we like them. Let your imagination run wild once in a while.

For instance: serve the peaches, stewed whole, on méringue pedestals, in a lake of red raspberry juice. Who knows? — your aesthetic senses may be wafted to heights never reached before.

STRAWBERRY AND ALMOND SOUFFLÉ (*for eight*):

Blanch 1½ cups of fresh almonds and sliver them lengthwise, paper-thin. Prepare 2 cups of thoroughly mashed strawberries, to which have been added 3 tablespoons of sugar. Now heat 1¾ cups of milk with three fourths of a cup of sugar. Make a smooth paste of 4 level tablespoons of flour and a little cold milk. Pour this gradually into the hot milk and cook two minutes. Remove from the fire and add, little by little, 2 level tablespoons of sweet butter and then the yolks of 8 eggs, well beaten, and a few drops of curaçao. Stir into this the strawberry pulp and most of the almonds. Now beat the whites of 12 eggs until stiff, and fold these into the first mixture. Put it carefully into two well-buttered glass soufflé cooking-dishes and sprinkle the tops of them with the rest of the almonds. Cook in a moderate oven for about twenty minutes. Two minutes before removing from the oven, sprinkle the tops with powdered sugar. Serve a bowl of thinly sliced and sweetened-to-taste strawberries with the soufflé.

PEARS IN COINTREAU, WITH FROZEN CREAM (*for eight*):

Peel 12 perfect, firm Bartlett pears, leaving them whole with their stems. Put immediately in cold water with a few drops of lemon juice so that they won't turn black. In the meantime, make a syrup of 4 cups of light brown sugar and 6 cups of water. Boil for a few minutes, then put the pears in and cook until tender and transparent, but not mushy. Fill a teacup with Cointreau, and when the pears are done, lift each separately and dip it in the Cointreau until well saturated. Put them into a big glass dish, piling in a pyramid if possible. Continue to boil the juice until moderately thick, then add the Cointreau in which the pears were dipped and pour gradually over the pears. Place in the refrigerator to chill.

An hour and a half before dinner is announced, empty a pint of thick cream into one of the trays of the refrigerator. When ready to serve the pears, this cream should be just crystallized and not quite stiff. Put it into a very cold silver bowl and pass with the pears.

SNAPDRAGON (*for twelve, or any number*):

If you have a secret longing to be a fire-eater, try this on Christmas Eve — but don't wear your best dress.

Cluster raisins from which the seeds have been removed are heaped in the center of a large silver platter. About 1 small cup of good strong previously heated cognac is poured over them. This is placed in the middle of the table. The host then strikes a match and lights the cognac, and with a silver spoon spreads the raisins all around the platter, and keeps ladling the burning brandy over the raisins to keep it lighted. The guests then dip their fingers in and swiftly retrieve a raisin at a time and pop it into their mouths. Be careful not to put in so much cognac that the blaze will rise high. It would be well to experiment with this dish previous to trying it out at the table.

SLICED ORANGES IN ORANGE SHERBET (*for eight*):

Peel 8 navel oranges. With a sharp knife cut off all the white part. Then carefully remove the pulp sections by slicing between the skins. Make a syrup by boiling half a cup of sugar and a cup of water. When cold, pour over the oranges and put in the refrigerator until ready to use. In the meantime, make some orange water ice. Boil 1 quart of water and 2 cups of sugar for five minutes. Add the grated rind of 2 oranges and 2 cups of orange juice and a quarter of a cup of lemon juice. Cool and strain. Freeze in the usual way, remove the dasher and pack. About an hour before you are ready for the dessert, make some Italian méringue by boiling 1 cup of sugar and half a cup of water until it forms a soft ball in cold water. Incorporate a very little of it at a time with the beaten whites of 3 eggs, stirring all the while. Continue to beat for two minutes on a very low fire. Cool.

Remove the top of the mold in which the orange ice is packed and stir this méringue into it. Also stir in well a quarter of a cup of curaçao. Pile this in a cold glass bowl and make a nest in the middle, in which you will put the oranges which were previously sliced.

CHERRIES IN CRACKED ICE (*for any number*):

Wash a big bowl of cherries and serve them in a big silver bowl filled with pounded ice.

ALMOND CREAM COATED WITH STRAWBERRY GELATINE (*for twelve*):

For this dessert you will need a one-quart mold and a two-quart mold of the same shape so that one will fit inside the other, leaving a space between them of about an inch. The dessert when finished will be an almond Bavarian cream with an inch coating of strawberry gelatine.

First make the gelatine. Stem and wash 2 quarts of strawberries. Mash them with a wooden mallet and add 2 cups of water and 1½ cups of sugar. Bring to a boil and simmer for a minute or two, skim and cool through a hair sieve. This should make about 4 cups of juice. Melt 3 teaspoons of gelatine in 1 cup of cold water. Heat the strawberry juice to boiling point and add the gelatine. Stir well and cool. Put 1¾ cups of it in the bottom of the big mold and place on the ice to set. When firm, place the second mold filled with ice in the center of the first, and pour the rest of the gelatine around it. Put aside to get quite firm.

In the meantime, make the almond cream. Soak 4 teaspoons of gelatine in half a cup of cold water. Dissolve 1 cup of almond paste in 2 cups of milk by heating to the boiling point, stirring until smooth and melted. Pour this onto the well-beaten yolks of 4 eggs, and add a pinch of salt.

Cook in a double boiler for a minute or two until it thickens slightly, then add the gelatine and 3 teaspoons of vanilla, stirring until the gelatine has completely dissolved; then cool. When it begins to set, whip for five minutes with a rotary beater, then fold in 1 pint of cream, whipped stiff.

By this time the strawberry gelatine should be set, quite stiff. Empty out the ice and put a little warm water into the small mold to loosen it. Remove it and fill the hole in the center with the almond cream. Place in the refrigerator to chill thoroughly and set. When ready to serve, dip the mold in warm water and turn out on a large platter. Decorate with whole strawberries and serve it with a bowl of strawberries, washed, stemmed, sliced, and sweetened with a syrup made of 1 cup of sugar and a half-cup of water.

STRAWBERRIES IN RED WINE (*for eight*):

Stem and wash 3 quarts of ripe strawberries, dry gently on a teacloth and pile the perfect ones neatly in 8 champagne glasses. Place each glass on a glass plate and place before the guests. Then pass a bowl of powdered sugar and a small carafe of red wine. The guests sprinkle some sugar over their berries and fill their glasses of strawberries with the wine.

STRAWBERRY TURNOVERS (*for eight or twelve*):

Make some puff paste with half a pound of sweet butter. Prepare this the day before, and set in the refrigerator, first wrapped in plenty of waxed paper and then in a teacloth. Early the next morning, roll it out to an eighth of an inch thickness and cut in three-inch circles. Place a teaspoon of good strawberry jam in the center of each. Paint one half of the edge with a beaten egg. Fold over and press the edges together. With a fork dipped in flour, mark the edges and pinch the tops. Paint with more egg the top surface, and place them carefully on a flat cooking tin. Place in the refrigerator again to chill thoroughly. Bake fifteen minutes or so in quite a hot oven, but watch carefully, as they burn easily. When cooked, remove from the oven and sprinkle copiously with confectioners' sugar. Serve cold. (*Note.* For recipe for puff paste see page 83.)

CHERRY TART (*for twelve*):

Sift 2⅔ cups of flour with 2 level teaspoons of sugar and 1 level teaspoon of salt. Work into this with the finger-tips 1 cup of butter. Bind together with 2 eggs beaten very slightly. Toss the paste on a floured board. Pat it out, and spread with 2 tablespoons of thick cream. Fold so as to enclose all the cream, and roll out. Fold again and set in the refrigerator to chill for three hours. Take out half of it at a time, roll to a size to cover a tart tin. Line the tin, trim and crimp the edges. Lay a piece of waxed paper in the bottom of the crust and fill with dried beans or little pebbles well washed. Put back in the refrigerator while you prepare the second tart. Brush the edges of both tarts with beaten egg, and cook in rather a hot oven until brown. Remove from the oven. Remove the pebbles and paper, and cool.

In the meantime, make the cream. Mix 1 cup of sugar with 4 tablespoons of flour and one eighth of a teaspoon of salt. Beat 4 whole eggs, and add them to the flour and sugar. Add slowly 2 cups of hot milk. Cook in a double boiler until very thick. Cool and add 1 teaspoon of vanilla. When very cold, stir in 1 cup of whipped cream, and spread this in the 2 tarts.

Pit plenty of big black juicy cherries. Make a thick syrup by boiling 2 cups of sugar with 1 cup of water for five minutes. Put the cherries in this and let them cook for half an hour. Remove them from their juice and lay them on a plate to cool. Boil down the syrup until very thick. Arrange the cherries on the two tarts so as to cover completely the custard, and glaze with the reduced juice.

STRAWBERRY TARTS WITH DEVONSHIRE CREAM
(*for eight*):

Mix together 1⅓ cups of flour, 1 level teaspoon of sugar, and half a teaspoon of salt. Sift several times. Then work in half a cup of butter with the finger-tips. Bind together with 1 beaten egg. Toss the paste on a floured board and pat or gently roll out. Spread over it a tablespoon of thick cream, roll it up, roll it out, then roll it up again. Set it in the refrigerator for two hours. In the meantime, wash and stem 2 quarts of strawberries. Pick out 48 of the most perfect, crush the rest, and add a cup of granulated sugar. Simmer gently for half an hour. Strain and continue to boil until greatly reduced and very thick. When ready to make the tarts, take a little of the paste at a time, roll it out into small circles, and line tiny individual tart tins. Crimp the edges and immediately put them back into the refrigerator so that they may keep very cold. When all are ready, brush the edges with beaten egg and set in a very hot oven. Watch carefully so that they won't burn. When brown, remove from the oven and place 4 strawberries in each. Then glaze with the strawberry syrup.

Serve with DEVONSHIRE CREAM made by putting 1 quart of raw certified milk and 1 pint of double cream in a shallow enamel pan. Set in a cool place for twelve hours. When this time is up, the cream should have risen to the surface. Now set the pan of milk in another pan of water and place this pan either on top of the oven part of a gas stove or on the very back of a coal stove; let the milk get gradually warm, not hot. Leave it on the stove until the cream crinkles and pulls away from the edge of the pan. When this happens, set the pan of milk in the refrigerator for at least twelve hours. Then carefully skim off the cream and place in a glass dish. It should be thick, slightly lumpy or clotted, and have a peculiarly delicious sweet taste.

SLICED FRUIT WITH ORANGE ICE AND ALMONDS (*for eight*):

First make a quart of orange ice by boiling a pint of water with 1 cup of sugar for five minutes; then add this to 1½ cups of orange juice and the juice of 1 lemon. Also add the grated rind of 1 orange. Strain, cool, and freeze in the usual manner. Remove the dasher and pack well. In the meantime, wash, pick over, and stem a pint of strawberries, a pint of raspberries, and a pint of blackberries. Also pit and quarter a cup each of ripe apricots and sweet plums. Make a boiled syrup of 1 cup of sugar and half a cup of water, and pour a little of this over all the different fruits, keeping them separate. Place in the refrigerator to chill. When ready to serve, peel and slice a few peaches and sprinkle them with powdered sugar. Turn the orange ice out into a not-too-shallow and plenty large platter, and place the different fruits in separate piles around the ice. Then sprinkle over all half a cup of blanched almonds left whole. Serve immediately on very cold plates. Kirsch may be passed with this.

PEARS À LA CUILLÈRE (*for eight*):

Wash eight perfect pears which have been well chilled. Cut a little slice off the bottom and with a sharp knife remove the core, but save the piece you cut off. Fill the pear with black currant jam mixed with kirsch, and replace the bottom. Place the pear, stem side down, in a glass of the right dimensions. The pear is eaten with a spoon, more kirsch being added if desired, while eating it.

COMPOTE OF FRUIT (*for eight*):

Wash 8 perfect, pink-cheeked peaches, 8 blue plums, 8 apricots, 8 pears, and 8 red plums. Make a syrup by boiling 2 cups of sugar with 1 cup of water for five minutes, then put the peaches whole into this. Let them boil a minute, then fish them out and let cold water run over them. The skin will pinch off, leaving the pink cheek. Put the peaches back into the syrup and boil until tender, not mushy. Put them on a platter to drain and in the same syrup place the pears which you have peeled and left whole. Cook until tender, then put them on a platter to drain, and into the same juice put the apricots left whole, the red and blue plums. Cook until they pop open. Then drain and put them on a plate. Continue to simmer the juice while you arrange the fruits on a large glass dish. When the juice has boiled down and is quite thick, cool and pour it over the fruits. Place in the refrigerator and serve very cold.

ORANGES MÉRINGUED (*for eight*):

Cut a slice off the navel end of 8 oranges, and with a spoon scoop out the pulp. Place the oranges in the freezing tray of the refrigerator, or as near the ice as possible, to chill them completely. Make a quart of orange ice (see page 194), and pack. Measure out 6 level tablespoons of granulated sugar, and separate the whites of 3 eggs. Place these in a large bowl in the refrigerator. Prepare 5 or 6 cups of chopped ice. Light the oven fifteen minutes before you are ready to prepare the oranges. Beat the whites of the eggs, slowly at first, add the sugar, little by little, continuing to beat until all the sugar has been used. It should be very stiff. Place in the refrigerator while you fill the oranges with the water ice. Place these on a bed of ice in an enamel pan. Put a big spoonful of méringue on each one, sprinkle with granulated sugar, and place in a very hot oven to brown. Remove from the pan and place each orange on a dessert plate and send to the table at once.

SLICED RAW PEARS IN ORANGE JUICE AND CURA-ÇAO (*for eight*):

Squeeze and strain 2 large glasses of orange juice. Sweeten with a tablespoon of powdered sugar and chill well. Fifteen minutes before serving, peel, core, and slice very thin 6 or 8 large, juicy ripe pears and sprinkle them with a good tablespoon of powdered sugar. Add 2 tablespoons of curaçao to the orange juice and pour over the pears. Serve in a white glass bowl. Cookies are good with this dish.

BANANAS WITH COCONUT CREAM (*for eight*):

This was and maybe still is the specialty of a very famous beauty specialist. I can't promise it will make you beautiful, but I know it's very, very good.

Grate 2 fresh coconuts. Place all the meat in a bowl and pour over it just enough boiling water to moisten it well. Let it stand an hour, mashing it now and then with a wooden spoon. Then put all this in a piece of strong linen and squeeze out all the milk. Make a second extraction, adding less water the second time. Add to the first milk and place in a bowl in the refrigerator, covering it carefully with another plate — and don't disturb it.

Half an hour before you are ready for the banana dessert, peel 8 bananas. Lay them in a buttered pyrex dish. Dot well with butter and pour over them a cup of pure honey. Place in a hot oven and cook until brown and well puffed. In the meantime, skim off all the thick white part of the squeezed coconut milk, which will have formed a cake on the surface. Place this in a pitcher and stir with a spoon to soften it, adding gradually some of the liquid part until it is the consistency of cream. Serve it with the baked bananas in place of real cream.

APRICOT JELLY (*for eight*):

Drain 2 cans of good peeled apricots and put them through a sieve. Squeeze the juice of 4 oranges and 2 lemons and add a cup of granulated sugar. Melt 4 tablespoons, or 4 envelopes, of gelatine in a cup of cold water, then add 2 cups of boiling water. Stir well and add to the fruit juice. Then add the apricot pulp. Mix well and place in a pretty mold. Place in the refrigerator to set. Turn out on a platter and garnish with blanched almonds. Serve with cream.

SLICED PEACHES IN PLUM JUICE (*for eight*):

Make a syrup of 1 cup of sugar with a quarter of a cup of water. When thick, pour it over a dozen red plums. Place on the fire and cook until the plums burst and the juice is red. Put several of the plums through a fine sieve and add to the juice. Place the juice on ice to chill thoroughly. Peel and slice 8 or 9 juicy peaches. Pour the plum juice over them and serve a small bottle of kirsch separately, to be poured on the fruit by each person, if desired.

BAKED APPLES PORCUPINE (*for eight*):

First blanch three quarters of a cup of almonds and split them in two. Dry in a warm place. Peel and core 8 green apples. Place them in a pyrex dish. Fill the cores with granulated sugar, in which you have mixed a little cinnamon. Dot with butter and bake until tender; but don't let them fall apart. Pour off the excess juice, if any, and reduce it by boiling. Pour it over the apples again. Make a stiff méringue of the whites of 4 eggs and 8 level tablespoons of sugar. Add a teaspoon of vanilla. Completely cover the apples with this and stick all the almonds into it. Sprinkle lightly with granulated sugar and place in a medium oven for five minutes, then increase the heat. As soon as brown, serve with thin cream.

PLUMP STRAWBERRIES (for eight):

Wash, pick over, and stem 2 quarts of strawberries. Make a syrup of 1 cup of sugar and a quarter of a cup of water. When thick, pour over the berries and let it cool completely. Place the berries on the fire again and let them just come to a boil. Remove from the fire and cool. Place in a glass dish on ice. Serve very cold.

STRAWBERRIES IN ORANGE JUICE (for eight):

Wash, pick over, and stem 2 quarts of juicy ripe strawberries. Make a syrup of half a cup of sugar and a quarter of a cup of water. Boil five minutes, cool slightly, and add 1½ cup of orange juice. Pour over the berries, and place in the refrigerator to chill.

COUPE (for twelve):

When I was sixteen, I went to the Blackstone Hotel in Chicago to a small luncheon party. I was very young, indeed, for my age, because I was so enthusiastic about the little méringue birds, perched on the coupe St.-Jacques, that I couldn't bear to eat it. I carried mine away with me, not inside of me, but wrapped in a paper doily. It was very sticky — and I finally ate it in the train on my way back to New York.

Make a quart of orange ice. (See page 194.) Also make some strawberry sherbet by crushing 2 quarts of strawberries which have been stemmed and washed, and adding 2 cups of sugar to them. Let them stand two hours, then add 2 cups of water to them and strain through a fine sieve. Dissolve 1 tablespoon of gelatine in a cup of boiling water. Add to the fruit juice. Cool and freeze. Pack both the orange ice and strawberry sherbet in ice and salt. Now make a dozen or so little méringue birds by beating the whites of 3 eggs, slowly at first, then increasing the speed until smooth and stiff; then add 12 tablespoons of granulated sugar, little by little. Drop by small spoonfuls on a white paper in oval shapes. Then, with a smaller spoon, drop on one end of the oval a smaller ball of the méringue to form the head of the bird. Put the remainder of the méringue in a pastry bag containing a flat saw-edged tip, and endeavor to make wings on the birds and a tiny tail. This is difficult, I admit; but remember, practice makes perfect. Insert a small piece of almond for the beak of the bird. Sprinkle with sugar and blow off all the excess. Place on a wet board and bake in a very slow oven at least an hour. When the birds are cold, melt a piece of chocolate, and, dipping a toothpick in the chocolate, make two little black spots for the eyes. In the meantime, you will have prepared a quart of raspberries and a quart of strawberries. Put some of each in the bottom of large champagne glasses. Then, when ready to serve, put a spoonful of orange ice and a spoonful of strawberry sherbet into each glass and perch a bird on each one. Serve at once.

STRAWBERRIES WITH WILD STRAWBERRY JAM (*for eight*):

Such a simple idea — but I confess it wasn't mine. I first encountered it Chez Jean.

Wash and stem 2 quarts of fine big strawberries. Place them in large champagne glasses. Pour over them, just before serving, a big spoon of wild strawberry preserve, which may be bought in some French importing food-specialty shops. Sprinkle a few shelled unsalted pistachio nuts over them and serve. A few drops of kirsch may be added.

PEACHES ON MÉRINGUE PEDESTALS (*for eight*):

First make the pedestals, using the same méringue as for the birds (see page 199); only this time, put it into a pastry bag and squeeze it out in a circle, leaving a hole in the center. The circles should be about three inches in diameter and quite thick through. Sprinkle with sugar and bake in a slow oven until dry. Wash 8 perfect peaches with pink cheeks. Make a boiled syrup of 2 cups of sugar and 1 cup of water. Put 8 fine peaches in this when it has thickened a bit. Remove in a minute or two and pinch off their skins. Put back into the syrup to cook until barely tender, so as not to lose their form. Let them cool in the syrup. Now crush a quart of red raspberries and add to them 1½ cups of the peach juice, boiling hot. Let them cool and strain through a fine sieve. Place the peaches and the raspberry juice in the refrigerator to chill thoroughly. When ready to serve, place the méringues on a large glass plate. Place a peach on each pedestal. Then pour the juice around and pass at once.

PEARS COOKED IN PORT (*for eight*):

Peel 8 fine pears, placing them immediately in cold water with a few drops of lemon, until all are peeled. Make a syrup of 4 cups of water and 1 cup of sugar and 1 cup of port. Place the pears in this and add the rind of half an orange cut in thin strips, using only the orange part. Cook until tender, then place in a glass dish. Strain the juice over them and serve hot or cold.

SUGARED CURRANTS (*for any number*):

Select very beautiful red or white currants. Wash them. Beat the whites of 2 eggs to a froth, then add half a cup of water. Fill a small bowl with powdered sugar, and first dip the currants, holding them by the stem, into the egg froth; then roll them well in the sugar. Be sure to cover them perfectly, dipping them in and out of the sugar. Lay them to dry and crystallize on a wire rack. Place on well-washed and dried grape leaves on a pretty plate.

CHERRIES COOKED IN RED WINE (*for eight*):

Cut the stems of some fine big red cherries halfway down. Place them in an enamel pan and pour over them 2 cups of good claret. Add a small stick of cinnamon and a cup of sugar. Put on a low fire and cook very slowly for ten minutes. Remove from the fire and let them cool in the juice. Then remove them one by one, placing them in a pretty dish, stems up. Put the juice back on the stove and reduce until quite thick, adding a tablespoon of currant jelly. When melted, pour over the cherries and serve very cold. Lady-fingers are good with these.

PRUNES IN RED WINE (*for any number*):

Wash prunes well and soak overnight in just enough water to cover them. The next morning, put them into an enamel pan with what juice there is left and add 2 cups of good claret. Simmer until the prunes are well cooked.

BLAZING PEACHES (*for eight*):

Cook 8 peaches whole as previously described (see page 195). Cool in their juice. Wash, stem, and crush 1 quart of strawberries, sprinkle with half a cup of sugar and let them stand two hours. Serve the peaches on a bed of crushed strawberries. Just before serving, heat half a cup of kirsch, being careful that it doesn't catch fire. Pour over the peaches and light it. Serve at once while blazing.

BANANA PUDDING (*for eight*):

Cream 4 level tablespoons of butter with 1 cup of granulated sugar; add the yolks of 6 eggs well beaten and 2 teaspoons of vanilla. Beat well until very creamy and light. Add 1¼ cups of sifted flour and 6 bananas sliced very thin. Mix gently. Beat the whites of 6 eggs to a stiff froth, gradually adding to the mixture. Turn the mixture into a well-buttered pudding mold, and set to bake in a moderately hot oven for forty minutes. Turn out onto a hot plate and pour over it the following sauce: Mix 8 tablespoons of raspberry jam with 2 tablespoons of sugar. Add a cup of water, 2 teaspoons of kirsch. Mix well for one minute, then place on the fire and boil for two minutes, stirring occasionally.

MELON GLACÉ À L'ORIENTALE (*for twelve*):

Use 2 very ripe cantaloupes; cut evenly in each a circular portion about 1½ inches from the top, making the openings about 3 inches in diameter; empty out the liquid and remove the seeds with a silver spoon. Take out the meat of the melons in small pieces, being careful not to break through the shell. Place the meat in a bowl, add an equal quantity of fresh pineapple cut in large dice; replace the fruit in the melon, add enough sliced bananas to fill, and add to each melon 2 level tablespoons of powdered sugar and 4 teaspoons of kirsch. Place the covers on the openings and seal them with butter. Let the melons remain packed in ice from two to three hours. When ready to serve, remove the butter carefully. Any other fruit combination may be used.

RICE PUDDING WITH APRICOTS (*for eight*):

Heat 4 cups of milk in a double boiler with two thirds of a cup of sugar. Add 2½ cups of cooked rice and a tiny pinch of salt. Cook for five or ten minutes until nice and creamy, then stir in the yolks of 6 eggs well beaten. Cook for several minutes longer, stirring well. Flavor with vanilla and pour into a baking-dish. In the meantime, soak some canned apricots halved, or stewed dried apricots, in a little apricot brandy. Lay these symmetrically on the pudding. Pour over them the brandy in which they were soaked. Beat stiff the whites of 4 eggs, and fold in 8 tablespoons of granulated sugar. Place this on top of the apricots, marking it with a spoon to make it pretty. Sprinkle lightly with granulated sugar, and bake in a moderate oven until delicately browned. Serve hot with cream that has been well chilled.

WATERMELON FILLED WITH FRESH FRUIT AND WATER ICE AND CHAMPAGNE (*for twelve*):

This should be served out-of-doors in a garden in the moonlight — on a very hot night.

Cut a large watermelon in half. With a large potato scooper cut from the center 2 or 3 cupfuls of watermelon balls. Put them immediately on ice, and then with a big spoon remove the rest of the pulp, leaving a shell about 1¼ inches thick. Place the shell on ice while you prepare the rest of the ingredients. First make a pitcher of syrup by boiling 2 cups of sugar with 1 cup of water for five minutes. Cool. When cold, pour a little over the watermelon balls. Now make a quart of orange ice — the same as given in the recipe for SLICED FRUIT WITH ORANGE ICE AND ALMONDS (see page 194). Freeze and pack. Then wash and stem a basket of fine strawberries. Dry them on a cloth and place in a bowl. Pour a little of the syrup over them and place in the refrigerator. Do the same with a pint of raspberries and a pint of blackberries. Wash and quarter 6 apricots and add a little syrup. Do the same with 6 red plums. When ready to serve the watermelon, remove it from the refrigerator and empty the water ice into the center, squashing it to make an even bed over the bottom. On this bed arrange the different prepared fruits in stripes, alternating a light-colored fruit with a dark-colored fruit. The middle section is reserved for some sliced peaches, which must be peeled, sliced, and sweetened at the last moment. The edge of the watermelon is sprinkled copiously with confectioners' sugar to make it look frosted. Sprinkle the top with blanched almonds. A small bottle of well-chilled champagne, in which 2 tablespoons of curaçao have been mixed, may be poured on just before serving, but is not essential.

Because of the nature of this dish, it must be placed on the table and served from there, as naturally it is too heavy to pass.

FROZEN STRAWBERRIES *(for eight)*:

Stem and wash 2 quarts of strawberries and crush them with a potato-masher. Add half a cup of sugar to each cup of pulp, and put in the refrigerator until juice is formed and the sugar is completely melted. Freeze in the usual manner in a freezer, or pack in the refrigerator tray, stirring it as it freezes.

FROZEN MÉRINGUED WHIPPED CREAM *(for eight)*:

Put the whites of 6 eggs into a big bowl with a pinch of salt. Beat slowly at first, then increase the speed until smooth and stiff. Then add 1½ cups of granulated vanilla sugar little by little. Drop by spoonfuls on white paper. Sprinkle with sugar, then tilt the paper so that the excess sugar falls off. Lay the papers on a wet board, and cook in a very slow oven for at least an hour. Remove from the papers and put in a warm dry place to dry even more.

Now make a syrup by boiling three quarters of a cup of sugar with one third of a cup of water until quite thick. Beat the yolks of 6 eggs well, then add the syrup gradually, and a cup of cream. Cook in a double boiler until a thick coating forms on the spoon. Put the mixture into a big bowl surrounded by ice and beat until cold, then add 4 cups of cream whipped not too stiff, and a teaspoon of vanilla. Break into this 5 or 6 méringues in fairly big pieces. Pack in the refrigerator tray or in a mold packed in ice and salt. Turn out and serve with a border of ripe red raspberries unsugared.

ALMOND SOUFFLÉ (*for eight*):

Blanch a quarter of a pound of sweet almonds and 2 bitter ones. Cut them in tiny slivers. Beat 6 egg-yolks until very creamy, then add 5 tablespoons of sugar, continuing to beat until very light. Then add three quarters of the almonds. Mix well and add a few drops of almond extract. Then beat stiff the whites of 7 eggs, and fold them carefully into the first mixture. Pour carefully into a buttered soufflé dish, and bake in a moderate oven for twenty minutes; then sprinkle with powdered sugar, and leave in the oven for three or four minutes longer. Serve immediately on hot plates and pass with it a bowl of slightly whipped cream flavored with a drop or two of almond extract, and containing the remainder of the slivered almonds. Serve a very sweet and very cold white wine with this.

DRIED FRUITS AND WALNUTS IN CREAM (*for eight*):

With scissors dipped in flour or boiling water cut in small pieces 8 uncooked dried prunes (the big soft kind), 8 dried figs, and a dozen dates. Wash half a cup of seedless raisins and soak awhile in a little lemon juice. Shell a dozen fine walnuts and break into little pieces. Drain the raisins and add to them the nuts, figs, dates, and prunes. Heat some good liquid honey and pour 2 tablespoons of it over the fruit. Mix well. Beat until just stiff 2 cups of cream and fold the fruit into it. Serve at once in a cold glass dish.

ENGLISH WALNUTS AND PORT (*for eight*):

Crack 2 pounds of fine English walnuts slightly and serve them in a silver bowl lined with galax leaves. Serve at the same time a fine bottle of port to be sipped while eating the walnuts. The nuts bring out the flavor of the port in a remarkable way.

XIII. SPECIALTIES OF MY FRIENDS

THIS little chapter is dedicated to all the friends here included, or not included, whose delicious food and culinary skill have been a constant inspiration and joy to me. Many of them are so talented that it is exceedingly difficult to select any one particular outstanding recipe from their repertoires. In fact, until I decided that originality should also be a reason for selection, I was at my wit's end trying to weigh the relative merits of various dishes.

JANET'S GREEN AND WHITE SPAGHETTI (*for eight*):
Put 2 big iron skillets on the fire. Into each of them put an eighth of a pound of butter and 3 tablespoons of olive oil. In the first pan, let 3 onions (which have been chopped into tiny pieces) swim around until they are golden brown. In the second pan, do the same thing with 1 bud of garlic cut in half. (This should not be cut any smaller because it's going to be thrown away.)

Now, while this golden-browning process is going on, fill 2 big deep pans with water and start them on their way to boiling.

Back to the skillets: put 1½ pounds of round steak, ground, into the garlic pan and let it get good and brown. Place a can of tomatoes in the onion pan, and, when they

come to a boil, turn the fire down so that they just simmer.
When the meat is brown and the tomatoes are simmering,
throw away the garlic and pour the contents of the meat
pan into the tomatoes. Salt and pepper this mixture, and
add 2 dashes each of sage and thyme and 2 pieces of bay
leaf smashed up a bit.

If your mixture is very wet (sometimes the tomatoes are
very watery), let it simmer down until there is very little
liquid left. Add several tablespoons of olive oil and some
more butter to make it good and rich. Then turn the fire
very low and put on a lid. The mixture should be rich
rather than wet, because oil and butter coat the spaghetti
nicely.

By now, the big water pans should be boiling. Cook a
hank of white Italian spaghetti in one pot, and a box of
Zucca's green spaghetti (colored with spinach) in the other,
and with plenty of salt. After the spaghetti is done, wash
it well with boiling water.

Then, on a big round hot bowl, drape the green spaghetti
around the edge and the white spaghetti in the middle.
At the last minute, pour the sauce on the white spaghetti,
and almost completely cover it with grated Parmesan cheese.

MARTHA'S BAKED TOMATOES (for six):

Cut off the tops of 12 tomatoes. Take out the pulp and
seeds. Boil them with 2 cut-up peppers until soft. Then
season with salt, pepper, 1 small cup of sugar, 2 pieces of
butter the size of 2 walnuts, place in the oven or in a covered frying-pan, and cook very slowly for about two hours.

HÉLÈNE'S POULET CRAPAUDINE:

Clean well a good young chicken. Cover it entirely with
grated bread crumbs, stuff it with 3 or 4 chicken livers, a

little butter, several leaves of fresh or pickled tarragon, salt and pepper, and sew it up.

Put the chicken into an iron cocotte with a heaping tablespoon of butter, and let it brown over a very low fire. When the chicken is golden brown, salt and pepper it, and cover the cocotte to let the bird cook over a slow fire.

When the chicken is cooked, take out the livers, rub them in 2 tablespoons of olive oil, a large spoonful each of parsley, chervil, and tarragon, chopped all together; add the juice of 1 lemon, the juice in which the chicken was cooked, and mix it all together. Be sure to keep your plate warm during this process. Serve the chicken on a very hot platter, and pour the sauce over it.

BAB'S ARROZ DE LA VALENCIANA (*for six*):

Cut up 1 good-sized chicken and put into a casserole, which has been on the stove, with 1 cup of sweet oil. Cook slowly so that the chicken will not get too dry. Cut up some raw ham in tiny slices and add to the chicken, also 6 or 7 small sausages (preferably *chorizos*, Spanish red sausages), or bits of pork.

In another pan, cut up tomatoes, or canned whole tomatoes, and sliced onions, and let these stew apart. Let some hearts of artichokes also cook apart.

Twenty-five minutes before serving, add to the chicken the tomatoes, 1 cup of cooked peas, hearts of artichokes, etc., and 4 small cups of rice, *dry*. After the rice has been well browned in the oil and mixture (about five minutes), add 8 cups of soup stock or water and cook on top of the stove for twenty minutes, then place in the oven until the rice is done.

Garnish with hard-boiled eggs, artichokes, bits of ham, and red — fresh or canned — peppers. If raw, the peppers should be freshly roasted on top of the stove or in the oven; then peel and add several pieces, or at least 1 whole pepper, when you add the other ingredients.

This should be served in a large, not too deep, earthenware dish.

ISABELLE'S GRATEAU DE MARRONS (*for six*):

Stir 6 ounces of spiced sugar (sugar in which a pinch of nutmeg and a fourth of a teaspoon of cinnamon have been well mixed) and a scant teaspoon of vanilla sugar (if this is not on hand, use half a teaspoon of vanilla) into the yolks of 3 eggs, to dissolve it. Add 8 ounces of peeled but uncooked chestnuts, crushed fine. Stir briskly to a white cream with a wooden spoon for ten minutes, then add the whites of the 3 eggs beaten to a froth, stirring all the time in the same direction. When well mixed, set in the oven for three quarters of an hour. To serve, turn out of the pan and cover with candied caramel surrounded by whipped cream.

MOFFAT'S POULET AUX CHOUX (*for eight*):

Take a slice of ham, about 1½ pounds, with a rim of fat around it. Cut it up into cubes, brown in a pan with a clove of garlic, a half-dozen scallions cut up fine. When some of the fat is fried out, put into the pan 2 chickens, about 2½ pounds each, trussed up as for baking. Brown the chickens a little in the ham fat. Into a deep casserole put a good-sized white cabbage quartered. Pour a pint of rich stock over this, and place the chickens and the ham and seasoning on top of the cabbage. Cover and cook in a moderate oven for about an hour and a half until tender. Add a glass of white wine and a pony of brandy just before serving.

SAM'S SPOON–BREAD (*for six*):

This is an exceedingly reliable recipe, provided you follow instructions carefully and remember that sour milk or buttermilk is absolutely necessary for success. Another necessary ingredient is white water-ground corn meal. And a word of warning: Do not be tempted to add more corn meal than the recipe calls for just because you think that the mixture to be baked looks hopelessly liquid to you. It should look that way.

Now for the ingredients: Take 1 cup of sour milk, add to it a third of a spoonful of baking soda and stir. Pour this into a mixing-bowl. Add to it 1 cup of sweet milk, then 1 cup of cold water; then 1 cup of corn meal in which has been sifted or folded 1 teaspoon of salt, 1 teaspoon of sugar, 1 teaspoon of baking powder. Separate the yolk from the white of 1 egg. Beat the yolk and add to the liquid and corn meal mixture. Beat the white of egg and fold in carefully. Melt about 1 tablespoon of butter in the bottom of a pyrex baking-dish, soufflé size, or else use a white enamel baking-dish. When the butter is slightly brown, remove from the stove and pour in the liquid mixture. Place the dish in a medium, not hot, oven, and allow to bake from thirty to forty minutes. If successfully concocted, this turns out to be moist and light in the middle, with a crispish brown crust and sides and bottom. It serves four greedy people, but can be made to do for six. Do not attempt a larger dish and double the amount of ingredients if you are serving more, but use two dishes and repeat the recipe.

LUCY'S PRALINÉ COOKIES (*for six or eight*):

Take the nut meats from paper-shelled almonds until you have about a half-cupful. Do not blanch the almonds, but brown them in a little butter till crisp over a slow blaze in an iron or aluminum frying-pan and then sprinkle them liberally with salt and drain on absorbent paper till cool. Then take a half-cup of butter and cream well. Add to it two thirds of a cup of yellow (light brown) sugar. Add 1 egg, well beaten, then add three quarters of a cup of flour in which you have sifted one fourth of a teaspoon of soda. Add 1 teaspoon of vanilla, and about a dessertspoon of maple syrup. Then add the browned almonds, which have been run through the meat-grinder, using the medium cutter so that the meats will not be too fine or too coarse. Stir well, and drop by small spoonfuls on a buttered cooky sheet, and cook for a few minutes in a medium hot oven. These cookies burn rather easily. They should be crisp and thin when baked.

AUDREY'S FILLET OF SOLE AU GRATIN (*for six or eight*):

Wash 1 spoonful of dried mushrooms in hot water, and then simmer them for an hour in 1 cup of water, until reduced to one half. Now make a thick sauce by browning 1 small carrot, half a knob of celery and a quarter of a clove of garlic, all cut very fine, in 1 tablespoon of chicken fat, then add 1 tablespoon of flour. Stir until smooth, then add a cup of beef broth, some salt and paprika, the juice of the dried mushrooms, and a few drops of Worcestershire sauce, and let this sauce boil slowly for half an hour. Chop 1 large onion very fine and stew it to a golden brown in a few spoonfuls of butter, then add 5 mushrooms, half a clove of garlic, half a teaspoon of chives, and 1 spoonful of parsley, all chopped very fine; some salt, a quarter of a lump of sugar, and paprika; and let it all stew for a quarter of an hour. Then cover the bottom of a gratin dish with these herbs, take the salted fish fillets from sole and arrange them on the dish over the herbs, folding under the pointed ends of the fillets. Sprinkle lightly with a little pepper and paprika, cover with small dabs of butter, pour in a wineglass of white wine, and cook in a hot oven for twelve to fourteen minutes. In the meantime, clean 18 good-sized mushroom buttons, removing the stems, and stew them in butter for twelve minutes. Now place these mushrooms over the fillets, pour their liquor into the finished sauce, from which the fat has been removed, mix in 1 spoonful of lemon juice, and strain it over the fish; then sprinkle lightly with cracker dust mixed with Parmesan cheese. Pour melted butter over the whole and bake in a hot oven for ten minutes.

PAT'S CODFISH (*for six or eight*):

Use dried codfish that you buy in wooden boxes. Soak over night 2 pounds of codfish. Boil, take out of the water, put in a pan with hot olive oil and a piece of garlic, sauté, then work it up with a Béchamel sauce. Season with salt, pepper, and nutmeg. Serve with boiled buttered potatoes.

MILDRED'S EGGPLANT (*for six*):

Peel and slice in quarter-inch slices 2 tender small eggplants. Fry in olive oil until a golden brown. Put the pieces on a plate in a warm place, and, in the oil in which they were fried, cook 2 small white onions until a golden brown. Sprinkle the onion over the bottom of a baking-dish. Then add a layer of the eggplant. Salt and pepper lightly and sprinkle with grated Parmesan cheese. Then add a layer of peeled and sliced tomatoes from which the pits have been removed. Dot with bits of butter, and then add another layer of eggplant, cheese, tomatoes, and so forth, until the dish is full. Top with plenty of Parmesan cheese and bits of butter. Bake in a medium oven for about an hour. Serve hot.

CLAUDINE'S CHICKEN PIE (*for six*):

Make a paste by mixing together 3 eggs, 1 glass of fresh or sour cream, a quarter of a pound of melted sweet butter, some salt, some soda, and enough flour to make a not-too-thick paste.

Now make a regular clear chicken soup from a 5-pound roasting chicken, with 3 carrots, 2 onions, and a little celery. When the chicken is cooked, take off all skin and bones and cut up the meat.

Take 3 pounds of round steak chopped, some salt, pepper, and 1 large onion cut in small pieces. Fry the onion and the chopped meat together in sweet butter, being careful not to brown the onion. Use the meat and all the juice from this in your pie.

When this is ready, mix in 3 chopped hard-boiled eggs. Grease a deep dish with sweet butter, powder with cracker meal, and spread part of the paste over the sides and bottom. Then put in a layer of chopped meat, then a layer of chicken, and repeat alternately, until the dish is full. Cover the pie with the rest of the paste and paint with the yolk of an egg and put in a moderately hot oven to bake about half an hour. Serve with chicken soup in cups.

CHASE'S BAKED SALMON (*for four*):

Buy a fine thick slice of fresh salmon, weighing about 2 pounds. If possible, use Gaspé Bay salmon, or a deep-colored salmon. Butter a pyrex baking-dish about 3 inches deep and not too large. Put 3 good slices of Bermuda onion around the edge of the dish, then 3 slices of lemon from which you have removed the pits. Lay the fish, which you have washed in cold water, in the center of the dish. Add 2 or 3 cloves and a small bay leaf. Then add enough cold sweet milk until it is level with the fish. Salt and pepper and place the dish in a moderate oven for twenty-five or thirty minutes, or until the salmon is perfectly cooked. Now beat the yolks of 3 eggs in a double boiler, and add slowly, stirring all the while over a low fire, about one third of a pound of sweet butter. Then drain the milk from the salmon and add it very gradually to the egg and butter, stirring with a wire whisk. Salt and pepper to taste, and add a little dash of cayenne. Don't let the water in the double boiler boil. When smooth and well mixed, pour the sauce over the fish and put back in the oven for a second or two. Remove and garnish around the edge with crisp watercress. Serve at once.

BETTY'S CURRIED SHRIMPS (*for four*):

Use 1 pound of shrimps, skinned, cleaned; put into boiling salted water and boil for half an hour. Take 2 tablespoons of butter, melt, and add 2 teaspoons of curry powder. Combine this with 2 tablespoons of flour, and add the water in which the shrimps were cooked. This should make about a pint of sauce. Add the shrimps, and keep in a double boiler until ready to serve. Garnish with toast points and serve on boiled rice, with chutney.

JEAN'S BABY LAMB (*for six or eight*):

First make half a cup of good tomato sauce, by simmering 1 pound of peeled and sliced tomatoes with 1 onion chopped fine, a little parsley, half a cup of white wine. Simmer for an hour; then pass through a sieve. Melt a tablespoon of butter and add to it a teaspoon of flour. Add the tomatoes, simmer for a little while longer, and add half a teaspoon of beef extract melted in a little hot water.

Now put a leg of baby lamb into an iron cocotte, with a tablespoon of butter and 3 or 4 white onions. Salt and pepper and add a cup of meat stock. Let this simmer gently for about an hour and a quarter. Then pour off the juice and reduce to a glaze by simmering in a separate little pan. In the meantime, add a little more butter to the lamb and let it get brown all over, turning it over and over. Then add 2 cups of meat broth, half a cup of tomato sauce, the reduced gravy, and 2 tablespoons of good cognac, and cook slowly for another hour and a half.

In the meantime, peel 2 dozen little white onions, and put them in a frying-pan with 2 tablespoons of butter. Sprinkle with a teaspoon of granulated sugar and cook them until they caramelize. Be careful not to burn them. Moisten them with a cup of meat stock and let them cook very slowly until tender throughout, but don't let them fall apart. Now let them cook fast to reduce the juice. Add them to the lamb, and cook for another ten minutes. Place the lamb on a big platter and garnish with the onions. Pour the gravy over all and serve at once.

EDGAR'S PLANKED SHAD (for six):

In the first place, you must have a good thick small seasoned oak plank to cook the fish on; and be sure it will fit in your oven. To season a plank, rub it well with olive oil and place in the oven until good and hot. Remove from the oven, cool, and repeat the process several times at least. Never wash the plank. It should just be well scraped with a dull knife, and wiped clean with olive oil.

Ask the fish man to bone a fine shad for you, unless you happen to know how to do it yourself. When ready to cook the fish, oil the plank well with olive oil and lay the fish, skin side down and open, on the plank. Place the plank in a moderate oven and cook the fish slowly for ten minutes, then sprinkle with melted butter and salt and freshly ground pepper, and continue to cook slowly for another ten minutes. Butter the fish again, and cook for ten minutes longer or until cooked through, depending on the size of the fish.

In the meantime, make some good fluffy mashed potatoes, by boiling 6 good-sized peeled potatoes in salted water. Drain, mash, and add hot cream until of the right consistency to go through a pastry bag.

Ten minutes before the fish is ready to serve, press the potatoes through the bag onto the board to form a border around the plank. Pour a little melted butter over them and place in the oven. If not brown when ready to serve the fish, place them under a hot blaze for a second. Garnish the fish with quartered lemons and parsley and serve at once.

RAY'S CRÊPES SOUFFLÉES (*for twelve*):

To make 24 crêpes of six inches in diameter, make a batter with 2 very fresh eggs, 1 cup of flour, 1¼ cups of milk, a pinch of salt, 1 tablespoon of sugar, 1 teaspoon of cognac, and 1 tablespoon of thick cream. Heat a 6-inch frying-pan, sprinkle with salt, and scour it with a piece of tissue paper. This prevents the crêpe from sticking. Place a small lump of butter in the pan and tilt it so that the whole surface is well buttered; then pour in very little of the batter and tilt the pan so that the whole bottom is covered with a thin coating. Cook until brown on one side, then flip it over with a knife and cook the other side. The crêpes should be very thin. Keep on making the crêpes, piling them one on top of the other until you have used all the batter.

When they are all cooked, lift them one by one and pile them again on another plate, so that they will not stick together, and will be easier for handling for the next process.

Put the pile of pancakes on a board, and with a sharp knife cut 4 2-inch nicks in the pancakes, so that what remains will be in the shape of a cross, like the Red Cross emblem.

In the meantime, make the following cream: Melt a tablespoon of butter and add to it 3 teaspoons of cornstarch, 3 teaspoons of rice flour, and 3 teaspoons of flour. Add to this 1 cup of hot milk, 2 tablespoons of granulated sugar, 1 tablespoon of thick cream, and half a vanilla bean. Cook in a double boiler slowly for fifteen minutes, stirring with care so that it will be very smooth. Remove from the fire, add the yolks of 3 eggs well beaten, 2 tablespoons of butter, and fold in last of all the well-beaten whites of 3 eggs.

Now lay all the crêpes out on a big board, and put a good teaspoon of the cream in the center of each cake. Then fold over the 4 flaps, making a little cushion. Place them, one next the other, on a slightly buttered silver-plated platter or baking-dish, and place in a moderate oven for eight minutes. Just before serving, cover with a little sauce, made by heating 3 large tablespoons of excellent kirsch with 2 large tablespoons of powdered sugar. Light it, and when burnt out, add, little by little, 4 tablespoons of sweet butter.

MR. C.'S SPANISH CHICKEN (for six):

Peel and slice fine 6 little white onions. Place 3 or 4 tablespoons of olive oil in a large iron frying-pan and when it

is hot add 1 clove of garlic and the onions and a young
chicken cut up as for fricassee. Salt and pepper and cook
until the chicken is light brown all over. Remove the
garlic and add 2 cups of washed and dried Spanish raw rice,
and a teaspoon of Spanish saffron pounded to a powder and
dissolved in a little boiling water. Cook all this, stirring
well, for about five minutes, then add a can of tomatoes, 4
cups of chicken broth, and half a pound of Spanish sausages,
chorizo by name, which have been washed in cold water and
scalded. Cook on top of the stove for ten minutes and then
place the pan in the oven uncovered for about half an hour.
In the meantime, cook separately 2 cups of shelled peas in
salted water. Empty the chicken and rice out onto a hot
platter and garnish with the peas, which you have seasoned well with butter, salt, and pepper. Serve with this,
on separate side dishes, canned red pimentos cold. Also
serve with this a light Spanish claret.

RUBY'S HOT COFFEE RUM (*for six*):

Make 6 cups of very strong coffee. Rub 6 lumps of sugar
on the rind of an orange until well saturated with the oil.
Place these in a chafing-dish with 6 cloves and several pieces
of broken cinnamon stick; also the rind of 1 orange, being
careful to use only the orange part. Now add enough
Jamaica rum to cover the sugar, and bring it to a boil. Stir
until the sugar has melted, but be careful that it doesn't
catch fire. Stir into this the black coffee, heat just to boiling point, then ladle it into small coffee cups.

EDDIE'S SPAGHETTI (*for six or eight*):

Mix in a bowl a half-pound each of raw ground veal,
beef, and pork, with a half-cup of chopped parsley, 1 raw
egg, and half a clove of garlic chopped very fine. Season

with salt and pepper and shape into little meat balls. Fry until yellow 1 large onion, sliced, in a teaspoon of lard and a quarter of a cup of olive oil. Do not allow the onion to brown. Then add the meat balls and cook until they turn white. Open 1 small can of tomatoes and mix with them 1 can of imported tomato paste dissolved in 2 cups of stock, or water. Pour this in on the meat balls, add 1½ bay leaves, 5 whole cloves, 1 teaspoon of sugar, 1 pinch each of red pepper, black pepper, and salt. Also add a quarter of a pound of peeled, sliced mushrooms. Allow the whole to cook slowly for three hours. (I generally cook it in the oven.)

Now for the spaghetti part. Put 1½ pounds of unbroken spaghetti into a large pot of boiling water and cook until just barely tender. When nearly cooked, salt it. Drain and dash a little cold water over it to wash off the starch. Mix the spaghetti with part of the sauce from which the meat balls have been removed. Add a handful of grated Parmesan cheese when mixing. Put on a large platter, garnish with the meat balls, and pour the rest of the sauce around the edge. Serve with this a bowl of grated cheese.

ANNE'S BRUSSELS SPROUTS EN CASSEROLE (*for eight*):

First peel and boil until tender in salted water 25 Italian chestnuts. Then pick off the faded leaves from 2 quarts of Brussels sprouts, wash carefully, and soak awhile in cold water. Drain, and pour over them plenty of boiling water. Add a tiny pinch of soda and cook until tender, adding a little salt when almost cooked. In the meantime, wash, dry, and peel 1 pound of mushrooms and slice them fine. Also make 3 cups of highly seasoned cream sauce, medium thick, using part cream. When the Brussels sprouts are cooked, drain well. Place them in a saucepan and add the chestnuts and a small piece of butter and the mushrooms. Mix lightly over a low flame to melt the butter, then place the whole in a casserole and pour over it the cream sauce and sprinkle over that three quarters of a pound of grated soft mild cheese. Place in a medium oven and bake about twenty-five minutes. Serve at once.

XIV. TEA AND COCKTAIL
PARTY ACCESSORIES

Tᴇᴀ-ᴘᴀʀᴛɪᴇs — the good old-fashioned kind — seem to have vanished into thin air, which is rather a pity. I still think it would be very cozy and restful to sit around the fire in the living-room, or around the dining-room table, and eat paper-thin bread and butter and wild strawberry jam, and cœur à la crême, and drink cup after cup of hot fragrant tea, and talk and talk. Instead of which we give a big cocktail party and everyone comes. There are a few hours of dense smoke — and great confusion — and then it's all over, and you really haven't seen or enjoyed anyone. Still, come to think of it, a sherry party or cocktail party is fun, too. Anyway, this chapter is dedicated to them both. Take your choice. You will find menus for both given in the menu chapter.

CŒUR À LA CRÊME:

This can be bought already prepared in a few French delicatessen shops, but a very good imitation can be made at home by working plain cottage cheese through a very fine sieve and putting it into a large heart-shaped aluminum mold which has had several holes punctured in the bottom and which has been lined with a piece of cheesecloth wrung out with a little cold water. Pack well and set in the re-

frigerator to chill. Turn out on a dessert plate, remove
the cheesecloth carefully, and pour a little cream over it.
Serve with Bar-le-Duc jelly or homemade strawberry jam
or wild strawberry jam.

PAIN SURPRISE:

The tea-table was lovely — the pink cloth, the pink and
red roses, the paper-thin china, the lovely silver, the plate
of dainty tarts, the most delicate of little cakes, and then,
right in the midst of it all, sat two loaves of bread — not
even sliced. To be sure, they had pink ribbons tied around
them, but we thought it seemed very odd, indeed. Lo and
behold, our hostess daintily lifted off the top of the bread
which had been previously invisibly cut — and the loaf
was filled with perfect little sandwiches. I bet five dollars
that a loaf of bread had been wasted accomplishing this —
I lost. Here is how it is done:

Buy a very fresh loaf of sandwich bread about fourteen
inches long. With a sharp knife carefully slice off the long
top crust in one whole piece. Insert a long pointed knife at
one corner between the crust and the soft part of the bread
until you strike bottom; then carefully saw all around the
bread. This will loosen the block of soft bread except for
the bottom. Now insert the knife not quite at the corner
between the lower crust and the side crust and push it in
until you hit the back crust; then carefully saw your way
across almost to the end. The block of white bread will
then easily come out intact, leaving a box of crust. Use this
bread for making the sandwiches, which, if properly cut,
will fit neatly back in the crust. When the lid is again put
on, it should appear to be in its original state. Tie a pretty
ribbon around it, wrap in wax paper, and keep in the refrigerator until ready for the tea-table.

CHOPPED MUSHROOM AND MAYONNAISE FILLING:

Wash a half-pound of choice mushrooms, dry well, remove the stems, and chop very fine. Mix with mayonnaise. Salt and pepper to taste.

TOMATO SANDWICHES:

Plunge 2 or 3 ripe tomatoes into boiling water, remove and peel, chill for two hours in the refrigerator. Cream some butter thoroughly, then spread lightly on the bread. Cover with thin slices of the tomatoes, sprinkle with salt and freshly ground black pepper. Tomato sandwiches ¡hould not be made too far ahead of time, as they get soggy.

CUCUMBER AND CHOPPED SWEET ONION FILLING:

Peel a young cucumber, slice thin, and soak for half an hour in ice-water. Do not salt. Drain well, dry on a tea-cloth, and chop with 5 or 6 pickled sweet onions. Spread bread with butter and some of the mixture. Salt and pepper lightly. These, also, should be made as late as possible.

CHOPPED WALNUT AND WATERCRESS FILLING:

Wash and remove leaves only from a bunch of fresh watercress, dry and chop fine. Add to it 2 tablespoons of finely chopped English walnuts and a very little mayonnaise. Salt to taste.

HAM AND HORSERADISH SANDWICHES:

Add 1 tablespoon of pickled horseradish to 3 tablespoons of well-creamed butter. Mix well and spread on white or brown bread. Lay thin slivers of cold boiled ham between each 2 slices of the bread.

STUFFED OLIVE AND SALTED ALMOND FILLING:

Blend a half-cup of minced, stuffed olives with a quarter of a pound of finely chopped salted almonds and 3 level tablespoons of mayonnaise.

CHOPPED EGG AND MAYONNAISE FILLING:

Hard-boil 3 eggs, chop fine, add a tablespoon of chopped watercress and 2 tablespoons of mayonnaise. Salt and pepper to taste.

SHRIMP AND HORSERADISH FILLING:

Peel and clean half a pound of freshly cooked shrimps. Run through the medium meat-grinder, add half a teaspoon of German mustard, 1 tablespoon of mayonnaise, 2 teaspoons of pickled horseradish, a few drops of lemon juice, and enough whipped cream to make of the right consistency to spread. Salt and pepper to taste.

THIN BREAD–AND–BUTTER:

To make thin bread-and-butter it is necessary to have a really sharp knife and plenty of thoroughly creamed butter. The crust of the bread should not be removed. Spread the loaf with butter and then slice off. It sometimes helps to plunge the knife into boiling water and wipe it off before making each slice. The bread should be laid on a platter, each piece underlapping the next by an inch, but left whole.

TOASTED MARMALADE AND BUTTER SANDWICHES:

Make 4 or 5 thin sandwiches well buttered and spread with orange marmalade. Remove the crusts and cut into pieces about 1 inch by 3 inches. These may be made in advance. Keep covered with a damp cloth till ready to toast. Then toast quickly on both sides and serve piping hot.

HOT CINNAMON TOAST:

Cut bread in quarter-inch slices and remove the crusts. Toast lightly and quickly. Butter well and sprinkle with powdered sugar and cinnamon mixed together. Cut in thirds, place on a buttered tin and put under the broiler for a moment to melt the sugar slightly. Serve immediately.

WATERCRESS SANDWICHES:

Wash and pick off the leaves only of 2 bunches of watercress. Dry and place in the refrigerator in a cloth overnight. In the morning, cream half a cup of sweet butter. Chop the watercress lightly, add a tablespoon of mayonnaise and salt to taste. Spread very thin white bread with a little butter and then with the watercress and mayonnaise, and put two pieces together. Trim carefully and cut in half lengthwise.

PECAN SANDWICHES:

Mix 1 cup of chopped pecans with 2 tablespoons of mayonnaise. Spread white bread sliced very thin with a little creamed butter, and then a layer of the nuts and mayonnaise.

BLACK WALNUT CAKE — TWICE-COOKED FROST-ING:

Cream a half-cup of butter, add gradually 1¼ cups of powdered sugar, beat until very light, add a half-cup of milk, 1 teaspoon of vanilla, and a few drops of almond extract. Now add 2 cups of flour which you have sifted three times with 2½ level teaspoons of baking powder. Add a pinch of salt to 5 egg-whites and beat until stiff but not dry, fold into the mixture carefully, then fold in very lightly a half-cup of well-floured, broken black-walnut meats. Pour into a well-buttered oblong cake tin and bake in an oven (375 degrees) for about twenty minutes. When cool, frost with icing made as follows:

Boil 1½ cups of granulated sugar with a half-cup of water until it forms a soft ball in water. Pour slowly onto the beaten whites of 2 eggs, add a little vanilla, a few drops of almond extract, and one eighth of a teaspoon of cream of tartar. Beat until smooth, then put the bowl over boiling water and continue to stir until the spoon grates on the bottom of the bowl. Spread evenly with a silver knife.

SCOTCH CAKES:

Cream 1 cup of butter well, then gradually stir in a half-cup of pulverized sugar and 2 cups of sifted flour. Add a few drops of vanilla and knead with the hands for ten minutes. Turn out onto a well-floured board and roll out to an inch thickness. Lay an inverted pie tin on it and trim to a perfect circle. Set it on a brown paper and place on a cooky sheet. Mark with the back of a knife in thin slices, as you would a pie. Bake in a moderate oven for about half an hour.

RICH ROLLED COOKIES:

Chop fine a few unsalted pecans. Cream a half-cup of butter, add one third of a cup of granulated sugar. Beat an egg well, add it to the butter and sugar, and add 1 teaspoon of vanilla. Sift into this three fourths of a cup of flour. Mix well and drop in tiny teaspoonfuls, far apart, on well-buttered baking-sheets. Spread thin with a wet knife and sprinkle a very few chopped nuts on each. Bake in an oven (375 degrees). When the cookies begin to brown around the edge, which is almost immediately, open the oven door, and with a palette knife remove, one by one, and roll, nut side out, immediately. If they are too much cooked or are allowed to cool, they will not roll.

COCONUT DROPS:

Mix a half-cup of Eagle Brand sweetened condensed milk and 2 cups of moist, shredded canned coconut together. Drop by tiny spoonfuls on a well-buttered pan about an inch apart. Bake in a moderate oven until a delicate brown.

WHITE PLUM CAKE:

Blanch half a pound of almonds, reserve 1 dozen of them for decoration of the cake, and shred the rest with a sharp knife. Scald a half-pound of Sultana white raisins and soak them until plump; then dry well. Cream 6 ounces of butter with 1 cup of granulated sugar, add the beaten yolks of 4 eggs and beat well. Sift 2 cups of flour with 1 teaspoon of baking powder, half a teaspoon of grated nutmeg, and a quarter-teaspoon of salt. Put a teaspoon of vanilla and half a teaspoon of lemon extract in a quarter of a cup of cold water. Add it alternately with the flour to the butter and egg mixture. When well mixed, add the raisins and the almonds, which have been lightly floured, and 1 cup of shredded coconut. Now fold in the stiffly beaten egg-whites, pour into a well-greased, oblong tin which has been carefully lined with buttered white paper. Bake in a moderate oven for about an hour.

HOT BUTTERED SCONES:

Wash and dry well a half-cup of currants. Mix and sift together 2 cups of pastry flour with 4 teaspoons of baking powder, three fourths of a teaspoon of salt, and 8 teaspoons of granulated sugar. Work into this 4 tablespoons of salted butter. Add the currants and then mix to a dough with about two thirds of a cup of milk. Divide into 6 parts, toss each piece onto a lightly floured board and put into a circle 4 inches wide and a half-inch thick. Bake on a hot griddle which has been very well buttered. When delicately brown on one side, turn with a pancake-turner. When cooked through, split and toast under a hot flame, spread with creamed butter, and serve on a napkin.

COOKIES:

Cream one third of a cup of butter with 1 cup of sugar. Add one third of a cup of milk in which has been dissolved one third of a level teaspoon of baking soda. Add 3 teaspoons of vanilla and enough flour to make a dough just stiff enough to handle. Toss one third of it at a time onto a floured board and roll out to a quarter of an inch. Sprinkle well with granulated sugar and cut out. Bake on well-buttered tins in a medium oven until a delicate brown.

PRALINÉ COOKIES:

First blanch a fourth of a cup of filberts and the same quantity of almonds. Dry them out in a warm oven for a few minutes. Butter a platter. Put half a cup of sugar into an aluminum saucepan with 6 teaspoons of cold water. Place on the fire and watch carefully. When the sugar begins to caramelize, remove from the fire, add the nuts, and pour out immediately onto the buttered platter. The sugar must be a pale golden brown. If it gets too dark, it will be bitter. When cold, break into pieces and run through the medium meat-grinder. Now cream a half-cup of butter with one third of a cup of sugar, 1 whole egg beaten well, and a teaspoon of vanilla. Mix well and add three fourths of a cup of flour in which has been sifted a saltspoon of salt. Add three tablespoons of the praliné and bake quickly, but watch carefully, as they burn easily. Remove from the tins immediately with a cake-turner.

CHOCOLATE CAKE:

Butter 4 shallow cake tins of the same size and shape. Cream a half-cup of butter with 1 ¼ cups of powdered sugar. Sift 2 cups of flour with a quarter of a teaspoon of salt and 2½ level teaspoons of baking powder. Add a half-cup of milk to the butter and sugar mixture, then the flour, and 2 teaspoons of vanilla. Beat well and fold in the stiffly beaten whites of 5 eggs. Put it into the tins. There should be not more than a half-inch of dough in each. Bake in an oven heated to about 375 degrees (quick oven) until a toothpick thrust in comes out clean. When cool, put the cakes together with frosting made as follows:

Beat the yolks of 4 eggs until light, add 3 cups of granulated sugar, and beat well. Add 1 cup of milk, 2 tablespoons of butter, and a tiny pinch of salt. Melt 8 squares of chocolate in a double boiler. Cook the first mixture, stirring hard until it boils up hard, then cook two minutes. Remove from the fire, add the melted chocolate, and 2 teaspoons of vanilla. Beat well until thick enough to spread.

HOT BACON BISCUITS:

Sift 1 cup of flour with a rounded teaspoon of baking powder and a level teaspoon of salt. Add a piece of butter the size of an egg. Work it in well with the finger-tips. Then bind together with milk into a stiff dough. Toss onto a floured board and roll out to a half-inch thickness. Cut with a cutter 1½ inches in diameter. Bake in a very hot oven. Split and butter and put a small piece of freshly fried bacon into each one. Place in a folded napkin and serve at once.

WALNUT MOCHA CAKE:

Cream a half-cup of butter with 1 cup of sugar. Add the well-beaten yolks of 2 eggs and a half-cup of milk. Add 1½ cups of flour in which has been sifted 2 teaspoons of baking powder and a pinch of salt. Mix well and add 2 teaspoons of vanilla and 1 cup of broken and lightly floured English walnut meats. Fold in carefully the stiffly beaten whites of 2 eggs, pour into a well-buttered loaf tin, bake in a moderate oven for about forty minutes, or until a toothpick inserted comes out clean. Ice when cold with frosting made by creaming a quarter of a cup of butter and gradually adding 1 cup of confectioners' sugar and a quarter of a cup of cocoa mixed together. Cream well, then soften with hot, very strong black coffee, and vanilla mixed. If it should get too thin, thicken with more sugar and cocoa. Spread unevenly on the cake and decorate with unbroken walnut halves.

GRANDMOTHER'S STRAWBERRY, PINEAPPLE, AND ORANGE CONSERVE:

This recipe makes about 6 glasses. Peel, core, and shred fine 1 pineapple. Pick over, stem, and wash 1 quart of strawberries. Remove the skin from 3 large navel oranges, keeping the skin as whole as possible. Remove the pulp from the oranges with a sharp knife, discarding as much of the pith as possible and save all the juice. Boil the peels in plenty of water until very tender, then remove from the water, and with a spoon scoop out as much of the bitter white inside as possible, leaving just the orange part. Then with a sharp knife sliver the skins into tiny thin strips about half an inch long. Now place the pineapple in a large white enamel pan and add a pint of water. Boil for twenty minutes. In the meantime, put the orange pulp and juice into another enamel pan with 2½ cups of sugar and boil for about fifteen minutes. Then add the rind and continue cooking slowly. When the pineapple is cooked, add the strawberries to it and 4½ cups of sugar. Let them come to a boil, then add the orange, and let it all boil together for about twenty-five minutes, or until thick and clear. Be sure to skim the jam while cooking and stir carefully to prevent sticking. Put into sterilized jars and seal the next day with paraffine.

EATSUM MILK WAFERS:

Eatsum Milk Wafers, lightly buttered and toasted in the oven, are delicious with sherry. They are also good with tea when buttered, toasted, and sprinkled lightly with confectioners' sugar.

POTATO CHIPS WITH CREAM CHEESE:

Place potato chips in the oven to crisp. Mix cream cheese with thick cream and a dash of paprika and add a few finely cut chives; when this is of the right consistency, put it into a pastry bag with a rosette tube and squeeze a small amount onto perfect chips.

RAW VEGETABLES:

Raw carrots, cauliflower, and celery are washed, peeled, and cut in fine strips, then crisped by placing in a bowl of ice-water. Serve on a plate with a small bowl of salt.

LIVERWURST APPETIZERS:

Prepare the night before using the liverwurst paste for the appetizers. Remove the skin from half a pound of best quality liverwurst and mash well with a fork. Add a quarter of a pound of fresh sweet butter and plenty of freshly ground black pepper. Cream well together and pack in a covered jar. Put in the refrigerator overnight. This mixture is spread between thin slices of French rolls, which are then toasted on both sides. Serve hot.

CREAM CHEESE BALLS BETWEEN TWO PECANS:

Make very small cream cheese balls with butter paddles, and put them between 2 unsalted pecans. Sprinkle lightly with salt.

SHRIMPS AND MAYONNAISE AND CHILI SAUCE:

Serve boiled shrimps which have been carefully shelled and meticulously cleaned, with a toothpick stuck in each, around the edge of a platter in the center of which you have placed a small bowl of stiff mayonnaise and one of chili sauce. The shrimps are daintily (we hope) dipped in one or the other by the guests. This sounds messy, but you will be surprised how well it works out.

TOMATO CHILI SAUCE:

Peel 12 tomatoes by first immersing in boiling water for a second. Cut them up in small pieces. Add 4 green peppers, from which you have removed the seeds and which you have chopped fine. Also add 2 big onions peeled and chopped fine, and 4 apples peeled and cut fine. Put all this into a big enamel pan and add 2½ cups of *light* brown sugar, a *pint* of vinegar, 2 level tablespoons of salt, 1 teaspoon of dry mustard, 1 teaspoon of celery seed, half a teaspoon of ground cloves, half a teaspoon of whole allspice, 1 tablespoon of ground cinnamon, a dash of freshly ground pepper, and half a level teaspoon of cayenne. Place on the fire and cook for two hours, or until thick and transparent. Stir very frequently with a wooden spoon. Put into sterilized pint jars and seal tight. This makes about 4 pints.

HOT SAUSAGE ROLLS:

Sift 1 cup of flour with half a teaspoon of salt. Work into this 3 ounces, or three quarters of a bar, of sweet butter. Moisten with ice-water and a few drops of lemon juice. Boil some frankfurters for five minutes, then peel them and slit them down the middle. Roll the paste out to about a quarter of an inch, cut in strips the same width as the sausages are long. Spread a little tarragon mustard on each piece of sausage, and roll up in the dough, wetting the edges to stick them together. Bake in a buttered tin about half an hour. Serve hot.

XV. HOT DRINKS

W<small>HAT</small> a difference a hot drink at the right moment can make in one's life! Have you ever been pulled from the brink of fatigue and despair by a steaming cup? It's seven o'clock in the morning, and oh, so cold! Wouldn't it be grand if someone would come and shut the window and bring us a cup of hot, hot tea with some thin bread-and-butter? It's eleven o'clock of a stormy day at sea and we are about to be revived with some hot bouillon. It's two-thirty and the perfect lunch has been passepartouted à la Whistler by the perfect cup of black coffee. We've reached the low hour of four o'clock, cold and blown by snow and sleet, while shopping. The answer? A cup of hot chocolate. Five-thirty, that moment when the day can be broken or rescued by the right cup of tea. We're contentedly uncomfortable after our gourmet dinner; the right rescue for a moment such as this is the right tisane. It's midnight, just one more log on the fire and a cozy hot toddy, or a nightcap, and good-night.

All of which goes to prove that every so often there comes a time in one's life when a hot drink is what we want more than anything in the world. One of the following recipes may help you over one of life's most difficult moments.

First of all, there are numerous tisanes, or herbal teas,

which, when taken after a meal in place of coffee or Sanka, are delicious, and refreshing. Some of the herbs or ingredients used may be bought in drugstores, the rest in health food shops or in the big groceries. I am giving you directions for making a few of my favorites.

MINT TEA:

Heat the teapot. Use 1 teaspoon of crushed dried leaves for each person, and add a cup of actively boiling water to each spoon of mint. Let this steep five minutes, and serve in teacups with a lump of sugar.

SWISS STRAWBERRY TEA:

This is made from the dried leaves of the strawberry plant. Use 1 heaping teaspoon to each cup of boiling water. Steep five minutes and serve with honey or brown sugar.

TILLEUL, LINDEN–TREE BLOSSOMS, AUX FLEURS D'ORANGER (*for two*):

For this you will need linden-tree blossoms and dried orange blossoms. Put a handful of the linden blossoms and a few orange blossoms into a hot teapot and cover well with boiling water. Steep five minutes and serve with sugar. If you have difficulty in getting orange blossoms, a few drops of orange flower water may be used instead. This is not a novelty; it is a well-known French drink, taken in place of coffee after meals.

CAMOMILE TEA (*for two*):

This is made by putting 1 pint of boiling water over 1 ounce of dried camomile flowers. Steep ten minutes, strain, and serve with honey or sugar.

HAGENBUTTEN TEA:

A most delicious German tea-drink from the seeds of the wild rose. The dried berries which contain the seeds may be bought in some German pharmacies. They are sometimes sold in berry form and sometimes in seed form. The berries must be opened and all the little seeds carefully removed. For four people use about 2 tablespoons of the little seeds. Place them in an enamel pan with 5 cups of water which is just ready to boil, cover and simmer very gently half an hour. Serve with sugar in teacups.

TURKISH COFFEE:

Boil 8 after-dinner coffee cups of water. Add to this 8 teaspoons of sugar and 12 teaspoons of pulverized Mocha coffee. Stir, put on the fire and, when it boils up, take it off. Do this three times. Then add a dash of cold water, and when settled serve in tiny cups.

CUBAN COFFEE (*for three*):

Heat 3 cups of rich milk to the boiling point in a large enamel pan. Put into it a half-cup of medium-ground coffee. Simmer for five minutes, then strain through a very fine sieve. Serve with sugar and whipped cream.

HOT EGG COFFEE:

For one portion, take the well-beaten yolk of 1 egg and 4 tablespoons of hot cream and a heaping teaspoon of sugar. Add a cup of hot, strong coffee. Beat the white of 1 egg. Fold it into the hot coffee. Serve at once.

VIENNA COFFEE (*for six*):

Put six cups of cold water into an electric percolator. Put 7 tablespoons of your favorite coffee, ground fine, into the top part of the pot and connect the plug. Cook from eight to ten minutes. To a half pint of cream add 1 eggwhite and beat well. Put a lump of sugar in the bottom of each cup and a good helping of whipped cream. Fill with hot coffee.

MOCHA CHOCOLATE (*for eight*):

Make 1 pint of strong black coffee. Heat the same quantity of rich milk to a boiling point. Pour milk and coffee from an equal height into a big pitcher. Sweeten to taste. Keep hot.

In a double boiler melt 2 squares of Baker's unsweetened chocolate with 3 tablespoons of cold water. Heat 4 cups of rich milk and 3 tablespoons of sugar to boiling point. Add melted chocolate and 1 teaspoon of vanilla. Stir well, then pour from a great height into the coffee and milk. Beat until frothy and serve with a little unsweetened whipped cream.

BRANDY COCOA (*for six*):

Mix 3 tablespoons of cocoa with 3 tablespoons of sugar. Dissolve to a cream with a half-cup of boiling water. Scald a quart of rich milk and add a few grains of salt. Add the cocoa to this and boil up once. Remove from the fire and stir in 3 tablespoons of good brandy.

MILK PUNCH:

Heat 1 quart of rich milk to the boiling point with a halfcup of sugar. Remove from the fire and add a half-cup of rum, a half-cup of cognac, and 1 teaspoon of vanilla. Stir well and heat again until very hot. Put silver spoons in 6 glasses and fill with the punch. Sprinkle with grated nutmeg or cinnamon. Serve with this heated wine crackers.

CAUDLE CUP (for six):

This is a drink that our ancestors offered callers on the arrival of the new baby. Boil for an hour 4 tablespoons of oatmeal in 2 quarts of water with several thin strips of lemon rind, a pinch of ginger, and several cloves. Strain and add to the gruel 2 wineglasses of sherry. Beat the yolks of 2 eggs well and gradually pour the hot gruel on them. Serve hot in glasses with a little grated nutmeg sprinkled on top.

NIGHTCAP (for four):

Beat the yolks of 4 eggs with 2 cups of rum and 2 teaspoons of allspice. Melt 4 tablespoons of sugar in 4 cups of boiling water and whip this into the eggs. Beat the whites stiff. Strain the hot egg mixture into tall glasses containing silver spoons. Top with beaten whites and sprinkle a little nutmeg on top.

POSSET (for three):

This is an old English drink. Add 2 strips of thin lemon rind to 3 cups of rich milk and heat to the boiling point. Squeeze and strain the juice of 3 lemons, add 3 tablespoons of sugar, and stir until the sugar melts, then add 1 tablespoon of brandy, a dash of nutmeg, and 12 blanched almonds chopped fine. Add to the hot milk, and beat with an eggbeater until frothy. Serve hot.

WASSAIL BOWL:

Also an old English drink partaken of on Christmas Eve. Core and roast 6 large apples without any sugar, until they are at the point of bursting, fleecy and white. Add a half-pound of light brown sugar to 1 pint of ale, and add to this 1 tablespoon each of ground ginger, nutmeg, and cinnamon. Heat very slowly, stirring meanwhile. Do not boil. When hot, add 1 quart of ale, a half-pint of Malaga wine, and a few strips of thin lemon rind. Put a hot apple in each of 6 mugs and fill with the warm ale.

TOM AND JERRY:

For 6 Tom and Jerrys, beat the whites of 6 eggs, then beat the yolks with eight teaspoons of granulated sugar until light and creamy, then fold this into the whites. Add a cup of Jamaica rum and a cup of brandy. Add to this half a teaspoon of cinnamon and the same amount of nutmeg. Pour into this gradually 3 cups of boiling water. Serve in earthenware mugs with a dash of nutmeg.

RUSSIAN TEA (for three):

Put 1½ teaspoons of green tea into a pan with a small stick of cinnamon, add 1 pint of milk and simmer over a low fire for five minutes. Strain through a fine sieve. Return to the pan and sweeten to taste with a lump of sugar rubbed on the rind of a lemon until well saturated. Beat the yolks of 2 eggs to a froth, then add the boiling milk gradually, stirring meanwhile. Serve hot.

RUM PUNCH (for six):

Put a quarter of a bottle of Jamaica rum into a bowl, add one eighth of a bottle of cognac, half a glass of Cointreau, and the thin rind of half a lemon and of half an orange. Also add half of an orange sliced thin and half a lemon. Sweeten to taste and add 4 cups of boiling water. Mix well and serve very hot.

SAUTERNE PUNCH (*for four*):

Put into an enamel pan a quart of sauterne, a cup of sugar lumps, the thin rind of 1 lemon, and 2 cloves. Dissolve the sugar in the wine, then heat very gradually until a white foam appears on top. Remove from the fire and remove the lemon rind. Add half a cup of heated cognac. Light the brandy and let it burn out. Put a thin slice of lemon into each glass and serve hot.

HOT CLARET PUNCH (*for four*):

Boil a cup of water with half a cup of powdered sugar and 2 pieces of broken cinnamon and 2 cloves. Add 2 lemons sliced very thin, and cover and let stand for ten minutes. Then add 3 glasses of claret and heat gradually, but do not boil. Serve very hot.

MULLED PORT (*for four*):

Stick an unpeeled orange full of cloves and roast it in the oven for about an hour, or until golden brown all over. Put 8 cloves, a 4-inch stick of cinnamon, a dash of nutmeg, and 2 strips of thin lemon rind into a cup of water and let it simmer gently until only half a cup of water is left. Then add a quart of old port and a glass of sherry. Let it heat very gradually, but don't boil. Sweeten to taste with a little sugar, and put it into a bowl, and add the roasted orange cut in quarters. Take it into the living-room and sit before the fire and ladle it into glasses containing silver spoons.

MULLED SHERRY (*for four*):

Put a piece of cinnamon 4 inches long into a cup of water with a dash of nutmeg and a few cloves and a small piece of bruised lemon rind. Simmer for a while, then add a quart of sherry and a wineglass of brandy. Heat carefully, but do not boil. Serve hot.

TWELFTH NIGHT CIDER (*for twelve*):

Bake 12 little apples with cinnamon and sugar, and keep hot. Put 3 quarts of hard cider or sweet cider into a porcelain-lined kettle. Add a teaspoon of vanilla and 2 tablespoons of sugar, a small piece of cinnamon, several cloves, a nutmeg tied in a little cloth, and a little thin lemon rind. Simmer for fifteen minutes, and pour into a punchbowl. Remove the spice bag and lemon peel, then add the baked apples and serve very hot.

MATÉ (*for two*):

This is a South American substitute for tea. It is prepared from the leaves of the Brazilian holly. Put a level teaspoon of maté into a small muslin bag, and pour on it a pint of freshly boiling water. Steep for a minute or two and serve with lemon and burnt sugar. (This last is made by putting a cup of sugar into a pan, moistened slightly with water, and cooked until it caramelizes a light brown. Don't cook too long. Pour onto a lightly buttered slab of marble or platter. Break in small pieces.) South Americans drink this with straws from cups made from gourds.

HOT ORANGE (*for four*):

Squeeze the juice of 3 oranges. Add half a cup of powdered sugar. Beat well 6 eggs, add the orange juice, and continue to beat. Strain, then add slowly 3 cups of boiling water. Serve in tall glasses with a dash of nutmeg on top.

TEA:

Soft water should be used, if possible, to make tea. If your water is very hard, add a tiny pinch of soda to it, and never boil the water for more than a minute or two. Put a teaspoon of your favorite tea to each person into a perfectly dry pot a quarter of an hour before it is required. Warm both the pot and the tea by placing them in the oven or before the fire. Then fill the teapot with boiling water and let it steep for five minutes.

HOT BISHOP (*for six*):

Take 1 teaspoon each of cloves, mace, ginger, cinnamon, and allspice. Simmer in a cup of water for forty minutes, then strain.

In the meantime, stick a few cloves in an orange and roast it in the oven for about an hour, or until it becomes golden brown. Rub 12 lumps of sugar on the rind of a lemon, until the lumps are well saturated with oil. Place them in a silver punchbowl with the juice of 1 lemon. Put three fourths of a bottle of port into a silver chafing-dish and add the spiced infusion. Heat slowly, but do not boil. Pour over the sugar in the punchbowl. Stir until the sugar melts, add the roasted orange and the rest of the bottle of port, and serve hot.

XVI. MENUS

THE hardest part of giving a party, in my opinion, is deciding what to have. There is always the danger of repetition. It's just possible that Mrs. Brown will remember that you gave her the shad roe mousse the last time she dined with you, and we shouldn't like to have that happen. The best way of avoiding this is to keep a little book giving the date of the party, the menu, and the guests. This you can consult the next time you invite Mrs. Brown. Another wise plan is to learn the food idiosyncrasies of your friends and at least make an effort to respect them. This can't always be done, but if you are conscious of serving a dish that Mrs. Brown imagines doesn't agree with her, then at least make up for it by having the next course something you know she will like. The following menus are mostly short, but in most cases will be adequate. Add or subtract from them as you please; but I hope they will make life a little easier for you.

GOURMET'S DINNER (*for eight*)

Caviar with Toast and Trimmings

Madrilène — Hot

Pheasants in Cream

Purée of Lima Beans and Peas

Romaine Orange and Almond Salad

Pears in Cointreau   Frozen Cream

INFORMAL DINNER (*for eight*)

Thin Pea Soup

Curried Duck — Apricot Chutney

Sliced Fruit with Orange Ice and Almonds

LUNCHEON PARTY (*for eight*)

Honeydew Melon — Powdered Ginger

Baked Chicken Custard

Carrots Vichy

Strawberry Tarts with Devonshire Cream

HOT WEATHER BUFFET PARTY (*for twelve*)

Vichisoise — Cold

Gnocchi — Hot

Cold Roast Duck

Cold Chicken under a Blanket

Cauliflower Salad — String Bean Salad

Watermelon Filled with Fresh Fruit

GARDEN SIT-DOWN PICNIC (*for eight*)

Cocktails, with Liverwurst and French Bread Toasted Canapés

Hot Boiled Lobster with Butter Sauce

Roasted Stuffed Capons — Cold
Potato and Truffle Salad

Cherry Tart — Coffee

COLD NIGHT BUFFET SUPPER (*for twelve*)

Black Bean Soup

Hot Hors d'Œuvres, consisting of:
Canned Red Pimentos, Stuffed — Hot
Baked Spiced Onions — Hot

Baked Eggs, Cecilia — Hot

Boiled Roasted Ham, Cumberland Sauce — Hot

(Mixed) Pots de Crèmes

LUNCH OR DINNER (*for eight*)

Spring Soup

Cauliflower with Cream Sauce, Buttered Crumbs

Veal Cooked in Chablis
Lettuce Salad

Oranges, Méringued

DINNER (*for eight*)

Cream of Soy Bean Soup

Lobster Mousse Surprise

Canards aux Olives

Chicory Salad

Pears in Cointreau — Frozen Cream

Rich Rolled Cookies

❈

FOR BRIEF LUNCHEON BEFORE THE MATINÉE (*for eight*)

Tomato Juice Frappé

Purée of Mushrooms and Endives

Apples Porcupine

❈

DINNER (*for eight*)

Veal Broth with Tapioca

Boiled Salmon with Cream Sauce and Potatoes

Squabs Stuffed with Pistachio Nuts
Asparagus Tips à la Française

Chicory and Escarole Salad
(Chicken liver Dressing)

The Queen's Custard

INFORMAL DINNER (*for eight*)

Boiled Turkey — Hot Broth

Mashed Potatoes

Spinach Ring with Mushrooms

Chocolate Pudding

SUNDAY LUNCH (*for eight*)

Eggs in Aspic

Roast Chicken Stuffed with Noodles

Spinach Salad

Bananas with Coconut Cream

FORMAL DINNER (*for eight*)

Potage Maigre Canadien

Beans with Cream and Egg Sauce

Roast Pheasants Basted with Gin and Juniper Berries —
Currant Sauce

Ray's Crêpes Soufflées — Sweet White Wine well chilled

INFORMAL SUPPER (*for eight*)

Cream of Chicken Soup

Cassoulet

Strawberries with Wild Strawberry Preserves

INFORMAL DINNER (*for eight*)

Beef Broth with Cabbage Toasts

Poached Leg of Lamb — Béarnaise Sauce
Boiled Potatoes

Lettuce Salad   Fines Herbes

Rich Chocolate Pudding — Mocha Sauce

FORMAL DINNER PARTY (*for twelve*)

Honeydew Melon à la Venice

Pea Soup with Whipped Cream and Croutons

Fish in Aspic with Watercress Sauce

Poulet Patron
String Beans in Butter

Mixed Salad — French Dressing

Praliné Custard

Strawberries with Little Mounds of Sugar

INFORMAL DINNER (*for eight*)

Cream of Tapioca Veal Broth

Canards aux Navets
Petits Pois à la Française

Romaine Salad — Hard-Boiled Egg Dressing

Pot de Crême Café

FOR MAN'S LUNCHEON OR DINNER (*for eight*)

Oyster Stew

Broiled Steak, Béarnaise Sauce
Potatoes Panier

Chocolate Ice Cream — Coffee Sauce

CHRISTMAS OR THANKSGIVING DINNER (*for twelve*)

Sherry

Potage de Curé

Roast Turkey with Ray's Stuffing, Cranberry Sauce
String Beans in Butter
Parsnip Fritters

Pumpkin Pudding — Scotch Cakes

Snapdragon

TEA PARTY (*for twelve*)

Pain Surprise

Large Plate of Thin Bread and Butter with
Cœur à la Crême and Wild Strawberry Jam

Coconut Drops   Chocolate Cake

COCKTAIL PARTY

Pain Surprise containing:
Chopped Mushroom and Mayonnaise Sandwiches
Ham and Horseradish Sandwiches
Hot Toasted Liverwurst Sandwiches

Cream Cheese Balls Between Two Pecans
Celery and Black Olives Soaked in Olive Oil

TEA PARTY (*for twelve*)

Pain Surprise containing:
Tomato Sandwiches   Cucumber Sandwiches
Hot Buttered Scones — Marmalade
White Plum Cake

COCKTAIL PARTY

Pain Surprise containing:
Chopped Walnut Sandwiches
Shrimp and Horseradish Sandwiches

Pain Surprise of Brown Bread containing:
Ham and Horseradish Sandwiches

Hot Sausage Rolls

Raw Vegetables

TEA PARTY (*for twelve*)

Hot Bacon Biscuits

Thin White and Brown Bread — Grandmother's Conserve

Hot Cinnamon Toast

Walnut Mocha Cake

COCKTAIL PARTY

Pain Surprise containing:
Chopped Egg and Mayonnaise Sandwiches
Stuffed Olive and Salted Almond Filling

Eatsum Milk Wafers, Buttered

Hot Bacon Biscuits

Potato Chips and Cream Cheese

Salted Nuts

TEA PARTY (*for twelve*)

Pain Surprise containing:
Watercress Sandwiches
Pecan Sandwiches
Hot Toasted Marmalade Sandwiches

Praliné Cookies — Chocolate Cake

COCKTAIL PARTY

Pain Surprise containing:
Tomato Sandwiches
Watercress Sandwiches

Shrimps and Mayonnaise and Chili Sauce

Raw Vegetables

DINNER (*for eight*)

Vichisoise — Hot

Soft Shelled Crabs — Amandines

Crown Roast of Lamb — Pink Apple Balls — Mint Sauce
Green Peas

Mixed Green Salad

Peaches on Méringued Pedestals

FORMAL PARTY (*for twelve*)

Consommé with Little Pieces of Alligator Pear

Boiled Deep-Sea Striped Bass

Boiled Potatoes

Fillet of Venison, Marinated

Purée of Marrons

Lettuce Salad — Fines Herbes — Camembert Cheese

Strawberry and Almond Soufflé

DINNER (*for eight*)

Cold Tomato Cucumber Soup

Scallops Amandine

Fondue de Poulet à la Crême

Noodles with Buttered Crumbs

Chicory Salad

Blazing Peaches

LUNCH OR DINNER (*for eight*)

Strawberries with Powdered Sugar

Curry of Chicken

Méringued Rum Cake

DINNER PARTY (*for twelve*)

Pea Soup with Buttered Crumbs

Shad Roe Mousse

Poulet en Cocotte (Double the recipe)

Lettuce with Fines Herbes

Compote of Fruit
or
Plump Strawberries (Double the recipe)

Lucy's Praliné Cookies

LUNCH (*for eight*)

Hors d'Œuvres of Marinated Mushrooms

Skate Wings with Beurre Noir

Boiled Potato Balls

Crême Bruler

LIGHT LUNCHEON PARTY (*for eight*)

Eggs Baked in Cream with Bacon

Asparagus — Parmesan Cheese — Brown Butter

Strawberries in Orange Juice

Rich Rolled Cookies

LUNCHEON PARTY (*for eight*)

Hors d'Œuvres of Radishes, Cucumbers, Green Peppers,
Coquilles de Beurre

French Bread

Veal Kidneys in Mustard

Asparagus, Egg, Watercress Salad

Sliced Oranges in Orange Sherbet

Coconut Drops

DINNER (*for eight*)

Smoked Salmon on Toast with Olive Oil, Coarse Pepper

Boula

Boned Squab Chickens en Casserole — Carrots Vichy

Crêpes Suzette

LUNCH BOX FOR MOTORING

Chicken Broth in Thermos — Hot

Fried Chicken

Watercress Sandwiches

Strawberry Turnovers

Black Coffee in Thermos

SUNDAY LUNCH OR INFORMAL DINNER PARTY (*for twelve*)

Cantaloupe with Parma Ham

Two Pigeon Pies

Baby Garden Lettuce with Hard-Boiled Egg Dressing

Iced Zabayonne

FRIDAY NIGHT DINNER (*for eight*)

Watercress and Potato Soup

Omelette de Curé

Boiled New Potatoes

Sliced Raw Pears in Curaçao and Orange Juice

Black Walnut Cake — Twice-Cooked Frosting

FRIDAY NIGHT DINNER (*for eight*)

Lobster Chowder

Salt Cod with Dried Beans

Lettuce with Fines Herbes Salad

Pears in Port

FRIDAY NIGHT INFORMAL DINNER (*for eight*)

Pumpkin Soup

Lobster and Salmon Pie

Provincial Potatoes

Caramel Rice Pudding

Classified Index

HORS D'OEUVRES AND FIRST-COURSE DISHES

Grilled sardines on toast, 1
Honeydew melons à la Venise, 1
Cantaloupe with Parma ham, 2
Radishes, cucumbers and green peppers, 2
Marinated mushrooms, 3
Canned red pimentos stuffed with rice and peas and ham, 3
Curried hard-boiled eggs, 4
Honeydew melon with powdered ginger, 4
Alligator pears à la Tahiti, 5
Strawberries with powdered sugar, 5
Tomato juice frappé, 5
Baked spiced onions, 5
Smoked salmon on toast with olive oil and coarse black pepper, 6
Caviar with toast and trimmings, 6

SOUPS — THIN

Consommé, 9
Beef stock, 10
Chicken broth, 10
Veal broth tapioca, 11
Madrilène, 11
Diet vegetable soup, 11
Beef broth with cabbage toasts and cheese, 12
Thin pea soup, 13
Spring soup, 13
Cold tomato cucumber soup, 13

SOUPS — THICK

Pea soup with whipped cream and croutons, 14
Cream of soy bean tapioca soup, 15
Cream of tapioca veal broth, 15
Minestrone, 16

SOUPS — THICK

Watercress and potato soup, 16
Vichichoise Meadowbrook, 17
Black Bean soup, 17
Pumpkin soup, 18
Oyster stew, 18
Cream of chicken soup, 19
Potage de Curé, 20
Lobster chowder, 20
Marie's potato soup, 21
Salmon and shrimp soup, 22
Potage maigre Canadien, 22
New England fish chowder, 23
Boula soup, 24

FISH

Fish in aspic, 28
Shad roe mousse, 30
Soft-shelled crabs almandine, 32
Lobster mousse surprise, 32
Fillet of flounder, 34
Skate wings with beurre noisette and capers, 35
Canned salmon curry, 36
Salt cod bénédictine, 37
Salt cod with dried beans, 37
Boiled deep-sea bass, 38
Truite saumonée braisée, 38
Boiled salmon, cream, egg, herb sauce, 39
Baked shad roe, 40
Trout with bacon, 40
Truites aux amandes, 40
Scallops almandine, 41
Lobster and salmon pie, 42
Hot boiled lobster, butter sauce, 44

EGGS

Fried eggs, 47
Poached eggs on toast, 47

EGGS

Coddled eggs à la coque, 48
Scrambled eggs, 48
Hard-boiled eggs, 49
Eggs on the plate, 49
Plain omelet, 49
Poached egg with pâté de foie gras, 50
Fried eggs with capers au beurre noir, 50
Eggs à la tripe, 50
Spanish eggs, 51
Eggs in tomatoes, 51
Veal kidney omelet, 51
Egg timbales with tomato sauce, 52
Eggs in spinach, 53
Eggs baked in cream with bacon, 53
Scrambled eggs with shrimps, 53
Stuffed eggs baked, 54
Curried eggs in brown rice, 55
Soufflé of chicken and cheese, 55
Chicken liver omelet, 56
Omelette de Curé, 56
Baked eggs — Cecilia, 57
Eggs in aspic, 58
Tabasco eggs, 59
Squiggled eggs, 59

FOWL

Pheasants in cream, 64
Canards aux olives, 64
Boiled turkey butter sauce, 65
Roast stuffed turkey, 66
Canards aux navets, 67
Poulet en consommé, 68
Chicken stew, 68
Garbure of squabs, 69
Baked chicken custard, 70
Roast pheasants basted with gin and juniper berries, 71
Poulet bonne femme, 72
Boned squab chickens en casserole, 73
Poulet à l'Espagnole, 73
Curry of chicken, 74
Cold boiled chicken Yorkshire style, 75
Chicken polenta, 76
Chicken en cocotte à la bonne à tout faire, 78
Roast chicken prunes and bacon, 79
Mexican chicken stew, 79
Poulet patron, 80

FOWL

Two pigeon pies, 83
Fried chicken, 86
Roast stuffed capons, 86
Cold chicken in a blanket, 87
Curried duck with apricot and date chutney, 88
Squabs stuffed with pistachio nuts, 89
Cold roast duck, 90
Fondue de poulet à la crême, 90
Roast chicken stuffed with noodles, 91
Roast turkey with Ray's stuffing, 92
Duck stuffed with green peas, 94
Duck à l'orange, 94
Boiled chicken with dumplings, 95

MEAT

Fillet of venison marinated, 99
Roast suckling pig with chestnut stuffing, 100
Apple sauce — horseradish sauce, 101
Poached leg of lamb, 102
Sauce béarnaise, 103
Boiled roasted ham hot, 104
Sauce for ham, 104
Civet de lapin, 104
Boeuf à la mode, 105
Blanquette de veau, 107
Kidney stew, 107
Veal kidney in mustard, 108
Veal cooked in Chablis, 109
Lamb à l'Alsace, 109
Cold ham, 110
A way of serving cold roast beef, 111
Crown roast of lamb etc., 111
Mint sauce, 112
Tripe — casserole, 112
Baked calf's liver, 113
Poupiettes of beef, 114
Broiled steak and sauce béarnaise, 114
Corned beef and cabbage, 115
Hot horseradish bread sauce, 116
Boiled tongue, 116
Mustard and bacon sauce, 116
Pot-au-feu, 117
Boiled leg of lamb with caper sauce, 117
Cold boiled bacon for breakfast, 118
Gigot braisé, 119

ALMOST NO MEAT

Tomato sauce, 121
Spinach and tongue in horseradish cream, 122
Cabbage stuffed with corned beef hash, 122
Another stuffed cabbage, 123
Artichoke hearts stuffed with ham and mushrooms — tomato sauce, 124
Purée of green peas in ham cornucopias, 124
Stuffed Bermuda onions, 125
Baked potatoes stuffed with beef, 125
Cabbage — potato and sausage, 126
Pancake delicacies, 126

VEGETABLES

Noodles with buttered crumbs, 129
String beans in butter, 130
Asparagus, browned butter, cheese, 130
Petits pois à la Française, 130
Potatoes panier, 131
Italian zucchini fan-shaped, 132
Parsnip fritters, 132
String beans, cream and egg sauce, 133
Baked beets in cream, 133
Provincial potatoes, 133
Red cabbage, 134
Purée of mushrooms with braised endives, 134
Asparagus tips cooked à la Française, 135
Cauliflower with cream sauce — buttered crumbs, 135
Carrots Vichy, 136
Purée of watercress, 136
Savoy cabbage, 137
Squash in cream, 137
Green peppers in olive oil, 137
Purée of onions, 138
Glazed turnips, 138
Purée of lima beans and peas, 138
Sweet potato pudding, 139
Purée of marrons, 139
Purée of spinach, 139
Vegetable curry, 140
Vegetable plate, 140
Tomato soufflé, 140
Cucumbers in cream, 141

VEGETABLES

Spinach ring with mushrooms, 141
French fried potatoes, 142
Mashed potatoes, 142
Boiled potatoes new and old, 143
Baked potatoes, 143

SALADS

Mixed salad — French dressing, 147
Celery salad — mustard dressing, 148
Cauliflower salad in French dressing, 148
Cucumber, tomato and radish salad, 148
Potatoes and watercress salad, 149
Chicory and escarole salad — chicken liver dressing, 149
Romaine salad — hard-boiled egg dressing, 150
Wilted salad, 150
Hot potato salad, 151
Vegetable salad, 151
Spinach salad, 152
Lettuce salad, 152
Chicory salad, 152
Hard-boiled egg salad, 152
Asparagus, egg and watercress salad, 153
Baby garden lettuce salad — hard-boiled egg dressing, 153
String bean salad, 153
Potato and truffle salad, 154
Romaine and orange and almond salad (Specialty of Ritz, London) 154

FILLING AND FATTENING FOODS

Gnocchi, 157
Polenta with sausages, 158
Spaghetti, 159
Cassoulet, 159
Ravioli, 160
Boston baked beans, 162
Southern baked beans, 163

CUSTARDS AND PUDDINGS

Praliné custard, 170
Crêpes Suzette, 171
The queen's custard, 173
Snow pudding, 174
Chocolate pudding, 174
Praliné cream, 175

CUSTARDS AND PUDDINGS

Tapioca pudding — zabaione sauce, 175
Bread pudding, 176
Caramel rice pudding, 176
Rice pudding, 176
Farina or cream of wheat pudding, 177
Pot de crême vanilla, 177
Pot de crême chocolat, 178
Pot de crême café, 178
Crême renversée, 178
Pumpkin pudding, 178
Rich chocolate pudding with mocha sauce, 179
Chocolate ice cream — coffee sauce, 180
Iced zabaione, 180
Méringued rum cake, 181
Boiled fig pudding, 182
Boiled apple dumplings, 183
Crême brûler, 183
Blazing baked Alaska, 184

FRUIT DESSERTS

Strawberry and almond soufflé, 187
Pears in Cointreau with frozen cream, 188
Snapdragon, 189
Sliced oranges in orange sherbet, 189
Cherries in cracked ice, 190
Almond cream coated with strawberry gelatine, 190
Strawberries in red wine, 191
Strawberry turnovers, 191
Cherry tart, 192
Strawberry tarts with Devonshire cream, 193
Sliced fruit with orange ice and almonds, 194
Pears à la cuillère, 194
Compote of fruit, 195
Orange méringued, 195
Sliced raw pears in orange juice and curaçao, 196
Bananas with coconut cream, 196
Apricot jelly, 197
Sliced peaches in plum juice, 197
Baked apples porcupine, 197
Plump strawberries, 198
Strawberries in orange juice, 198
Coupe, 198

FRUIT DESSERTS

Strawberries with wild strawberry jam, 200
Peaches on méringued pedestals, 200
Pears cooked in port, 201
Sugared currants, 201
Cherries cooked in red wine, 201
Prunes in red wine, 202
Blazing peaches, 202
Banana pudding, 202
Melon glacé à l'Orientale, 203
Rice pudding with apricots, 203
Watermelon filled with fresh fruit and water ice — and champagne, 204
Frozen strawberries, 205
Frozen méringued whipped cream, 205
Almond soufflé, 206
Dried fruits and walnuts in cream, 206
English walnuts and port, 206

LIST OF SPECIALTIES OF MY FRIENDS

1. Janet's green and white spaghetti, 209
2. Martha's baked tomatoes, 210
3. Hélène's poulet crapaudine, 210
4. Bab's arroz de la Valenciana, 211
5. Isabelle's grateau de marrons, 212
6. Moffat's poulet aux choux, 212
7. Sam's spoonbread, 213
8. Lucy's praliné cookies, 213
9. Audrey's fillet of sole au gratin, 214
10. Pat's codfish, 215
11. Mildred's eggplant, 215
12. Claudine's chicken pie, 216
13. Chase's baked salmon, 216
14. Betty's curried shrimps, 217
15. Jean's baby lamb, 217
16. Edgar's planked shad, 218
17. Ray's crêpes soufflés, 219
18. Mr. C's Spanish chicken, 220
19. Ruby's hot coffee rum, 221
20. Eddie's spaghetti, 221
21. Anne's Brussels sprouts en casserole, 222

TEA AND COCKTAIL PARTY ACCESSORIES

Coêur à la crême, 225
Pain surprise, 226
Chopped mushroom and mayonnaise filling, 227
Tomato sandwiches, 227
Cucumber and chopped sweet onion filling, 227
Chopped walnut and watercress filling, 227
Ham and horseradish sandwiches, 227
Stuffed olives and salted almond filling, 228
Chopped egg and mayonnaise filling, 228
Shrimp and horseradish filling, 228
Thin bread and butter, 228
Toasted marmalade and butter sandwiches, 228
Hot cinnamon toast, 229
Watercress sandwiches, 229
Pecan sandwiches, 229
Black walnut cake — twice-cooked frosting, 229
Scotch cakes, 230
Rich rolled cookies, 230
Coconut drops, 231
White plum cake, 231
Hot buttered scones, 231
Cookies, 232
Praliné cookies, 232
Chocolate cake, 233
Hot bacon biscuits, 233
Walnut mocha cake, 234
Grandmother's strawberry, pineapple and orange conserve, 234
Eatsum Milk Wafers — buttered, 235

CANAPES

Potato chips with cream cheese, 235
Raw vegetables, 235
Liverwurst sandwiches toasted, 235
Cream cheese balls between two pecans, 236
Shrimps and mayonnaise — and chili sauce, 236
Hot sausage rolls, 237

HOT DRINKS

Mint tea, 240
Swiss strawberry tea, 240
Tilleul, or Linden-tree blossoms, aux fleurs d'oranger, 240
Camomile tea, 240
Hagenbutten tea, 241
Turkish coffee, 241
Cuban coffee, 241
Hot egg coffee, 241
Vienna coffee, 241
Mocha chocolate, 242
Brandy cocoa, 242
Milk punch, 242
Caudle cup, 243
Nightcap, 243
Posset, 243
Wassail bowl, 243
Tom and Jerry, 244
Russian tea, 244
Rum punch, 244
Sauterne punch, 245
Hot claret punch, 245
Mulled port, 245
Mulled sherry, 245
Twelfth Night cider, 246
Maté, 246
Hot orange, 246
Tea, 247
Hot Bishop, 247

Alphabetical Index

Alaska, blazing baked, 184
Alligator pears, à la Tahiti, 5
Almond, and strawberry soufflé, 187
   cream, coated with strawberry gelatine, 190
   romaine and orange salad, 154
   salted and stuffed olive filling, 228
   soufflé, 206
   with orange ice and sliced fruit, 194
Almost no meat, 121–26
Appetizers, 1–6
   liverwurst, 235
   potato chips with cream cheese, 235
   raw vegetables, 235
Apple, baked, porcupine, 197
   balls, pink, 111
   dumplings, boiled, 183
   sauce, 101
Apricot jelly, 197
   with rice pudding, 203
Artichoke hearts, stuffed with ham and mushrooms with tomato sauce, 124
Asparagus, browned butter, and cheese, 130
   egg and watercress salad, 153
   tips, cooked à la Française, 135
Aspic, eggs in, 58
   fish in, with watercress sauce, 28
Audrey's fillet of sole, au gratin, 214

Bab's arroz de la Valenciana, 211
Bacon, and mustard sauce, 116
   biscuits, hot, 233
   cold boiled, for breakfast, 118
Baked beans, Boston, 162
   southern, 163
Banana(s), with coconut cream, 196
   pudding, 202

Bass, deep-sea striped, boiled, 38
Bean(s), baked, Boston, 162
   baked, southern, 163
   lima, purée of, and peas, 138
   soy, tapioca soup, 15
   string, cream and egg sauce, 133
   string, in butter, 130
   string, salad, 153
Béarnaise sauce, 103
Beef, à la mode, 105
   broth, with cabbage toasts and cheese, 12
   cold roast, a way of serving, 111
   corned, and cabbage, 115
   pot au feu, 117
   poupiettes of, 114
   stock, 10
Beets, baked in cream, 133
Betty's curried shrimps, 217
Biscuits, hot bacon, 233
Bishop punch, hot, 247
Black bean soup, 17
Black walnut cake, twice-cooked frosting, 229
Boeuf, à la mode, 105
Boula soup, 24
Brandy cocoa, 242
Bread and butter, thin, 228
Bread pudding, 176
Bread, spoon, Sam's, 213
Broth, beef, with cabbage toasts and cheese, 12
   chicken, 10
   veal tapioca, 11
Brussels sprouts, en casserole, Anne's, 222

Cabbage, potato, and sausage, 126
   red, 134
   savoy, 137

Cabbage, stuffed, another, 123
  stuffed with corned beef hash, 122
Cake, black walnut, twice-cooked
    frosting, 229
  chocolate, 233
  méringued rum, 181
  Scotch, 230
  walnut mocha, 234
  white plum, 231
Calf's liver, baked, 113
Camomile tea, 240
Canapés, 235–37
  cream cheese balls between two
    pecans, 236
  hot sausage rolls, 237
  liverwurst sandwiches toasted, 235
  potato chips with cream cheese, 235
  raw vegetables, 235
  shrimps and mayonnaise, and chili
    sauce, 236
Canards, aux navets, 67
  aux olives, 64
  See also Duck
Cantaloupe, with Parma ham, 2
Caper(s) sauce, 117
  with skate wings and beurre noisette,
    35
Capons, roast stuffed, 86
Caramel rice pudding, 176
Carrots, Vichy, 136
Casserole, boned squab chicken, en, 73
  Brussels sprouts, Anne's, en, 222
  tripe, en, 112
Cassoulet, 159
Caudle cup, 243
Cauliflower salad, with French dress-
    ing, 148
  with cream sauce and buttered
    crumbs, 135
Caviar, with toast and trimmings, 6
Celery salad, with mustard dressing,
    148
Chase's baked salmon, 216
Cheese, and chicken soufflé, 55
  cream, balls between two pecans,
    236
Cherry(ies), cooked in red wine, 201
  in cracked ice, 190
  tart, 192
Chicken, and cheese soufflé, 55
  Bab's arroz de la Valenciana, 211
  baked chicken custard, 70
  boiled with dumplings, 95

Chicken, broth, 10
  cold boiled, Yorkshire style, 75
  cold, in a blanket, 87
  curry of, 74
  En cocotte à la bonne à tout faire, 78
  fondue de poulet à la crême, 90
  fried, 86
  Hélène's poulet crapaudine, 210
  Mexican stew, 79
  Moffat's poulet aux choux, 212
  pie, Claudine's, 216
  polenta, 76
  poulet à l'Espagnole, 73
  poulet bonne femme, 72
  poulet en consommé, 68
  poulet patron, 80
  roast, prunes and bacon, 79
  roast stuffed capons, 86
  roast, stuffed with noodles, 91
  soup, cream of, 19
  Spanish, Mr. C's, 220
  stew, 68
Chicory, and escarole salad, with
    chicken liver dressing, 149
  salad, 152
Chili sauce, tomato, 236
Chocolate, brandy cocoa, 242
  cake, 233
  ice cream, with coffee sauce, 180
  mocha, 242
  pot de crême, 178
  pudding, 174
  pudding, rich, with mocha sauce, 179
Chowder, fish, New England, 23
  lobster, 20
Chutney, apricot and date, 89
Cider, Twelfth Night, 246
Cinnamon toast, 229
Civet de lapin, 104
Claret punch, hot, 245
Claudine's chicken pie, 216
Cocktail and tea party accessories,
    225–37
Cocoa, brandy, 242
Coconut, cream, with bananas, 196
  drops, 231
Cod, salt, bénédictine, 37
  salt, with dried beans, 37
Codfish, Pat's, 215
Coeur à la crême, 225
Coffee, cuban, 241
  hot egg, 241
  rum, Ruby's hot, 221

Coffee, sauce, 180
  Turkish, 241
  Vienna, 241
Cold ham, 110
Conserve, grandmother's strawberry,
  pineapple and orange, 234
Consommé, 9
Cookies, 232
  Lucy's praliné, 213
  praliné, 232
  rich rolled, 230
Corned beef, and cabbage, 115
  hash stuffing in cabbage, 122
Coupe, 198
Crabs, soft-shelled almandine, 32
Cream, almond, coated with straw-
    berry gelatine, 190
  coconut, with bananas, 196
  coeur à la crème, 225
  crème brûler, 183
  crème praliné, 175
  crème renversée, 178
  Devonshire, 193
  frozen, with pears in cointreau, 188
  horseradish, 122
  pot de crème, café, 178
  pot de crème chocolat, 178
  pot de crème vanilla, 177
  whipped, frozen méringued, 205
Cream cheese, balls between two pe-
    cans, 236
  with potato chips, 235
Cream of wheat, or farina, pudding,
  177
Crème, brûler, 183
  café, pot de, 178
  chocolat, pot de, 178
  coeur à la, 225
  praliné, 175
  renversée, 178
  vanilla, pot de, 177
Crêpes, soufflés, Ray's, 219
  Suzette, 171
Cuban coffee, 241
Cucumber(s), and chopped sweet on-
    ion filling, 227
  in cream, 141
  tomato and radish salad, 148
  with radishes and green peppers, 2
Currants, sugared, 201
Curry(ied), of chicken, 74
  duck, with apricot and date chut-
    ney, 88

Curry(ied), eggs, hard-boiled, 4
  eggs, in brown rice, 55
  salmon, canned, 36
  shrimps, Betty's, 217
  vegetable, 140
Custard, 167–85
  baked chicken, 70
  praliné, 170
  the queen's, 173

Devonshire cream, 193
Duck, à l'orange, 94
  canards aux navets, 67
  canards aux olives, 64
  cold roast, 90
  curried, with apricot and date
    chutney, 88
  stuffed, with green peas, 94
Dumplings, boiled apple, 183

Edgar's planked shad, 218
Egg(s), 47–59
  à la tripe, 50
  asparagus and watercress salad, 153
  baked, Cecilia, 57
  baked in cream with bacon, 53
  chopped and mayonnaise filling,
    228
  coddled, à la coque, 48
  coffee, hot egg, 241
  curried, hard-boiled, 4
  curried, in brown rice, 55
  fried, 47
  fried, with capers au beurre noir, 50
  hard-boiled, 49
  in aspic, 58
  in spinach, 53
  in tomatoes, 51
  omelette de Curé, 56
  on the plate, 49
  poached, on toast, 47
  poached, with paté de foie gras, 50
  salad, hard-boiled, 152
  scrambled, 48
  scrambled, with shrimps, 53
  Spanish, 51
  squiggled, 59
  stuffed, baked, 54
  tabasco, 59
  timbales, with tomato sauce, 52
Eggplant, Mildred's, 215
Endives, braised, with purée of mush-
    rooms, 134

Escarole, and chicory salad, with chicken liver dressing, 149

Farina, or cream of wheat, pudding, 177
Fig pudding, boiled, 182
Fillings, 157–63
  chopped egg and mayonnaise, 228
  chopped mushroom and mayonnaise, 227
  chopped walnut and watercress, 22
  cucumber and chopped sweet onion, 227
  shrimps and horseradish, 228
  stuffed olive and salted almond, 228
Fish, chowder, New England, 23
  in aspic, with watercress sauce, 28
Flounder, fillet of, 34
Fondue de poulet à la crême, 90
Force-meat, for ravioli, 161
Fowl, 64–95
Fritters, parsnip, 132
Frosting, twice-cooked, 229
Fruit(s), 187–206
  compote of, 195
  dried, and walnuts in cream, 206
  fresh fruit and water ice and champagne in watermelon, 204
  sliced, with orange ice and almonds, 194

Gigot, braisé, 119
Gnocchi, 157
Grandmother's strawberry, pineapple, and orange conserve, 234

Hagenbutten tea, 241
Ham, and horseradish sandwiches, 227
  and mushrooms in artichoke hearts with tomato sauce, 124
  boiled roasted, hot, 104
  cold, 110
  cornucopias, containing purée of green peas, 124
  Parma, with cantaloupe, 2
Hash, corned beef, stuffing, in cabbage, 122
Hélène's poulet crapaudine, 210
Hors d'oeuvres, 1–6
Horseradish, and ham sandwiches, 227
  and shrimp filling, 228
  cream, 122
  sauce, 101
  sauce, hot bread, 116

Hot bacon biscuits, 233
  bishop punch, 247
  boiled lobster, butter sauce, 44
  boiled roasted ham, 104
  claret punch, 245
  coffee rum, Ruby's, 221
  drinks, 240–47
  egg, 241
  horseradish bread sauce, 116
  orange punch, 246
  potato salad, 151
  rolls, 237
  scones, buttered, 231

Ice, orange, with sliced fruit and almonds, 194
  water, and fresh fruit and champagne in watermelon, 204
Ice cream, chocolate, with coffee sauce, 180
Isabelle's grateau de marrons, 212

Jean's baby lamb, 217
Jelly, apricot, 197

Kidney, stew, 107
  veal, in mustard, 108

Lamb, à l'Alsace, 109
  baby, Jean's, 217
  boiled leg of, with caper sauce, 117
  crown roast of, with pink apple balls, mint sauce, 111
  gigot braise, 119
  poached, leg of, 102
Lapin, civet de, 104
Lettuce, baby garden, with hard-boiled egg dressing, 153
  salad, 152
Lima beans, and peas, purée of, 138
Linden-tree blossoms, or tilleul, aux fleurs d'oranger, 240
Liver, baked calf's, 113
  chicken, omelet, 56
Liverwurst appetizers, 235
Lobster, and salmon pie, 42
  chowder, 20
  hot boiled, butter sauce, 44
  mousse surprise, 32
Lucy's praliné cookies, 213

Madrilène, 11
Marie's potato soup, 21

Marinated mushrooms, 3
Marmalade and butter sandwiches, toasted, 228
Marrons, Isabelle's grateau de, 212
  purée of, 139
Martha's baked tomatoes, 210
Maté, 246
Meat, 99-126
Melon(s), cantaloupe with Parma ham, 1
  glacé à l'Orientale, 203
  honeydew à la Venise, 1
  honeydew with powdered ginger, 4
Méringued, oranges, 195
  rum cake, 181
Mexican chicken stew, 79
Mildred's eggplant, 215
Milk punch, 242
Minestrone soup, 16
Mint, sauce, 112
  tea, 240
Mocha, chocolate, 242
  walnut cake, 234
  sauce, 179
Moffat's poulet aux choux, 212
Mousse, lobster surprise, 32
  shad roe, 28
Mr. C's Spanish chicken, 220
Mulled port, 245
Mulled sherry, 245
Mushrooms, and ham, in artichoke hearts with tomato sauce, 124
  chopped, filling and mayonnaise, 227
  marinated, 3
  purée of, with endives braised, 134
  with spinach ring, 141
Mustard and bacon sauce, 116

New England fish chowder, 23
Nightcap, 243
Noodles, with buttered crumbs, 129

Olive, stuffed, and salted almond filling, 228
Omelet(te) de Curé, 56
  chicken liver, 56
  plain, 49
  veal kidney, 51
Onions, baked spiced, 5
  purée of, 138
  stuffed Bermuda, 125
  sweet, chopped, and cucumber filling, 227

Orange(s), ice, with sliced fruit and almonds, 194
  méringued, 195
  punch, hot, 246
  romaine and almond salad, 154
  sliced, in orange sherbet, 189
Oyster stew, 18

Pain surprise, 226
Pancake delicacies, 126
Parma ham with cantaloupe, 2
Parsnip fritters, 132
Pat's codfish, 215
Pea soup, thin, 13
  with whipped cream and croutons, 14
Peaches, blazing, 262
  on méringue pedestals, 200
  sliced in plum juice, 197
Pears, à la cuillère, 194
  cooked in port, 201
  in cointreau, with frozen cream, 188
  sliced raw, in orange juice and curaçao, 196
Pears, alligator, à la Tahiti, 5
Peas, green, purée of, in ham cornucopias, 124
  petits pois à la Française, 130
  purée of, and lima beans, 138
Pecan, sandwiches, 229
Peppers, green, in olive oil, 137
  green, with radishes and cucumber, 2
Petits pois à la Française, 130
Pheasants, in cream, 64
  roast, with gin and juniper berries, 71
Pie, chicken, Claudine's, 216
Pig, roast suckling, with chestnut dressing, 100
Pigeon pies, two, 83
Pimentos, canned red, stuffed with rice and peas and ham, 3
Pink apple balls, 111
Polenta with sausages, 158
Popovers, 44
Port, and English walnuts, 206
  mulled, 245
  pears cooked in, 201
Posset, 243
Pot au feu, 117
Potage de Curé, 20
  maigre Canadien, 22

Potato(es), and truffle salad, 154
  and watercress salad, 149
  and watercress soup, 16
  baked, 143
  baked, stuffed with beef, 125
  boiled, 143
  cabbage and sausage, 126
  chips, with cream cheese, 235
  French fried, 142
  mashed, 142
  panier, 131
  provincial, 133
  salad, hot, 151
  sweet, pudding, 139
Poulet, à l'Espagnole, 73
  aux choux, Moffat's, 212
  Bonne femme, 72
  Crapaudine, Hélène's, 210
  en consommé, 68
  fondue de, à la crême, 90
  See also chicken
Poupiettes of beef, 114
Praliné, cookies, 232
  cookies, Lucy's, 213
  cream, 175
  custard, 170
Prunes, in red wine, 202
Pudding(s), 167–85
  banana, 202
  boiled fig, 182
  bread, 176
  chocolate, 174
  chocolate, rich, with mocha sauce, 179
  farina, or cream of wheat, 177
  pumpkin, 178
  rice, 176
  rice, caramel, 176
  rice, with apricots, 203
  snow, 174
  sweet potato, 139
  tapioca, zabaione sauce, 175
Pumpkin, pudding, 178
  soup, 18
Punch, caudle cup, 243
  hot bishop, 247
  hot claret, 245
  hot orange, 246
  maté, 246
  milk, 242
  mulled port, 245
  mulled sherry, 245
  nightcap, 243

Punch, posset, 243
  rum, 244
  sauterne, 245
  Tom and Jerry, 244
  Twelfth Night cider, 246
  wassail bowl, 243
Purée, of green peas, in ham cornucopias, 124
  of lima beans and peas, 138
  of marrons, 139
  of mushrooms, with endives braised, 134
  of onions, 138
  of spinach, 139
  of watercress, 136

Queen's custard, the, 173

Radish(es), cucumber and tomato salad, 148
  with cucumbers and green peppers, 2
Ravioli, 160
  force-meat for, 161
  sauce for, 162
Ray's crêpes soufflés, 219
Red cabbage, 134
Rice, brown, with curried eggs, 55
  pudding, 176
  pudding, caramel, 176
  pudding with apricots, 203
Rich chocolate pudding, 179
Rich rolled cookies, 230
Romaine, orange and almond salad, 154
  salad, with hard-boiled egg dressing, 150
Ruby's hot coffee rum, 221
Rum, cake, méringued, 181
  coffee, Ruby's hot, 221
  punch, 244
Russian tea, 244

Salad(s), 149–54
  asparagus, egg and watercress, 153
  baby garden lettuce, with hard-boiled egg dressing, 153
  cauliflower, and French dressing, 148
  celery, with mustard dressing, 148
  chicory, 152
  chicory and escarole, with chicken liver dressing, 149
  cucumber, tomato, and radish, 148

Salad(s), hard-boiled egg, 152
  hot potato, 151
  lettuce, 152
  mixed, with French dressing, 147
  potato and truffle, 154
  potatoes and watercress, 149
  romaine, orange and almond, 154
  romaine, with hard-boiled egg dressing, 150
  spinach, 152
  string bean, 153
  vegetable, 151
  wilted, 150
Salad dressing, chicken liver, 149
  French, 147, 148
  hard-boiled egg, 150, 153
  mustard, 148
Salmon, and lobster pie, 42
  and shrimp soup, 22
  boiled, cream, egg, herb sauce, 39
  canned, curry, 36
  Chase's baked, 216
  smoked, on toast, with olive oil and coarse black pepper, 6
Salt cod, bénédictine, 37
  with dried beans, 37
Sam's spoon-bread, 213
Sandwiches, ham and horseradish, 227
  pecan, 229
  thin bread and butter, 228
  toasted marmalade and butter, 228
  tomato, 227
  watercress, 229
Sardines, grilled on toast, 1
Sauce, béarnaise, 103, 114
  butter, 44
  caper, 117
  coffee, 180
  cream, egg, herb, 39
  for ham, 104
  for ravioli, 162
  for tongue, 112
  horseradish, 101
  hot horseradish bread, 116
  mint, 112
  mocha, 179
  mustard and bacon, 116
  tomato, 77, 121
  tomato chili, 236
  zabaione, 175
Sausage, potato and cabbage, 126
  rolls, hot, 237
  with polenta, 158

Sauterne punch, 245
Savoy cabbage, 137
Scallops amandine, 41
Scones, hot buttered, 231
Scotch cake, 230
Shad, planked, Edgar's, 218
  roe, baked, 40
  roe mousse, 30
Sherbet, orange, with sliced oranges, 189
Sherry, mulled, 245
Shrimp, and horseradish filling, 228
  and mayonnaise and chili sauce, 236
  and salmon soup, 22
  Betty's curried, 217
  with scrambled eggs, 53
Skate wings, with beurre noisette and capers, 35
Snapdragon, 189
Snow pudding, 174
Sole, Audrey's fillet of, au gratin, 214
Soufflé, almond, 206
  crêpes, Ray's, 219
  of chicken and cheese, 55
  strawberry and almond, 187
  tomato, 140
Soup(s), 9–24
  beef broth, with cabbage toasts and cheese, 12
  beef stock, 10
  black bean, 17
  boula, 24
  chicken broth, 10
  chicken, cream of, 19
  chowder, fish, New England, 23
  chowder, lobster, 20
  consommé, 9
  madrilène, 11
  minestrone, 16
  oyster stew, 18
  pea, thin, 13
  pea, with whipped cream and croutons, 14
  potage de Curé, 20
  potage maigre Canadien, 22
  potato, Marie's, 21
  potato and watercress, 16
  pumpkin, 18
  salmon and shrimp, 22
  soy bean tapioca, cream of, 15
  spring, 13
  tomato and cucumber, cold, 13
  veal broth, 11

Soup(s), veal broth, cream of tapioca,
    15
  vegetable, 11
  Vichichoise Meadowbrook, 17
Soy bean tapioca soup, 15
Spaghetti, 159
  Eddie's, 221
  Janet's green and white, 209
Spanish chicken, Mr. C's, 220
Spinach, and tongue in horseradish
    cream, 122
  eggs in, 53
  purée of, 139
  ring, with mushrooms, 141
  salad, 152
Spoon-bread, Sam's, 213
Spring soup, 13
Squab, boned chicken, en casserole,
    73
  garbure of, 69
  stuffed, with pistachio nuts, 89
Squash, in cream, 137
Steak, broiled, and béarnaise sauce,
    114
Stew, chicken, 68
  chicken, Mexican, 79
  kidney, 107
  Oyster, 18
Strawberry(ies), and almond soufflé,
    187
  frozen, 205
  in orange juice, 198
  in red wine, 191
  plump, 198
  tarts, with Devonshire cream, 193
  tea, Swiss, 240
  turnovers, 191
  with powdered sugar, 5
  with wild strawberry jam, 200
Stuffed olive and salted almond filling
    228
Surprise, pain, 226
Sweet potato pudding, 139
Swiss strawberry tea, 240

Tapioca, pudding, zabaione sauce,
    175
  soy bean soup, 15
  veal broth, 11
  veal broth, cream of, 15
Tarts, cherry, 192
  strawberry, with Devonshire cream,
    193

Tea, 247
  camomile, 240
  Hagenbutten, 241
  mint, 240
  Russian, 244
  Swiss strawberry, 240
  tilleul, or Linden-tree blossoms aux
    fleurs d'oranger, 240
Tea and cocktail party accessories,
    225–37
Thin bread and butter, 228
Tilleul, or Linden-tree blossoms, aux
    fleurs d'oranger, 240
Toast, cinnamon, 229
Tom and Jerry, 244
Tomato(es), and cucumber soup, cold,
    13
  cucumber and radish salad, 148
  chili sauce, 236
  eggs in, 51
  juice, frappé, 5
  Martha's baked, 210
  sandwiches, 227
  sauce, 77, 121, 124
  soufflé, 140
Tongue, and spinach in horseradish
    cream, 122
  boiled, 116
Tripe en casserole, 112
Trout with bacon, 40
  See also Truite
Truffle and potato salad, 154
Truites aux amandes, 40
  saumonée braisé, 38
  See also Trout
Turkey, boiled, butter sauce, 65
  roast stuffed, 66
  roast, with Ray's stuffing, 92
Turkish coffee, 241
Turnips, glazed, 138
Twelfth Night cider, 246

Veal, broth, tapioca, 11
  broth, cream of tapioca, 15
  cooked in Chablis, 109
  kidney in mustard, 108
  kidney omelet, 51
  See also Veau
Veau, blanquette de, 107
  See also Veal
Vegetable(s), 129–43
  curry, 140
  plate, 140

Vegetable(s), raw, 235
  salad, 151
  soup, diet, 11
Venison, fillet of, marinated, 99
Vichichoise Meadowbrook soup, 17
Vienna coffee, 241

Wafers, Eatsum Milk, 235
Walnut(s), black, cake; twice cooked
    frosting, 229
  chopped and watercress filling,
    227
  English, and port, 206
  in cream, and dried fruit, 206
  mocha cake, 234
Wassail bowl, 243

Water ice, and fresh fruit and cham-
    pagne in watermelon, 204
Watercress, and chopped walnut fill-
    ing, 227
  and potatoes salad, 149
  hard-boiled egg and asparagus
    salad, 153
  purée of, 136
  sandwiches, 229
Watermelon, filled with fresh fruit and
    water ice and champagne, 204
White plum cake, 231

Zabaione, iced, 180
  sauce, 175
Zucchini, Italian, fan-shaped, 132